Contested Terrain

THE NEW AMERICAN CANON

The Iowa Series in Contemporary Literature and Culture

Samuel Cohen, series editor

Contested Terrain

SUBURBAN FICTION AND U.S. REGIONALISM, 1945–2020

Keith Wilhite

UNIVERSITY OF IOWA PRESS, IOWA CITY

ISBN 978-1-60938-857-7 (pbk)
ISBN: 978-1-60938-858-4 (ebk)

Design by Shaun Allshouse

Printed on acid-free paper

Cataloging-in-Publication data is on file with the Library of Congress.

For Jennifer

Contents

Acknowledgments

This book has been a work in progress for most of my professional life, and along the way I have benefitted from the insights and suggestions of advisors, colleagues, and friends. My work on suburban literature and culture started with my dissertation, and though the focus has shifted and most of the exemplary texts have changed, I remain indebted to my earliest readers, especially Tom Lutz and Barbara Eckstein. I am also grateful to those who read selections and offered comments that, by now, they have surely forgotten. Thank you to Harry Stecopoulos, Nick Yablon, Loren Glass, Garrett Stewart, and the members of my writing cohort at the University of Iowa: Jeff Charis-Carlson, Sean Scanlan, Erica Still, and Jeffrey Swenson.

The transformation from dissertation to book has been arduous, but I would like to thank the anonymous readers at *American Literature* and *Modern Fiction Studies* who helped to sharpen my thinking about the suburbs as "region" and to envision how the articles first published in those journals might provide a foundation for this book. Susanne Hall and Mike Ennis, friends and former colleagues in the Thompson Writing Program at Duke University, provided additional insight, encouragement, and moral support at pivotal moments in the development of this project. I am thankful to you both. A travel grant from the Thompson Writing Program also helped to fund my research at the Harry Ransom Center, University of Texas at Austin.

Two symposia dedicated to suburban literature, history, and culture proved beneficial in honing my ideas: the 2013 "Cultures of the Suburbs International Research Network" in Hempstead, New York, and "Suburbia—An Archaeology of the Moment: Suburbs in the Arts and Literature of the English-Speaking World" at Université Toulouse–Jean Jaurès in 2017. Both forums afforded that rare opportunity to spend entire days engaged in collegial conversations with writers and scholars of suburban studies, and it was a privilege to take part in those discussions.

My colleagues at Siena College have likewise offered encouragement throughout the writing process, and I am grateful for the opportunities I have had to talk through my ideas about suburban fiction at our department colloquia. I feel lucky to be part of such an affable, creative, and productive group of teacher-scholars. Thanks especially to Erich Hertz for our conversations about *The Virgin Suicides*. Two summer research fellowships from Siena's Committee on Teaching and Faculty Development helped to support the writing of this project. I want to thank Sam Cohen for seeing the potential in my book proposal and the editorial staff at the University of Iowa Press, especially Meredith Stabel, Tegan Daly, Susan Hill Newton, and Susan Boulanger. I offer heartfelt thanks to the peer reviewers whose generous readings, thoughtful critiques, and skeptical questions helped me to reconsider the stakes of reading suburban fiction as "regional writing."

My deepest gratitude goes to Jennifer Warnecke for her patience, her sense of humor, and her enduring support throughout the highs and lows of this project. This book is also dedicated to the memory of our fathers, Joseph Wilhite (1944–2018) and Gregory Warnecke (1930–2020), and my mother, Judith Wilhite (1943–2022).

An earlier version of chapter four was published as "Face the House: Suburban Domesticity and Nation as Home in *The Virgin Suicides*," *Mfs* 61, no. 1 (2015): 1–23, reprinted by permission of Johns Hopkins University Press. Other chapters include revised sections from previously published articles, and I am grateful to the following journals and editors:

"Contested Terrain: The Suburbs as Region," *American Literature* 84, no. 3 (2012): 617–44, sections reprinted by permission of Duke University Press.

"One House at a Time: Democratic Citizenship and Domestic Security in *Clybourne Park*," *MidAmerica* 47 (2020): 8–20, sections reprinted by permission of the Society for the Study of Midwestern Literature.

Introduction

The Suburbs as Region

"Contestation is the real story of suburbia."
—Dolores Hayden, *Building Suburbia* (2003)

A T ABOUT THE HALF-WAY point in the film *Mr. Blandings Builds His Dream House* (1948), a remarkable exchange takes place between Mr. and Mrs. Blandings and their building inspector. The couple (Cary Grant and Myrna Loy) would like to rehab the old house on the property they have purchased in rural Connecticut. According to their real estate agent, this is no ordinary plot of land: they stand on the very ground where General Gates stopped to water his horses during the Revolutionary War. In other words, as the realtor proclaims, when you buy this home and property, "you're buying a piece of American history."[1] Despite this storied past, building contractors and friends alike declare the structure irreparable and advise the Blandingses to tear it down. Finally, to make the situation perfectly clear, the inspector places an empty picture frame on a wooden barrel and invites the couple to look through it. The house leans severely on its foundation and, at last, Mr. and Mrs. Blandings are made to see that their hope of rehabbing the old house is impossible. As the home tilts beyond the margins of the frame, they opt to build a new "dream house" on their historic property.

The film is based on the 1946 novel of the same title by Eric Hodgins; the novel was, in turn, developed from Hodgins's short

1

story "Mr. Blandings Builds His Castle," which was originally published in the April 1946 issue of *Fortune* magazine. We can read all three as exemplars of an emerging postwar discourse about, and popular interest in, the new suburban "dream house," creating a synergy between postwar suburban narratives and advertising, extending to the construction of model Blandings homes across the country.[2] The story is premised on the idea that urban space is too cramped, too crowded, and, ultimately, too anti-family. The movie expects viewers to overlook the fact that, by New York standards, the Blandingses' apartment does not appear all that small, and that the family lives in enough material, if not always spatial, comfort to employ a house servant. The couple's relocation from New York City to "the country," just a short train ride away from Mr. Blandings's advertising office, participates in what was already a well-known tradition in the 1940s, namely conflating "what later historians would term a 'suburban' ideal" with country living and country architecture.[3] In this way, *Mr. Blandings* serves as an early advertisement for a compulsory postwar suburban dream. It seems only fitting, therefore, that the novel ends with the Blandings house featured in the Christmas issue of the magazine *The Home Lovely*. "Our problem was to create a home of modern implications in a community dominated by fine old colonial farmhouses that had stood the test of Revolutionary days," Mrs. Blandings tells the editors, adding that they sought the "*sine qua non* of all normal couples' ideals and ambitions, the Home of One's Own."[4] Multifamily, urban living is unfit for the "ideals and ambitions" of the postwar nation; only a privately owned, modern home, built on the foundations of America's Revolutionary-era principles, will suffice to fulfill the desires of a "normal" family.

A half-century later, the season one finale of *Arrested Development* offered a more sardonic assessment of this suburban dream. As devotees of this critically acclaimed—if insufficiently popular—television comedy know, *Arrested Development* begins on a yacht with a retirement party for George Bluth Sr. (Jeffrey Tambor), who is stepping down from his post as president and CEO of the Bluth Company, a real estate development firm based in Newport Beach, California. After passing a literal scepter to his wife, Lucille (Jessica Walter), George is arrested for defrauding investors and, with that, the season's assorted conflicts and fiascoes are set in motion. With George in prison, the management of the Bluth Company falls not to the profligate and besotted Lucille, but to the only dependable member of the family, Michael (Jason Bateman). To varying degrees, the first season revolves around Michael's reluctant stewardship of the company as he tries to triage his parents' and siblings' myriad dysfunctions.

In the season one finale, "Let 'Em Eat Cake" (June 6, 2004), we learn that the initial charges of fraud and embezzlement do not accurately reflect the scope of George's malfeasance.[5] The Bluth Company had illegally constructed grand, suburban-style houses in Iraq, and the incriminating paper trail was never destroyed because, as George belatedly explains to Michael, "Saddam owed us money." Earlier in the episode, Michael gained some insight into the company's misdeeds when a local news broadcast was preempted by a special report on the "Mini-Palaces of Saddam." As an embedded reporter walks through one of several houses recently seized by U.S. troops, she delivers the shocking detail "that these homes appear to be American built." Indeed, the place does seem familiar. As Michael peers at the screen, he asks his niece, Maeby (Alia Shawkat), "Does that look a little like our kitchen island?" At that instant, a spindle falls from a staircase in the Iraqi "mini-palace," reprising a similar mishap in the Bluth model home only moments before. The episode cuts to sequential shots of the same suburban house: first, to the familiar image of the Bluth model home, isolated on its dune-like plateau, surrounded by plot markers for houses that were never completed due to the company's financial insolvency; and second, to Michael's television, an identical image of the Bluth's "Sea Wind" unit, nestled in the barren hillsides of Iraq, a cloud of black smoke rising in the background.

These two sagas of home building—one from the immediate post–World War II era, the other amid the Iraq War and a housing bubble becoming difficult to ignore—offer accessible snapshots of the key eras that frame this study of postwar suburban culture. *Mr. Blandings* explicitly links the move from city to suburb with the revolutionary origins of the country, stamping a national imprimatur on the outflow of residential living that will inaugurate and normalize the ensuing decades of suburban sprawl. The novel and film gloss what I contend the literary narratives across the postwar era reveal in more depth, namely suburban development as a domestic nation-building project that promotes privatism—an increased emphasis on private property, the private realm, and the pursuit of individual and family interests—in counterpoint to the emergent economic and military imperialism of the United States after World War II.[6]

The mirror image of the Bluth house in *Arrested Development* offers a more cynical appraisal on the preceding half-century of sprawl. The placement of the Sea Wind unit in an unfinished subdivision in Newport Beach and somewhere on the outskirts of wartorn Baghdad produces an uncanny effect. The house is both here and there, domestic and foreign, creating an unnerving sense of dislocation underscored throughout the series by the slow decay of the model home that threatens to displace the Bluth family. The comedy of the scene inheres in this uncanny effect and the revelation it delivers, played to wry perfection by Bateman. Yet, as a development firm, the Bluth Company is also complicit in the speculative practices that inflated the real estate bubble and contributed to increased foreclosure rates and, eventually, the Great Recession that settled over the country from 2007 to 2009. From today's vantage point, every exterior shot of the Bluth model home, standing in a desolated landscape, presages these residential and economic crises. If one takes this reading a step further, the juxtaposition of the two Sea Wind units—one in America, one in Iraq—also encourages the viewer to see the suburban "mini-palace" in an international context and to acknowledge that in 2004, in a very real sense, the United States was at war in an oil-rich region of the Middle East to preserve an unsustainable mode of living in America's suburbs. The Iraq War, a radical enactment of neoconservative foreign policy, finds its domestic counterpart in a neoliberal conception of suburban privatism: a worldview that forsakes "social solidarity" in the name of "individualism, private property, personal responsibility, and family values."[7]

Contested Terrain: Suburban Fiction and U.S. Regionalism, 1945–2020 argues that postwar suburban narratives invite us to read for the regional, national, and even transnational contexts of our residential geographies and domestic spaces. As I will show, these narratives owe a debt to and extend a tradition of U.S. literary regionalism, even as the literature itself interrogates the limits of regional writing in a suburban age of universal standardization. For decades, cultural geographers, urban historians, and city planners have been tracking the transnational, indirect costs of U.S. suburbs, yet literary scholars have often settled for reading suburban fiction as reiterations of prevailing critiques from the 1950s and 1960s. The problem is not that we have been reading these works on their own terms (that is, reading literature as literature), nor am I suggesting we abandon aesthetic interests and get in line with our colleagues in the social sciences. But I am intrigued by our preoccupation with an image of the suburb as a reified artifact of Cold War cultural critique, a preoccupation that tends to produce totalizing, ahistorical accounts of suburban settings. Our theoretical frameworks have shifted with the times, but most readings remain beholden to traditional notions of suburban banality, neuroses, and disillusionment. Lingering beneath contemporary perspectives on the alienating suburban "nowhere" is the eerie homogeneity captured in William Garnett's aerial shots of 1950s Lakewood, California.[8] As D. J. Waldie suggests, these photographs have "framed all future views of [Lakewood] and of suburbs generally."[9]

For more than a half-century, this perspective has encouraged authors, filmmakers, and critics to adopt a disparaging approach to suburbia, one codified early on by John Keats's *The Crack in the Picture Window* (1956), as we continue to supplement appraisals of suburban insularity and conformity initially advanced by David Riesman's *The Lonely Crowd* (1950), William H. Whyte's *The Organization Man* (1956), Lewis Mumford's *The City in History* (1961), and Betty Friedan's *The Feminine Mystique* (1963). Artists and critics alike have framed suburbia as a landscape that is at once pastoral and gothic. Cul-de-sacs of proper houses and families, the standard-bearers of a national nostalgia, must all give up their secrets of violence, adultery, sexual repression, and bourgeois estrangement.[10]

I would maintain that even Catherine Jurca's *White Diaspora* (2001), the most insightful and expansive account of suburban literature to date, reads early twentieth-century representations of "dispossession" through the prism of postwar criticism, presenting suburbia as an ironic space of white middle-class "alienation," "*self*-loathing," and perceived "victimization."[11] Similarly, Robert Beuka's adaptation of Foucault's heterotopia updates familiar tensions between utopian fantasies and dystopian realities. The suburbs, though, are not simply "a heterotopic 'mirror' to mainstream American culture."[12] They are the social, political, and economic spaces that produce and perpetuate mainstream American culture. Foucault's heterotopia simply supplants suburban topography with an inherently contradictory notion of space.[13] In brief, even if we agree that Levittown and Lakewood are no longer the models for developers, novelists, or filmmakers, our contemporary critical approaches to suburban narratives often tend to rehearse the initial attacks leveled against these communities.[14]

More recent studies have set out to complicate and reframe this discussion. In her analysis of early twenty-first-century literature, Kathy Knapp reads a resounding sense of "unexceptionalism" that contrasts "the narrative of American innocence and resolve swiftly marketed by the mass media and the Bush administration" after the September 11 attacks.[15] Taking up works by writers such as Richard Ford, Jonathan Franzen, Chang-rae Lee, and Philip Roth, she argues that the white, middle-class everyman in these novels does not exhibit the familiar postwar sense of ennui and victimization. "These everymen are brought low by sickness, financial ruin, and devastating loss," and they offer "a different set of lessons to a humbled middle-class readership" in the post-9/11 era.[16] Indeed, Knapp persuasively suggests that these novels "advance an aesthetic of contingency that inaugurates a new suburban literary tradition, the basis of which is connectedness rather than alienation."[17] Although not staking a claim to a new literary tradition, Karen Tongson adeptly challenges the enduring representation of homogeneous suburbia through an exploration of "queer of color regionalisms in the United States."[18] Focusing on the suburbs of Southern California, her eclectic study exposes an array of racial and sexual diversity obfuscated by cultural discourses that enshrine a white, heteronormative image of suburbia. Leveraging previous work in the fields of suburban studies and queer theory, Tongson reroutes the discussion toward "the spatial *imaginaries* perpetuated, disseminated, and culturally produced in a range of representational media, such as performance, popular music, literature, television, and new media, as well as the genre of criticism itself."[19]

Of late, there has also been a trend toward revisionist approaches to midcentury and contemporary literature set in the American suburbs. Joseph George reads suburban fiction through a phenomenological lens, discovering instances of "critical hospitality" in intimate interactions that create opportunities for complexity and diversity.[20] Drawing on the insights of Emmanuel Levinas and Roberto Esposito, he argues "that suburban fictions repeatedly imagine a different type of community possible within domestic spaces, one in which critical hospitality refuses individualistic interactions and prompts intersubjective identity construction."[21] In *The Literature of Suburban Change* (2020), Martin Dines intends "to give time back to the suburbs by examining the ways writers have exploited different narrative forms to articulate more complex stories that demonstrate how suburbs, and their pasts, are still in production."[22] I read in Dines's project a complementary perspective, at least insofar as we both contend that the suburbs are more interconnected across broader geographic scales than scholars have previously acknowledged. Whereas my project takes aim at the contested terrain of suburban nation building and its ties to national identity, Dines discovers, across a variety of literary genres, writers concerned "with the matter of who gets to tell whose story, with conflicting accounts of changing circumstances, and with contested histories."[23]

The focus on placeless suburbs, cultural dystopias, and middle-class alienation has usefully exposed a dominant facet of the literature, and my project builds upon these previous studies, as well as the new directions proposed by Tongson, Knapp, and Dines. Drawing on a cross-section of literary texts and political contexts from 1945 to 2020, *Contested Terrain* proposes a more expansive treatment of suburban fiction as the latest, perhaps final outpost in the tradition of U.S. regionalism. Although I may be accused of simply substituting one outmoded methodology for another, such a critique depends on misreading regionalism as either a subliterary genre or, as Roberto Dainotto suggests, a pernicious political ideology that opposes modernity and suppresses difference in the naive pursuit of "grounded, rooted, natural, authentic values shared by a true community."[24]

Admittedly, for many American readers, the term *regionalism* will conjure an array of stock or antiquated images: Mark Twain's Mississippi River towns and Willa Cather's midwestern prairies; William Faulkner's Yoknapatawpha or the Louisiana local color of George Washington Cable and Kate Chopin; Sarah Orne Jewett's deceptively quaint New England coastal villages; the romantic western vistas of John Muir or the fatal borderlands of Cormac McCarthy's bygone Southwest. The critical suspicion that regionalism promotes an anti-modern, pastoralized vision of vanishing landscapes explains, in part, the contemporary resistance to (or indifference toward) regional literature. Moreover, if one thinks of regionalism strictly as a literary genre—as opposed to a geopolitical structure or a critical response to place—then the works we classify as regional writing had their heyday over a hundred years ago, from the mid-nineteenth to the early twentieth century. Viewed in historic and generic terms, literary regionalism worked "alongside realism and naturalism as a parallel tradition of narrative prose," eventually inspiring the "revolt from the village" writers in the 1920s, like Sinclair Lewis and Sherwood Anderson, and the entrenched defiance of the southern Agrarians in the 1930s.[25] More cynically, one might cite regionalism as just one of the literary forms that preceded modernism, when things really started to get interesting.

Figured in these terms, there are temporal and spatial obstacles to reading postwar and contemporary suburban narratives as participating in a tradition of U.S. regional writing. Regionalism does not seem to jibe with the modern conditions that make suburban living possible, much less the postmodern geographies and late-capitalist economies of present-day multinational corporations. Indeed, it would seem suburbia's standardization and fractal expansion have displaced the natural landscape and, along with it, the possibility of regional specificity. By the 1950s, suburbia had already assumed a dominant position on the ground and in the cultural imagination, so much so that in *Howl* (1956) Allen Ginsberg could invoke the "invisible suburbs" as synonymous with "Moloch whose love is endless oil and stone," the key elements for fueling the cars and paving the landscapes of our suburban nation.[26] For this reason, I share the same anxiety Tom Lutz expresses in his argument for literary value when he acknowledges, "Regionalism may seem an odd place to look for an ethos of cosmopolitan openness to difference and an odd place to stake a claim for the continued relevance of the literary for contemporary culture."[27] Douglas Reichert Powell's study of "critical regionalism" echoes this basic conundrum: "Since the high period of modernism in the 1950s, 'regional' has been a pejorative term . . . to apply to cultural work. The word 'regionalism' may denote 'local color' but it connotes 'provincialism.'"[28] His assessment updates Lucy Lippard's contention that we continue to equate regionalism with "corny backwater art flowing from the tributaries that might eventually reach the mainstream but is currently stagnating out there in the boondocks."[29] To call oneself a regional writer, or to argue on behalf of regionalism as a critical methodology, risks being labeled subliterary or intellectually obsolete.

In opposition to such withering appraisals, *Contested Terrain* demonstrates that regionalism, as both a literary discourse and a method of geopolitical analysis, clarifies the fraught relationship between isolationism and imperialism that has shaped U.S. residential geography and, in turn, helps us rethink the role literary texts play in uncovering the historical project of suburban nation building. Indeed, although our key texts differ dramatically, my project shares with Tongson's an interest in the links between region and empire. She writes that "the Southern California suburbs from Orange County to the Inland Empire have functioned as a conceptual and topographical nexus for an American empire bound up with histories of sexuality, race, and desire."[30] As I formulate it, in postwar America, geography and politics coalesce around a conceptual and topographical commitment to the imperial reach of suburban privatism. In this project, I hope to show that regionalism, perhaps ironically, offers the best way for literary scholars to address more fully the central paradox of postwar suburban development.

The physical and conceptual development of the suburbs embodies a dialectic impulse: an isolationist strategy in an era of global expansion and an imperialist, land-grab campaign within U.S. metropolitan regions. With the nation facing a housing shortage after World War II, government agencies and programs such as the Federal Housing Administration (FHA), the Home Owner's Loan Corporation (HOLC), and the G.I. Bill guaranteed and subsidized low-interest mortgages for newly constructed houses in the suburbs. According to Kenneth Jackson, such programs enabled "sixteen million soldiers and sailors of World War II [to] purchase a home after the defeat of Germany and Japan."[31] These federal programs also condoned discrimination through prejudicial loan practices and redlining, a rating system that favored "new, homogeneous" neighborhoods and "undervalued neighborhoods that were dense, mixed, or aging," resigning cities to residential blight and economic decline.[32] The Housing Acts of 1949 and 1954 further reduced affordable urban housing and entrenched racial and economic segregation while shifting federal subsidies to private developers.[33] In effect, the government created the expectation among white Americans that a suburban home was both an entitlement and a marker of middle-class standing. Aided and abetted by government subsidies and technological advancements—such as the automobile, superhighways, and assembly-line production tactics—suburban development has altered our understanding of domestic space. Alongside the rhetoric of America's ever-expanding global dominance, the emphasis on privacy and private property ushered in a new, informal geography that calculated national security and personal worth to the scale of the detached, single-family home.[34] After World War II, the suburban home emerged as the predominant geo-cultural ideal in the U.S., underwritten by federal policies and disseminated through written and visual media.

Over the past seventy-five years, from the postwar housing boom to the foreclosures of the Great Recession, suburbia has become our primary, noncontiguous, *national region*, and I am contending that we read suburban narratives as a form of regional writing that locates the political subject within the competing ideologies of privatism and globalism. In this way, my project also aligns with more recent efforts by scholars to rethink, trouble, and expand our understanding of genre. In *Contemporary Drift* (2017), Theodore Martin aims to historicize the very concept of "the contemporary" in literature and film, and he tethers that project to what he calls "the historical drag of genre."[35] As a discernible period, the contemporary is notoriously ambiguous—ranging anywhere from post-1945 to post-1980 to post-9/11—but the formal legibility of genre, with its iterative tropes and conventions, provides Martin with "an alternative methodology for historicizing the present."[36] He writes,

"Genres lead distinctly double lives, with one foot in the past and the other in the present; they contain the entire abridged history of an aesthetic form while also staking a claim to the form's contemporary relevance."[37] My inquiry into postwar suburban literature undertakes a similar reconsideration and, in this case, a revitalization of an often marginalized or "feminized" genre.[38] As Martin contends, genres carry the past with them, and one of the through lines for this project will be to consider how writers both inhabit and reinvent the genre of regionalism across an era of increasing spatial complexity. *Contested Terrain* advocates for the contemporary relevance of regionalism as a recognizable literary aesthetic and a critical perspective attendant to the differing geographic scales of the built environment, from suburban homes and neighborhoods to metropolitan regions and the nation. Far from provincial or sub-literary, the works examined herein evince a regional attunement to the ways local suburban topographies reflect and refract national contests over residential rights and racial containment, sexuality and domestic security, urban sprawl and sustainability, privatism and globalism.

This methodological commitment to read suburban fiction in terms of an ostensibly outmoded genre, to read through a regionalist lens and, in the process, to broaden the literary terrain of regionalism also dovetails with Kristin Jacobson's account of the paradigm shift in domestic fiction that began in the late-twentieth century. While nineteenth-century domestic fiction typically positioned the household as a stable, ordered, and normative force in American society, Jacobson argues that "neodomestic fiction represents and promotes a politics of instability and heterogeneity."[39] Her project makes at least two essential interventions. First, her focus on spatiality uncovers connections across historical eras and between aesthetically disparate texts—realist, modernist, and postmodernist—that take the household as their focal point. "What remains," Jacobson writes, "despite these aesthetic changes, is a collection of novels that feature a domestic setting and the processes involved in making home."[40] The second intervention owes a debt to the work of Judith Butler on "gender performance" and to the concept of "relational space" advanced by feminist geographers as an ideological corrective to "separate spheres or other hierarchical binaries."[41]

Jacobson troubles the gender politics of the private realm, discovering in neodomestic fiction both masculine and queer domesticities that "challenge and recycle conventional domestic structures."[42] I read a similar transhistorical significance in the iterative and adaptive tropes of regionalism that operate alongside and within the more "serious" genres, from realism to postmodernism. My exemplary texts embody a reconstructed or submerged regional aesthetic that advances a critical response to the changing geopolitical structures of postwar American society. The fault lines of postwar suburban development—including race, gender, and sexuality—reveal themselves as central to the literature's suburban settings and to the project to construct and define the nation.

Working across seventy-five years of literary and cultural history, my project will demonstrate how suburban fiction updates and revises long-standing regionalist approaches to the crossroads of the domestic and the foreign and to the intersection of local and more global concerns: the geographic containment of racial difference and the repressive construction of a common national identity; the charged insularity and normative force of the heterosexual domestic sphere; the immanent geographic inequalities of neoliberalism; the environmental threats posed by exurban sprawl; and the potential economic and political perils of our attachment to the cultural ideal of the single-family home. Now that "[m]ore Americans reside in suburban landscapes than in inner cities and rural areas combined," the suburban nation-building project has come to fruition, and in a far from simple way.[43] As physical and conceptual sites, the suburbs provide a contested terrain for evolving U.S. demographics and shifting ideations of American identity, where an individual's desire for a secure, respectable house vies with a developer's quest for profits, and where cultural critics, literary writers, and urban planners explore the limits of regional discourse in the modern and contemporary period.[44]

Although it is true that the material reality of suburban standardization marks an end to U.S. regional distinction as it has been traditionally conceived, this does not mean that regional writing disappears, nor am I suggesting that standardization equates to global homogeneity. As Jon Teaford writes, "There is no 'one' suburbia, and there never has been."[45] Suburbs include residential subdivisions and industrial parks, working-class neighborhoods and wealthy enclaves, strip malls and vast gallerias. In part, my appeal to critical regionalism reflects this material reality of residential life in contemporary America. The urban planners Peter Calthorpe and William Fulton note that "most of us are citizens of a region—a large and multifaceted metropolitan area encompassing hundreds of places that we would traditionally think of as distinct and separate 'communities.'"[46] You may live in a suburban neighborhood but commute downtown or to an exurban industrial park for work. Your employer may have exclusively local ties but, more typically, businesses rely on metro-regional, national, and international networks. If you are not lucky enough to have restaurants or a movie theater within walking distance of your home, then you probably drive to yet another community for socializing and entertainment. This interwoven, multifaceted mode of living creates ripple effects within the economy and produces indirect costs for the environment.[47] As Calthorpe and Fulton continue, "Metropolitan life throughout the nation now rests on a new foundation of economic, ecological, and social patterns, all of which operate in unprecedented fashion at a regional scale."[48]

I read for the ways suburban literature embodies the interconnected scales of home, region, and nation, as well as the way the literature recasts the form and meaning of regionalism as a response to the complexities of postwar suburban nation building. Reichert Powell suggests that "to discuss region is inherently to draw connections, comparisons, articulations, and overlaps with other places, because that is what region is: a rhetoric that connects specific local sites to a variety of other kinds of place constructions of various scales and motives."[49] In the chapters that follow, I will consider how the literary texts inhabit or exemplify a reconstructed regional aesthetic, but I will also foreground regionalism as a methodology for exploring spatial and rhetorical "overlaps" in suburban fiction, as well as the contested patterns and fault lines that emerge. Judith Fetterley and Marjorie Pryse write, "As both a literary and a political discourse, regionalism . . . becomes the site of contestation over the meaning of region, one that reveals the ideological underpinnings of regionalization."[50] My project frames both suburban topography and suburban fiction as "site[s] of contestation." As a form of

regional writing, suburban fiction lays bare the power relations that
underlie domestic spatial formations and the national and international politics that make our patterns of residential living possible.
As Roger Keil maintains, the single-family, "one-story house has its
origins in the distinctive imperialist history of Britain's colonization
of India," and this history has been "kept alive as American consumerism was subsequently projected into the world with iconic
images of suburban bliss; that America was ready to follow up the
image with deeds was made clear whenever its armies put 'boots on
the ground' to safeguard the empire's global interests in defense of
the suburban dream at home."[51] As a method of literary and geopolitical analysis, regionalism clarifies the ways suburban narratives
expose supposedly "placeless" homes and neighborhoods as contested sites within a matrix of metro-regional, national, and transnational concerns.

Building on a tradition of scholarship, *Contested Terrain* argues
that suburban literature remains rooted in a conception of region as
"a mode of analysis, a vantage point . . . that provides a location for
critique and resistance," as Fetterley and Pryse contend, but this literature also adapts and reinvents this analytic mode in response to
evolving patterns of suburban and metro-regional development.[52]
Moreover, as an iteration of regional writing, suburban literature
corresponds with urban planning discourses and ecological narratives that elucidate the "regional scale" and global cost of suburban
living. From the beginning, as Lutz contends, regional writing took
as its subject the limning of geographic and social communities in
relation to "local and global concerns [that] were not opposed to,
but completely enmeshed in, literary aesthetics."[53] Read as regional
writing, suburban narratives reconstruct this "enmeshed" history of
the local, global, and literary in the context of modern and present-
day suburbia. As a national region, the suburbs invoke the dialectic contest between isolationism and imperialism and between the
domestic and the foreign at the scales of the single-family home,
the metropolitan region, and our suburban nation more broadly
conceived. As this study shows, suburban fiction offers a parable
of the private home as the apotheosis of Amy Kaplan's "manifest
domesticity": a revision of "the nation as home" for the postwar era,
"inextricable from the political, economic, and cultural movements

of empire."⁵⁴ Suburban nation building and suburban domesticity enact an ongoing process of inclusion and exclusion, an expansion and contraction that monopolize the residential landscape and remaps borders between the public and the private in accord with prevailing notions of security and vulnerability.⁵⁵ Across postwar U.S. literature, we read how suburbs are produced by local, national, and transnational politics, and in turn, how suburban spaces reproduce the disguised politics of geography.

In inviting us to read suburban narratives as heir to this U.S. regional tradition, I am also suggesting we rethink what it means to talk about regional writing in an era defined by what Neil Smith calls the "rhetorical spacelessness" of American imperialism. According to Smith, since 1945 the "American Empire [has] defined its power ... through the more abstract geography of the world market rather than through direct political control of territory."⁵⁶ The twenty-first century wars in Iraq (2003–2011) and Afghanistan (2001–2021) call into question the extent to which U.S. foreign policy actually relinquished the "direct political control of territory," but such a challenge would not diminish the importance of "abstract geography" to the United States' postwar ascension as a global power. The flow of capital, workers, and industrial pollution across intra- and international borders has obviated traditional notions of contiguous regions, reaping rewards for affluent and upper-middle-class Americans while mostly sequestering the indirect costs of suburban living and the expansion of metropolitan regions.

Indeed, if there were ever a territory constructed for the era of "rhetorical spacelessness," it would be suburbia as it has come to occupy the economic, political, and cultural landscapes of the United States. Globalization and suburbanization inspire similar fears of the placeless while repressing the politics of space for its "beneficiaries," and I would argue that such symmetry exists because the topography of suburban privatism now dominates our understanding of space.⁵⁷ Whether through the "exporting" of suburban-style habitation on U.S. military bases, or in America's de facto support of oil-rich totalitarian regimes, or in the global dissemination of fast-food culture, the politics of space that underwrite suburban sprawl connect the private homes in which most Americans live to a more complex geographic network than the façades of these homes would feign reveal.[58] Yet, such material and ideological repressions almost always hold out the possibility for a new kind of spatial "awakening." According to Lawrence Buell, "acts of writing and reading will likely involve simultaneous processes of environmental awakening—retrievals of physical environment from dormancy to salience—and of distortion, repression, forgetting, inattention."[59] Regionalism provides a literary and geopolitical discourse for unearthing these repressed sites, for shaking off our spatial amnesia and making room for a more complete purview of the places we inhabit and the future possibilities of our suburban nation.

To develop this line of thinking, *Contested Terrain* offers a diverse cross section of suburban literature published between two major housing crises: from the housing shortage and suburban boom after World War II through the housing bubble, defaults, and foreclosures that precipitated the Great Recession. More specifically, I examine suburban literature as a site where the meanings of home, region, and nation are contested. In some of the literary examples that follow, suburban homes and neighborhoods serve as the primary site of conflict, while in other cases they function as a countervailing force to impress upon readers how ideologies of privatism, domesticity, and national security adjust in relationship to the single-family household. The year 1945 provides an obvious starting point for such an inquiry: it marks the end of the war, the beginning of the Cold War and, in terms of domestic geopolitics, the escalation of suburban development and the increased involvement of the federal government in residential policy and planning. Beyond these well-documented details of U.S. urban history, the year 1945 also serves as a turning point in the history of American political and economic imperialism. According to Smith, the end of World War II inaugurated America's "second moment" of empire, a period that he sees as ending with the Gulf War in 1991.[60] Smith claims that "in the global map of the postwar world, different territories were now linked more by economic and political relations than by strictly physical territorial relations of distance, size, and location. A relational geography mediated by politics and economics superseded the absolute geography of the nation-building and colonial eras."[61] The precedence of "relational" over "absolute" geography collapses physical distances and helps to disguise the footprints of U.S. imperialism through the subtler pathways of global capitalism. In short, empire building through international markets allows for geopolitical control without the impropriety of colonial-era military occupation.

To be sure, America's rise as a global power has not proceeded unchallenged or unimpeded after World War II, nor has the government abstained from war and other military action when deemed beneficial to national interests. But as the abstract geography of the global market came to dominate the postwar era, and with the ascendancy of neoliberal economic policies in the 1970s and 1980s, the United States accumulated wealth and power at a scale few other countries could hope to equal. As David Harvey suggests, "uneven neoliberalization"—the ability of certain countries like the U.S. and U.K. to navigate the relational geography of global capitalism—tends "to increase social inequality and to expose the least fortunate elements in any society . . . to the chill winds of austerity and the dull fate of increasing marginalization."[62] This period of international power and economic prosperity made possible the domestic project of suburban nation building. The imperial politics of "rhetorical spacelessness" underwrite the expansion of suburban privatism across the country in the postwar era, not in the crude sense that the nation becomes a homogeneous collection of private empires, a "geography of nowhere," but rather in the way homes and neighborhoods disguise and repress the geopolitical networks that make suburban living possible.[63] What Smith labels the "second moment" of empire enables the rise of suburbia as a national region and the suburban home as the new geographic scale of national identity.

Although the Great Recession does not prove as tidy an endpoint, it does provide another threshold moment in American history, and certainly no one would argue it suffers from lack of political significance. The election of Barrack Obama in 2008, the country's first African American president, promised—even if it did not deliver—the end of neoliberal economic policies and the Bush Doctrine of foreign policy. Corporate interests continue to dictate political and economic policies, and the steady upward redistribution of wealth exacerbates income inequality, a process that escalated under President Donald J. Trump and promises to endure during the tenure of his anti-labor judicial appointees.[64] The literature that emerges in the wake of the Great Recession provides a moment to reflect on the neoliberal policies that took root in the 1970s, became the country's dominant ideology during Ronald Reagan's presidency, continued unabated throughout the 1990s, and came to ugly fruition as "naked class power" under Bush II.[65] In other words, as I discuss in the final chapter, the literature that takes on the recent housing crisis and the ensuing economic downturn suggests we have arrived at a pivotal moment from which to scrutinize the cultural ideal of the suburban home.

The following chapters are organized around such critical junctures and points of contention in the entwined history of residential politics and suburban literature in the United States: race, restrictive covenants, and residential rights; compulsory domesticity, "queer" desires, and national security in the Cold War era; the rise of neoliberalism and the emergence of the postmodern metropolis; New Urbanism and the call to remake suburbia for the new millennium; the housing crisis, Great Recession, and the so-called "end of the suburbs."[66] Part one of the study considers how literature positions the single-family home as a contested site within Cold War politics concerning race, sexuality, and national security. The first chapter examines two works of literature on either side of the 1948 Supreme Court decision *Shelley v. Kraemer*, which declared the enforcement of racial covenants unconstitutional. Considered the first U.S. novel to address race and suburbia, Sinclair Lewis's *Kingsblood Royal* (1947) stages a confrontation between Neil Kingsblood, who has recently learned his great-great-grandfather was Black, and his white neighbors in Sylvan Park. The novel skewers the purportedly sympathetic attitudes of upper-midwestern liberals toward racial equality, but beneath Lewis's trademark satire lies an incisive portrait of "whiteness" as the cornerstone of suburban nation building. In Lorraine Hansberry's *A Raisin in the Sun* (1959), though the suburban neighborhood remains offstage, the violence and politics of metro-regional residential segregation frame the play. While *Raisin* remains tightly focused on the blighted living conditions available to African Africans on the South Side of Chicago, my reading situates the Youngers' move to Clybourne Park within the context of Black residential "pioneering" in the urban North. The play registers an inflection point that will come to exemplify the discursive history of race and suburbanization. From the pre- to the post-*Shelley* era, we read how a discourse of domestic security and (white) suburban citizenship adapts to changing demographic trends.

Chapter two considers how formal and informal networks of surveillance enable the disciplining of queer desires as a localized response to threats of national security in Patricia Highsmith's *The Price of Salt* (1952) and Richard Yates's *Revolutionary Road* (1961). In the latter, Yates invokes clichés about suburban provincialism that expose Frank Wheeler's feckless nature, but these banalities ultimately make way for the novel's more thoroughgoing exploration of the suburbs as a regulatory terrain. To elaborate on this claim, I redirect our attention to the novel's two sacrificial and "maladjusted" characters: April Wheeler, who rebels against the feminine mystique of marriage and motherhood, and the institutionalized John Givings, whom I suggest the novel positions as a "queer" figure, exiled from the consumer capitalism of modern suburbia and, thus, a threat to national security. In Highsmith's novel, the love affair between Therese Belivet, a set designer and store clerk, and Carol Aird, an elegant suburban housewife, challenges the Cold War ideal of heteronormative domesticity. Highsmith sends her lovers on the road where they discover temporary spaces of respite—the car, cafés, bars, hotels—from the insular, gendered-realms of the postwar suburban home. As the expression of a desire to escape one's provincial setting, their road trip offers a queer reenactment of a familiar regionalist trope, even as the novel remains hyperaware of public prohibitions against "subversive" same-sex desire. Although this chapter's tight focus on domesticity may seem oblique to the project's interest in the metro-regional scale of exurban sprawl, I argue that the suburban home as a regulatory domain is central to the project of building and defining the postwar nation.

Part two considers the impact of neoliberal policies on suburban nation building as the country transitions to the post–Cold War era. In the third chapter, I explore the complicated, arguably ongoing transformation from the modern to the postmodern metropolis that coincided with the rise of neoliberalism in the 1970s and 1980s.

There is a certain symmetry between suburban privatism and the emphasis on privatization at the core of neoliberal ideology, and in part, this chapter considers how the rapid exurban sprawl of this era serves as a domestic counterpart to the international propagation of neoliberalism.[67] The main focus of chapter three, however, is the tension between the modern and postmodern metropolis and, more specifically, the ways Don DeLillo's *White Noise* (1985) and Jonathan Franzen's *The Twenty-Seventh City* (1988) engage with evolving residential, metro-regional, and national geographies. Both novels attend to the regional complexity of conurbation at various geographic scales, from suburban homes and neighborhoods to the seemingly borderless environments threatened by airborne toxins. Although *White Noise* renders more adeptly the fluid boundaries of postmodern geography, *The Twenty-Seventh City* does capture the apparent inevitability of neoliberalism and the way it exploits existing racial divides, undermines collective action, and promotes uneven geographic development, even as the novel itself evinces a nostalgia for modern, map-able regions. While DeLillo and Franzen might bristle at the label "regional writing," my analysis uncovers a submerged regional aesthetic at work in their varied attempts to limn the shifting geopolitical structures of the postmodern metropolis—an aesthetic attunement to place that usefully recalibrates regionalism's traditional topographic and discursive terrain.

The fourth chapter also addresses a transitional space, in this case the threshold of the post–Cold War era. Jeffrey Eugenides's *The Virgin Suicides* (1993) provides an exemplary case study for the ways literature casts suburban neighborhoods as nodal points for regional, national, and even international concerns as the twentieth century draws to a close. Set in 1970s suburban Detroit, the story of the Lisbon sisters' demise is narrated in retrospect by the young boys who, now middle-aged men, cleave nostalgically to their childhood neighborhood and the events that transpired between Cecilia Lisbon's first suicide attempt and the suicides of her sisters. Although rarely an affect associated with "serious" suburban fiction, nostalgia is a familiar trope of regionalism that Eugenides works within and against to expand the narrative's historical and geographical terrain. The novel continually pushes us back in time and pulls us into the contemporary moment of the novel's production in the early 1990s, transforming the 1970s into a crossroad for the novel's retrospective analysis of postwar suburban domesticity. Taking this broader historical context into account, I argue that the narrators' wistful focus on the Lisbon family and home evolves into a meditation on isolation, containment, and the ideological privileging of suburban domesticity. The novel positions the reader to "read regionally" across the scope of postwar twentieth-century urban development and to anticipate questions of sustainability and suburban living that will preoccupy the early twenty-first century.

The final part of Contested Terrain weighs literary attempts to represent suburban development in the new millennium and efforts to respond, however tentatively, to the housing crisis and Great Recession. Chapter five examines how literary narratives might establish a mode of thinking about suburban regionalism and domestic nation building in the early twenty-first century, at a time when New Urbanism was in vogue and something of a popular groundswell existed around the ideas of smart growth and sustainable planning. Antipathy toward suburbia may be as old as suburbanization, but at the turn of the century, a desire on the part of both residents and planners to rein in sprawl coincided with the realization that, according to Calthorpe and Fulton, "We [were] at a turning point in the life of metropolitan America. We [had] outgrown the old suburban model."[68] This chapter principally addresses Chang-rae Lee's Aloft (2004) and Richard Ford's The Lay of the Land (2006). Although working at different registers, both novels respond to the spatial effects of residential sprawl, domestic privatism, and the suburb as a symptomatic fact of twenty-first century U.S. life. They display an attention to the evolving patterns and indirect costs of residential development, and they demonstrate a need for a more sustainable scale of living. I am particularly interested in how these novels navigate suburbia's changing demographics and the shifting signifiers of race, class, and place across a more heterogeneous (if still segregated) suburban nation. In Aloft and Lay of the Land, the suburbs emerge as a contested, "transnational" region for renewed debates about the domestic and the foreign.

The concluding chapter begins with a layperson's introduction to the 2008 housing crisis that precipitated the Great Recession before turning to Patrick Flanery's *Fallen Land* (2013) and Jung Yun's *Shelter* (2016). Each novel explores the fissures and disrupted links among suburban homeownership, upward class mobility, and national ideas about democracy and freedom. We can read these family dramas, in which strained relationships and acts of violence figure prominently, as stand-ins for a more global rift that disarticulates homeownership from domestic stability and national security. In complementary ways, *Shelter* and *Fallen Land* adopt a regional aesthetic that harkens back to and critiques nineteenth-century ideas about the moral influence of architecture and design. The housing crisis provides an occasion for Yun and Flanery to reflect on and update literary approaches to the suburb as region and the fault lines of suburban nation building, including the isolationism and violence of the domestic sphere, the legacy of racial containment, and the environmental imperialism of suburban sprawl.

Collectively, the following chapters examine how postwar suburban development has reshaped metropolitan regions across the country under the cover of political, geographic, and economic inevitability. The indirect costs of these residential neighborhoods have been obfuscated and naturalized by decades of increased privatization, racial segregation, the federal subsidizing of the single-family home, and the presumed homology between suburbia and middle-class values. Considering the suburbs as a noncontiguous, national region allows us to rethink Dainotto's skeptical query: "Are not regions, quite literally, a translation of 'central' desires into an imagined periphery?"[69] The suburbs mark the translation of a once peripheral desire for "country living" into an imagined, national totality. Since World War II, suburban nation building has translated narratives of American exceptionalism, self-determination, and democratic values into a spatial matrix of houses and subdivisions in sprawling municipalities built to repress the connections between the local and the global, between the places we live in and the world at large.

Read as the heir to a U.S. tradition of regional writing, as works attuned to the complexity and interconnectedness of place, suburban literature can offset this geopolitical amnesia. Francesco Loriggio argues that "once we admit that worlds are plural and coexist, however much they may encroach on one another, we also admit that the question of what regionalist fiction is becomes not a secondary question, but very nearly the question of what fiction is."[70] In the era between World War II and the Great Recession, in which suburbia dominates U.S. residential geography, politics, and culture, suburban fiction seems precisely the place to look in response to that question. In the analyses that follow, I intend to show how suburban narratives renew, destabilize, and expand our understanding of region—as a geographic site for nation building and as "a location for critique and resistance"—and regional writing from the postwar era to the twenty-first century.

An uncertain future of housing crises and economic recessions, persistent environmental degradation, and the existential threat of global pandemics may eventually precipitate the end of the suburbs, but until then, we cannot put the genie of metro-regional sprawl back in the bottle. We need to work with the environments that we have and conceive new understandings of space. Literary narratives have a role to play in this process. *Contested Terrain* spotlights a set of cultural texts that invite us to read regionally, to attend to the ongoing negotiations between the domestic and the foreign, and to recognize the political, cultural, and geographic forces that have transformed once peripheral suburbs into a national region. Acts of writing and reading offer possibilities for a new spatial awareness that, in turn, can help us reimagine the enduring importance of place in a seemingly placeless global culture.

PART I

Cold War Battle Lines and Prohibitions

(1940s–1960s)

1

Moving Out, Moving In

Race, Residential Rights, and Domestic Security

I N FEBRUARY 1945, the popular magazine *House & Garden* published a special issue dedicated to the topic of "Building." A few years earlier, during the initial days of America's involvement in World War II, the magazine had dissuaded readers from taking on new projects and, instead, advocated for the dutiful conservation of resources. The pages of *House & Garden* abounded with ads and articles connecting democratic values—private property, freedom, self-reliance—to the war effort. In September 1942, for example, the publishers ran an ad for Celotex Building Products promoting the home as the domestic frontline. The ad opposes a frowning Uncle Sam, hand raised to halt "the building of a new home (unless it is a war necessity)," with a smiling Uncle Sam who "says YES! — To keeping your home in good repair and up-to-date."[1] The company encourages homeowners to repair roofs, add insulation, and transform attics into additional bedrooms and to send away for a free copy of the "American Home-Owners Wartime Guide." In the August 1942 issue, *House & Garden* ran a counter-advertising campaign by May Oil Heating Equipment. With a red "X" scrawled across the image, the "Ad. Dept" is instructed to "kill this ad" because the "plant [is] 100% on war work!" Homeowners are encouraged to defer the dream of purchasing "fine May products" until "the war is won!"[2] The ad typifies what Horkheimer and Adorno observed about wartime industry and consumer culture more broadly, namely that "commodities which can no longer be supplied continue to be advertised merely as a display of industrial power."[3] Throughout the war, such displays aligned with the magazine's promotion of a suburban, do-it-yourself mindset, conflating democratic citizenship and domestic security in ways that companies were eager to capitalize on.[4]

As early as 1944, however, the emphasis on austerity yields to a wave of patriotic spending, and *House & Garden* is not alone in driving the discourse. In January 1944, *House Beautiful* declares, "[Our soldiers] are fighting so that we may live with our loved ones, in surroundings as comfortable and beautiful as those shown on these six pages, in a society where the economic and political values make such a life possible."[5] The editor, Elizabeth Gordon, does the work of mapping the superiority of American economic and political values onto a set of architectural designs for mini-mansions, complete with sketches for a servant's room over the garage. By January 1945, the magazine offers a more modest version of the American postwar suburban dream—what Dolores Hayden has referred to as "a triple dream, house plus land plus community."[6] In the article "A Proper Dream House: For Any Veteran," a smaller headline assures readers that "A Good Small House Can Be a Private Kingdom in Itself," and the caption under the enclosed architectural plan advises "[v]eterans who wish to buy or build their own homes [to] apply for a loan under the 'G. I. Bill of Rights.'"[7] Writing for the magazine, Irene Moore notes, "This skillfully landscaped, two-bedroom home has great meaning for a veteran—or for any man—who despairs of achieving the good life on an average [quarter-acre] suburban lot."[8] Federally subsidized "private kingdoms" serve as the guarantees of an expanding white middle class, but they are also the spoils of war: a symbol of "the American ideal of good living," Moore continues, "one of the ideals these veterans have fought for."[9]

The February 1945 "Building" issue of *House & Garden*, though, offers the most unapologetic hymn to suburban nation building. In the provocative article, "Looking Forward," the editors advise readers to look to the future by attending to the sensibilities of the home:

> It would be a healthy thing if all of us, before we begin our
> postwar planning, would take time out to check our position

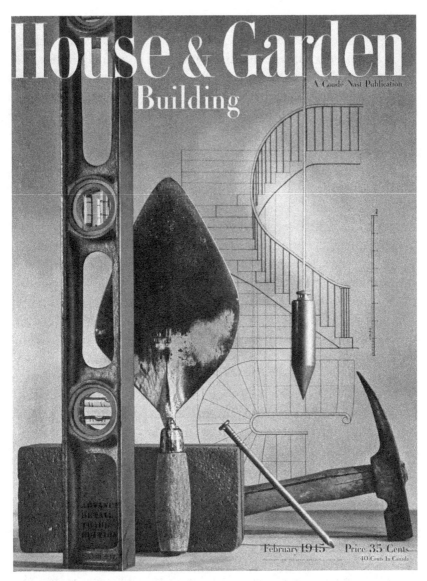

Suburban nation building: *House & Garden*, February 1945. Rolf Tietgens, *House & Garden* © Condé Nast.

and see whether we are facing forward or backward. Do you visualize your new house as a sort of formal façade behind which you will arrange the pattern of your daily life as best you can? Or do you feel that a carefully considered solution of your individual problem will suggest the form your house should take? Will your house be built to fit you, or will you be trimmed to fit a house? To a much greater degree than many of us realize, it's up to us what kind of house we'll get.[10]

The house that "fit[s] you" also secures your fitness as an individual. The "Building" issue invites you to contemplate whether your home is "too small" and provides readers with helpful plans for constructing new additions and "stretching" a kitchen to suit the proper, forward-looking home and family.[11] The magazine facilitates the conflation of industry, consumerism, politics, and the domestic sphere in which, as Horkheimer and Adorno have observed, "the images and texts of advertisements are, at a cursory glance, hardly distinguishable from the editorial section."[12] In this same issue, an ad for GE's "All Electric Kitchen," specifically designed for "After-Victory Homes," juxtaposes the remodeled kitchen with scenes of family togetherness. Commentary about "gadget-blessed" appliances "designed for the future" shares space with a note on the son's military service—"Next to Charlie, our G.E.'s the best soldier in the family"—and the ad concludes with a reminder to tune in to "The G-E House Party" weekdays on CBS.[13] In other words, although V-E Day was still three months away, the discourse had turned decidedly postwar, synergized across print and television, as advertisers locate suburban homeownership within the discourse of national identity and future prosperity.

To state the obvious, what *House & Garden*, *House Beautiful*, and other magazines of their ilk did not explicitly promote was the racial exclusivity of this vision. While architectural plans, building projects, and household renovations could be scaled to accommodate more modest budgets, they could not accommodate or imagine racially inclusive residential communities. In magazines from the 1940s, "African Americans were nearly always depicted in inferior or service positions," as adjuncts to the consumer goods that signify white, suburban, middle-class citizenship.[14] On the ground, beyond the world of magazine images, racial covenants restricting property ownership had been a fact of urban and suburban development since the late-nineteenth century, though as Carol Rose and Richard Brooks point out, "these racialized 'deed restrictions' and 'covenants' became much more prevalent all over the country after the turn of the twentieth century, at a time when the whole country was urbanizing rapidly and African Americans in particular were moving out of the rural South and into major cities."[15] Deeds for houses in the Levittown development on Long Island, New York—a leader in providing homes for World War II veterans and the standard-bearer for the initial wave of postwar suburbanization—contained a clause restricting homeownership and residency to "members of the Caucasian race," making an exception only for "the employment and maintenance of other than Caucasian domestic servants."[16] Clarifying his position during an interview with the *Saturday Evening Post*, William Levitt notoriously noted that "if we sell one house to a Negro family, then ninety to ninety-five per cent of our white customers will not buy into the community. That is their attitude, not ours. We did not create it, and we cannot cure it. As a company, our position is simply this: we can solve a housing problem, or we can try to solve a racial problem. But we cannot combine the two."[17] Although by the early 1950s, suburbs such as Ronek Park, a development on Long Island, were available to African Americans, options were decidedly constrained.[18] Such material restrictions, however, did not limit the desire among African Americans to imagine themselves into the era of postwar national prosperity, and the single-family, suburban house as a symbol of stability, autonomy, and refuge crossed class and racial lines.[19]

Ann Petry cleverly addresses this point in *The Street* (1946). Although scholars have read Petry's debut novel in terms of its urban naturalism and gothic undertones, *The Street* also contains, early in the text, a crucial flashback to Connecticut where Lutie Johnson had previously worked as a domestic servant for the Chandler family.[20] The flashback is triggered by an advertisement for kitchen products and design. The first thing Lutie notices about the ad is "a girl with incredible blond hair" standing next to a "smiling man in a navy uniform."[21] The centerpiece of the image is "a kitchen sink . . . whose white porcelain surface gleamed under the train lights. The faucets looked like silver" (28). Lutie concludes that "[i]t was . . . a miracle of a kitchen. Completely different from the kitchen of the 116th Street apartment she had moved into just two weeks ago. But almost exactly like the one she had worked in in Connecticut" (28). Set in 1944, *The Street* stages a spatial conflict between two distinct versions of home: the claustrophobic 116th Street apartment in Harlem, where Lutie currently lives with her son, and the spacious, private house in Lyme, Connecticut, for which the kitchen ad serves as a metonym. Although, at first, Lutie struggles with being away from her husband, her son, and their "small frame house" in Jamaica, Queens (29), she eventually becomes enthralled with the Chandlers and their conversations about "new markets" and their presumptuous desire to become "'filthy' rich" (43). As Petry writes, "she came more and more under the influence of their philosophy" and, after a while, only returned to her home in Queens every other month (44).

Print media plays an important complementary role in conscripting Lutie to the Chandler "philosophy" and their suburban way of life. "For in those two years with the Chandlers she had learned all about Country Living. She learned about it from the pages of the fat sleek magazines Mrs. Chandler subscribed for and never read. *Vogue, Town and Country, Harper's Bazaar, House and Garden, House Beautiful*" (50). Lutie is a complex and sympathetic character because she is acutely aware of her deterministic urban environment, but here Petry invites readers to see how an ideology of "Country Living" sets the terms for Lutie's urban tragedy. *The Street* perceptively captures the deleterious effects of an incipient postwar consensus on its working-class, Black protagonist, a consensus that designates the suburban home and nuclear family as the primary markers of a forward-looking national identity. Although it would have been unavailable to Lutie—the magazine did not debut until fall 1945—*Ebony* would do much the same to promote "a vision of suburban life that many middle-class African Americans could appreciate and to which they might aspire."[22] In the 1940s and 1950s, the United States embraced suburban nation building for its white citizenry—economically through federal loan programs and government redlining practices; on the ground through real estate development, racial covenants, and neighborhood associations;

and culturally through television, film, and advertising—that, in turn, forged the links among personal worth, national identity, and the geographic scale of the single-family home.

Now, to note that overtly racist policies and practices distinguished the initial era of postwar suburbanization is a truism, not an argument. Building on that historical reality, this chapter explores how 1940s and 1950s literature addresses the legacy of white supremacy at this pivotal moment of residential development, revealing the way whiteness grounds the ideology of the forward-looking nation and establishes the terms for democratic citizenship and domestic security. The near-universal promotion and underwriting of suburban living alongside the existence of restrictive racial covenants ensured the single-family home would emerge as the latest battle line on which the U.S. would contest ideas about race, citizenship, and residential rights. To locate these concerns more specifically, this chapter reads Sinclair Lewis's *Kingsblood Royal* (1947) and Lorraine Hansberry's *A Raisin in the Sun* (1959) as exemplars of a regionalist response to the complex, interconnected patterns of metropolitan residential development and the geographic containment of racial difference in midcentury America. As Fetterley and Pryse have argued in response to nineteenth- and early-twentieth-century American literature, "Regionalism becomes a site where questions of race and questions of gender find mutual and dynamic articulation for both white writers and writers of color," adding that regionalism "also reveals whiteness itself to be a standpoint constructed against the 'otherness' of characters."[23] This chapter argues that Lewis and Hansberry reinvent and reconstruct a regionalist critique of "whiteness" as immanent to the forward-looking nation at a critical juncture in the history of residential politics.

Notably, *Kingsblood Royal* and *A Raisin in the Sun* were published on either side of the landmark Supreme Court decision *Shelley v. Kraemer* (1948), which resolved that racial covenants, when enforced by the state, violate the Equal Protection Clause of the Fourteenth Amendment. The particulars of this case and the responses to the decision are salient to this inquiry and warrant a brief account. The lawsuit pitted the Shelleys, an African American family who had purchased a house in St. Louis, Missouri, in 1945, against their white neighbors. Unbeknownst to the Shelleys, the house was subject to a covenant, dating back to 1911, that prevented "the occupancy as owners or tenants of any portion of said property for resident or other purpose by people of the Negro or Mongolian Race."[24] The lower courts had sided with the respondents, represented by Louis Kraemer, claiming that, as a private arrangement among the neighborhood residents, the covenant did not constitute an infringement upon federal rights. While the Supreme Court agreed that private individuals may accept and voluntarily enter into racially restrictive agreements, the justices concluded that judicial action to uphold such covenants "bears the clear and unmistakable imprimatur of the State" and, therefore, represents a discriminatory act in defiance of the right to equal protection. In his unanimous opinion, Chief Justice Fred Vinson writes, "We have noted that freedom from discrimination by the States in the enjoyment of property rights was among the basic objectives sought to be effectuated by the framers of the Fourteenth Amendment. That such discrimination has occurred in these cases is clear. Because of the race or color of these petitioners, they have been denied rights of ownership or occupancy enjoyed as a matter of course by other citizens of different race or color."[25]

The response among lawyers and legal scholars was generally positive, but Brooks and Rose note that "[w]hether favorably disposed to the decision or not, commentators overlapped in two forecasts of things to come: that white homeowners would try to evade the decision and keep their neighborhoods white, and that the real estate industry would try to accommodate them."[26] In the popular press, both sides of the divide over property rights and citizenship were swift to make their voices heard. On May 15, 1948, the editors at the *Chicago Defender* hailed the decision against racial covenants as a civil rights triumph for African Americans and a great leap forward toward the goal of "full citizenship for all Americans," but their forecast that the Court "[had] laid the ground work for the building of interracial peace and goodwill" overestimated the real-world impact of the legal decision.[27] Indeed, in an article published just one day earlier, writers at *U.S. News & World Report* fretted over property values and ginned up grassroots resistance. "Real Estate: Exclusive . . . Restricted" outlines ways to preserve the racial homogeneity of neighborhoods without running afoul of the

Shelley decision. In addition to instituting "occupancy standards" and encouraging "the threat of damage suits" against neighbors who violate "the covenant's terms," the article lists several forms of "social" and "financial" pressure that can be applied to maintain a neighborhood's all-white population, including "methods of harassment."[28] Such practices were consistent across all levels of society, from working-class suburbs to more exclusive enclaves.[29]

Kingsblood Royal examines this intersection of economic class and the color line in the mid-1940s, and Lewis frequently references racial exclusivity in the vernacular of social constraint: "social exile," "social fences," "social death," and "social prejudice."[30] The novel tells the story of Neil Kingsblood, a former Army captain and up-and-coming cashier at Second National Bank who, while researching his genealogy, discovers that his mother's great-great-grandfather, Xavier Pic, was a "full-blooded Negro" (64). Although initially dismayed by the realization that he is 1/32 Black and his daughter, the "golden Biddy," 1/64 Black (65), Neil eventually warms to the idea that he is something other than "a one-hundred per cent. normal, white, Protestant, male, middle-class, efficient, golf-loving, bound-to-succeed, wife-pampering, Scotch-English Midwestern American" (43). The rest of the white community in Grand Republic, Minnesota is not as keen to accept Neil's biracial identity, and the novel ends with a violent confrontation and the family's expulsion from the exclusive suburb of Sylvan Park.

Trading satire and genealogical intrigue for midcentury urban realism, Hansberry's *Raisin in the Sun* also examines the insidious nature of purportedly "social" tactics to preserve homogeneous neighborhoods and the rights of white citizens to control their communities. Hansberry brings both personal history and a record of political activism to the topic of residential segregation. As a child, her family was harassed and temporarily driven from their home in a predominantly white neighborhood; as an adult in the early 1950s, working for Paul Robeson's progressive newspaper *Freedom*, she wrote articles about the housing crisis for minority populations, slum clearance policies, and discriminatory lending practices.[31] The first Broadway play written by an African American woman, *Raisin* reflects a continuation of Hansberry's political commitments. Set on the South Side of Chicago "between World War II and the present," the play explores how a rural, pre–Great Migration conception of home inspired the postwar era of residential pioneering by African Americans living in northern cities.[32] Lena "Mama" Younger's desire to secure "a nice house" and "a yard with a little patch of dirt" must withstand the social and financial pressure leveraged by the Clybourne Park Improvement Association (92). While Neil Kingsblood and his family eventually succumb to pressure and abandon Sylvan Park, the Youngers decide to move to Clybourne Park and begin the arduous task of staking a claim to improved domestic living in a hostile, predominantly white space. Taken together, *Kingsblood Royal* and *Raisin in the Sun* offer a primer on the postwar suburban house as both a transracial cultural ideal of domestic stability and the frontline in an ongoing battle for white supremacy and residential rights. These two works exhibit a regional aesthetic that frames racial containment as central to the topography of suburbia and to the construction, both materially and ideologically, of the forward-looking, postwar nation. Read as works of critical regionalism, as responses to the complex geopolitics of place, these literary texts expose the legal and extralegal means used to enshrine a suburban vision of domesticity as the inalienable right of white citizenship. From the fashionable Sylvan Park to the working-class Clybourne Park, Lewis and Hansberry detail the pernicious adaptability of this vision across the 1940s and into the post-*Shelley* era.

Land of the Noble Free

To begin at the end: *Kingsblood Royal* closes with an armed conflict and a forced eviction. As the police stand idly apart from the crowd, the Kingsbloods, aided by friends and allies from the African American neighborhood of Five Points, try to defend their home in Sylvan Park. Lewis sets the confrontation against an idyllic landscape:

> The background of suburban street could not have been more placid, with the branches in a gently moving screen across the cool lamplighted windows over the way. But against this background, the menace grew rapidly. Dozens and then scores of men and excited women filled the yards opposite, oozed into

> the street. Aggressive men pushed forward in the center, men
> whose killer faces were the more grotesque above their pert
> ties, their near-gentlemanly tweed jackets. (345)

That first sentence reads like a caption for a magazine photo: a
neighborhood in arcadian twilight. The repressed "menace" erupts
from within that tranquil scene, and Lewis depicts the threatening crowd as "a dark cataract of hate" set loose from their ties and
tweedy restraints (345). If *House Beautiful* figured suburbia and the
single-family home as the prototypical symbols of our "economic
and political values," as the territory the soldiers were fighting to
preserve, then *Kingsblood* intends to show readers what that war
looks like on the home front.

We can trace the origins of this violent clash to the novel's
opening pages. We are first introduced to Neil Kingsblood, Grand
Republic, and the "picture-window real-estate development called
Sylvan Park" through the detached and blinkered perspective of
some touring New Yorkers (6). The Blinghams—husband, wife,
daughter—seem preternaturally blind to their surroundings as the
narrator ironically draws the reader's attention to everything the
family fails to notice about the town, its architecture, and its inhabitants. Edward Watts reads this traveling family as an embodiment
of the colonial "Eastern gaze," casting the Midwest as "primitive
Other" and recalling the historical displacement of heterogeneous
populations by the Anglo-Saxon East.[33] Situating *Kingsblood* within
the context of Lewis's past work, Jennifer Delton argues that the
"obnoxious" views of the Blinghams "signify Lewis's suspicion
that his old critique of American provinciality had lost much of
its power by 1947," and that "[o]nly something as real, as raw, as
dangerous as the racial ideologies most white Americans still took
for granted" could hone that former line of criticism.[34] Indeed,
immediately after dropping the disengaged lens provided by the
Blinghams, Lewis turns to the problem of race and residential
development. The real estate developer Mr. William Stopple adver-
tises the Kingsbloods' suburb as the fulfillment of "the American
Way of Life," but he "privately advises [clients] that Sylvan Park is
just as free of Jews, Italians, Negroes, and the exasperatingly poor
as it is of noise, mosquitoes, and rectangularity of streets" (10). The

links among single-family homes, economic prosperity, and racial exclusivity—including a reminder about who counts as "white" at this historical moment—announce the novel's focus, and the rest of the narrative arcs inevitably toward that climactic confrontation and forced eviction.

Lewis also scales these metro-regional concerns to the private realm where Neil and Vestal Kingsblood are "having an amount of servant trouble that seemed improbable with so tolerant a couple" (7). Sylvan Park's restrictive covenant, as in Levittown, does not extend to domestic servants, and the Kingsbloods employ "a young lady of color," Belfreda Gray, as a live-in maid. A peculiar paranoia characterizes the household, leaving Neil and Vestal worried that Belfreda, and the Black race more generally, are "laughing at them" (26). Racial epithets trip easily off their tongues, and Neil's interactions with Belfreda are informed by racist beliefs—fostered over a lifetime, polished in the military—and a familiar exoticism of racial difference. Neil's uncertain fascination with Belfreda will prove a trial run for his enthrallment with Sophie Conrad, a nurse from Five Points to whom he ascribes "the tempting strangeness of a mythical Africa" (149). Yet early in the narrative, his belief that Blacks "don't quite belong to the same human race" parries his unspoken attraction to the domestic help (14). For good measure, Vestal shares a similar frisson when faced with the "animal beauty" of Belfreda's beau, Borus Bugdoll, anticipating the ambivalence she will come to feel for her biracial husband (25). Neil's obsession over their "servant trouble" leads to a restless night remembering the irreverent "black roustabouts in uniform in Italy" and a childhood classmate, Emerson Woolcape, who looked white but confessed to being "part Negro," a fact that overshadows all his other attributes: "Still and all, when you knew that, you *thought* of him as being black" (16).[35]

Given the heavy-handed introduction to the Kingsblood family and the general lack of subtlety on matters of race, it is not surprising that *Kingsblood Royal* fared poorly with critics at the time of its publication. In comparison to Lewis's superb novels of the 1920s, which had earned him a Nobel Prize, *Kingsblood* was considered subliterary, and reviewers assailed the novel's inauthentic characters, unbelievable story line, and thematic simplicity.[36] In his 1948 review for *Commentary*, James Baldwin declared it "a new low, even for the American liberal middlebrow," and he dismissed it as "an ill-tempered, tasteless, condescending novel."[37] More recently, however, critics have read *Kingsblood* as a significant entry in the tradition of the "passing novel" and as a representative of "*transracial* movement" wherein a character adopts "a given racial identity, regardless of whether or not that identity represents the character's 'real' racial classification."[38] In other words, even though his ability to "try on" Black identity signifies his "privileged position," as Andrea Newlyn explains, "Neil's transracial crossing and embodiment nevertheless also challenge dominant notions of racial identity as fixed, stable, or innate categories and indentificatory positions."[39] In a complementary fashion, Delton argues that the novel "tied an existing critique of American society to notions of whiteness and blackness and sin and salvation," and that "Lewis did in the end overturn the traditional assumption of black sin and white salvation."[40] In response to the novel's purportedly unbelievable story line, Edward Dauterich draws on historical records and census data to show how Lewis's Grand Republic offers a realistic portrait of a "sundown town," likely modeled on Duluth, Minnesota, where three African Americans had been lynched in 1920.[41]

Whether Lewis had the Duluth lynching in mind or not, his novel does adeptly capture the treacherous nature of racism masquerading as progressive liberalism in northern cities. In a particularly extraordinary sequence, Lewis outlines an "American Credo" about African Americans, forged by the midwestern "standardbearers of democracy" (193). In compact, staccato paragraphs, he dissects racist assumptions about Black intellect, industry, and sexuality as supported by spurious science and promoted under the banners of eugenics and ethnography. As Neil Kingsblood surveys the residents gathered at the Sylvan Park Tennis Club, he realizes that the most treacherous sentiments were those that passed as sympathetic: "while I'm all for equal rights and maybe social equality some day for you darkies, when the time is right, can't you see that *now isn't the time for it?*" (198). When it was simply a matter of ending the lynching epidemic, everyone could agree on civil rights, but "[n]ow, [Negroes] were demanding every human right, and whites who were self-admiringly willing to give them a dish of cold potatoes were sometimes unwilling to give them room at the workbench and the polling booth" (328). Such insidious sentiments raise questions that strike at the heart of democratic citizenship: who counts as an American, and who may avail themselves of the rights of citizenship?[42]

Taken as a whole, then, the more contemporary critical response to Lewis's novel suggests that, despite its occasionally leaden rhetoric and drift toward caricature, *Kingsblood Royal* offers a lacerating, even radical critique of racism and upper-midwestern liberalism in the 1940s, one that warrants further attention for its insights into identity and citizenship. I want to add to this reevaluation by examining *Kingsblood* as an example of regional writing that locates and critiques whiteness as the cornerstone of postwar suburban nation building. Lewis's novel embodies a regional interest in the crossroads of the domestic and the foreign where blackness figures as a threat to white domestic tranquility and, by extension, national security. We see this quite clearly as the narrative draws to a close. Neil expresses frustration at his family's inability to "admit that they were, by the very definitions they had all maintained, Negroes," and he derides "the white mythology about the delights of exclusive clubs and polite churches and invitations to dull houses," customs and practices that inform notions of "good society" from Sylvan Park to more elite enclaves (323). *Kingsblood Royal* takes aim at this "white mythology" of suburban culture and the way it had come to define and codify citizenship in the postwar era. Just as the novel destabilizes traditional assumptions about racial identity, it also unsettles our assumptions about genre and the supposed provincialism of midwestern "local color." Lewis's narrative frames the suburbs as an emergent national region defined by its political, cultural, and economic investment in whiteness as constructed against a foreign "otherness."

To develop this idea, I want to focus on three contested patterns pertaining to race and place in the novel: racial segregation and displacement (both residential and economic); the domestic realm as sanctuary and quarantine; and social and legal clashes to preserve white residential rights at the expense of Black domestic security. In an effort to understand his newfound Black identity, Neil seeks out the counsel of Reverend Brewster, whose own path from Columbia and Harvard to Grand Republic allows Lewis to gloss the city's patterns of racial succession. Dr. Brewster's first "church had been a shanty in Swede Hollow," Lewis writes.

> In his dozen years here he had seen the Negro island expand from three or four hundred to two thousand; had seen over-timid or over-bumptious dark immigrants from the Carolinas and Texas turn into citizens; . . . Swede Hollow became over-crowded with Finns and Poles and Scandinavians; rents were grossly raised (by favorite customers of the Second National Bank); and Dr. Brewster led his own flock and most of the other Negroes from Swede Hollow to the brick-fields and swamps where the Five Points was to rise. (96)

The novel details familiar lending practices and blockbusting techniques that force African Americans into less desirable areas, and the reference to the Second National Bank indirectly implicates Neil in the formation of the neighborhood. Five Points exists as a temporary stronghold within patterns of racial displacement, but Lewis notes the requisite transformation of this "dark" population "into citizens," underscoring the contested nature of the term for Black residents.

Once in Five Points, Neil is initially struck by the uncanny nature of the shopping district, a "familiar huddle" of storefronts, so similar to those found in "that Anglo-Saxon city, Grand Republic," rendered unfamiliar by the lack of a single "white face on the crowded sidewalk" (92). He notes the vaguely threatening appearance of the inhabitants, the foreign sounding "dialect from the Deep South," and a residential street where "behind neat stucco cottages, with tidy small lawns, there was such a diminutive jungle slum as he had not known could exist in the enlightened Northern States" (92). As Neil wrestles with the possibility of "turning black" (92), especially if it would mean relocating his family to Five Points, he determines, "The street was more alien . . . than Italy in wartime, and it seemed to him that every dusky face, every rickety wall, hated him and would always hate him, and he might as well go home" (93). Yet, as a harbinger of Neil's eventual transracial crossing, this sense of the un-American and "alien" gives way to recognition. Approaching Ebenezer Baptist Church, Dr. Brewster's congregants dispel his initial perception of the neighborhood: "he was among people who, though their faces were more beloved of the sun, were like any other group of middle-class church-going Americans" (93). For the moment, at least, markers of class and religion assuage the sense that Neil has tripped behind enemy lines.

Serving as Neil's liaisons in Five Points, Emerson Woolcape—the classmate who looked white but was not—and his parents, John and Mary, initiate him into "race-talks": sessions where members of the community, free of the white gaze, are at liberty to discuss what it means to live Black in the purportedly progressive North. One of the most ardent speakers is Clem Brazenstar, a southerner working for the Urban League who challenges Neil's assumptions about the lack of racial violence in the North. He calls attention to "the job-ceiling" that keeps African Americans under-employed or displaced from the workforce and the methods of harassment they encounter in factories and at restaurants. Addressing Neil directly, Clem argues that "in this democratic Northern town, they don't lynch Negroes—not often—but they tell us every day that we're all diseased and filthy and criminal. And do they believe it? Hell, no! But they make themselves believe it and then they make other people believe it and so they get rid of us as rivals for the good jobs that they'd like themselves" (142–43). This charge lays bare the economic violence of exploitative labor practices and the social pressures that perpetuate inequality, but Clem also suggests how a commitment to the white mythology of democratic, middle-class citizenship coalesces around and defines itself against a willfully erroneous notion of the "diseased and filthy and criminal" Black population.

As Neil adjusts to his biracial identity, houses take on a more central role in the novel, on both sides of the color line. After Neil receives a promotion at work, Vestal begins planning for a new house. Victory over Japan has ended World War II and, as if heeding the advice of *House & Garden*, she has designs on a newly built "house that would then dignify their position" (161). Lewis writes that "while Vestal was properly glad that their friends would be coming home from the South Pacific, she confessed to an equal delight that now the manufacturers would turn from arms to unimaginable domestic treasures: plastic dressing-tables and crystal coffee-pots and automatic dish-washers" (162). Neil cannot fully embrace his wife's vision for the postwar consumer industrial complex, and he begins to bristle amidst the suburban comfort and security represented by his home, his job at the bank, his beautiful wife, and her desire to possess a new gas stove, a yearning so keen she channels Thomas Wolfe: "It's a jewel of a stove, a rose, an eagle, a Bedlington of a stove, a stone, a leaf, a door, and I love it more than I do virtue—at least, it's more practical" (162). Vestal's encomium to domestic consumerism may affirm that "the Model Kitchen . . . had replaced the buffalo and the log cabin as a symbol of America" (12), but beneath the apparent calm of the Kingsblood household, Neil entertains a "longing for the cool, humorous, devastating talk of Ash and Clem and Sophie" in Five Points (163).

Vestal's desire to design a proper "After-Victory Home" lies in stark contrast to the Woolcapes' house, which appears more like a hideout than a haven. Although John and Mary, who are both light-skinned, claim not to experience much discrimination in Grand Republic, that is partly due to their self-imposed house arrest, staying home evenings instead of risking unwelcome encounters. "Yes, we love our home," John says, "and here we're safe" (144). As the Woolcapes' son, Ryan, a sergeant in the Army, explains, the North has substituted "quarantine" for Jim Crow legislation (143). The Woolcapes' domestic refuge against the physical, social, and economic perils of Jim Crowism serves as a touchstone in Neil's efforts to understand race. Again invoking the comity of shared class proclivities, he determines that "[t]here was no reason why a man of average perception should have been astonished that the house of middle-class Negroes with ordinary good taste and neatness should be exactly like the house of any other middle-class Americans with ordinary taste and neatness" (107). The lack of a "voodoo altar" or "leopard skin" inside the Woolcape house forces Neil to acknowledge his racist assumptions (107), but his realization also suggests something more fundamental about race and the "middle-class" home in the postwar imaginary. Just as the Kingsblood house in Sylvan Park affirms and gives order to his sense of whiteness, Neil expects the Woolcape house to help him differentiate what it means to be Black, only to confront a kind of class determinism in matters of decorum that belies the supposed logic of the residential color line. Indeed, the repeated reference to the "middle-class" suggests that any imagined racial crossing depends upon an equally imaginary (and unlikely) lateral move in economic status. Neil, and perhaps Lewis himself, cannot fathom one without the other.

After Neil publicly announces he has "Negro blood," precipitating his social and economic ostracism, Lewis enacts the expected reversal: the Kingsblood cottage turns from sanctuary to quarantine amidst a call for cultural purity. Now that the war has ended, the returning veterans and the bluebloods of Sylvan Park redeploy their wartime rhetoric to preserving the integrity of their hometown. At the annual Federal Club holiday celebration, members lament the increasing presence of Blacks in the community and endorse more aggressive segregationist policies. One of the town luminaries, Major Rodney Aldwick, cites the scourge of "Negro agitators" (225) and "local traitors" (226), including Ryan Woolcape, Sophie Conrad, Reverend Brewster, and Clem Brazenstar, whom he misnames "Brazenstein" to inflect the anti-Semitic strains of his speech. In closing, Aldwick rouses the troops: "those of us who faced the enemy guns" will not feel at ease "until we are assured that you are going to preserve for us what we fought to preserve for you—the pure, clean, square-dealing, enterprising, freely-competitive America of the Founding Fathers!" (227). This already jarring speech is even more disturbing when cast alongside the contemporaneous jingoism in popular magazines like *House Beautiful*. As quoted, the editorial positioned U.S. soldiers as warriors fighting to ensure domestic tranquility and economic prosperity amidst America's "comfortable and beautiful" neighborhoods. By echoing such popular sentiments about cultural preservation and free enterprise in a speech otherwise committed to bellicose race-baiting—and delivered at the pointedly named Grand Republic Federal Club—Lewis reminds readers of the "pure, clean" white nationalism taking root in the suburbs of this forward-looking nation.

In the ensuing weeks, after Neil loses his job and the family is relegated to "a social concentration camp" (290), the house in Sylvan Park becomes a cathectic site in his racial crossing. In other words, in the face of the social and legal harassment precipitated by the public confession of his "blackness," Neil stakes his sense of identity and self-worth to the defense of the domestic realm. On separate occasions, the mayor of Grand Republic and the developer of

Sylvan Park each encourage the Kingsbloods to move. The mayor's direct provocation—"we don't want any of you niggers horning into decent white neighborhoods, corrupting the kids and frightening the women" (238)—contrasts with the developer's subtler attempts to encourage the family to relocate to the ethnically diverse neighborhood of Canoe Heights (239). This effort to evict the Kingsbloods is part of a broader effort in Grand Republic to drive the Black population back to the South. The Neighborhood Committee becomes the primary instrument of pressure and harassment in this crusade, citing the unfortunate "social prejudice" in Sylvan Park (303) and persistent fears about "lowering the social tone of the community" (304). Lewis shows how the end of the war and the return of U.S. veterans amplify the conflict over the residential color line:

> Sant Tabac [stop all Negro trouble, take action before any comes] . . . cannot be credited with all the discharges of Negroes in Grand Republic. The return of the white soldiers, the strikes, the conversion of factories from tanks to suspender buckles, and the general conviction, richly cultivated by the radio and the comic strip, that all Negroes are amusing but bungling fools, were greater elements, but all of them worked sweetly together to start the epidemic of firing Negro workers, which began on All Fools Day. (316)

Sant Tabac hopes to spur a reverse Great Migration, but what is most notable here is the synchronicity across political, economic, and social spectrums to intimidate the Black community. As the novel makes clear, neighborhood associations complement postwar transformations in industry, such as the conversions of factories and the "economic murder" of African Americans (315), while popular discourse (radio, comic strips) perpetuates racist stereotypes and provides ideological cover for racial displacement and material upheaval.

In turning his attention to the direct costs of the postwar suburban idyll for the non-white citizens of Grand Republic, Lewis continues to expand the scope of the novel's regional complexity. A lynching in the South sends tremors through Five Points, and as more African Americans are dismissed from their jobs, conflicts between the police and unemployed "street-corner gangs" erupt (318–19). Reluctantly, residents relocate to other cities, including Dr. Ash Davis, who sells his sleek modern house—a "revolt from all the Cape Cod and Tudor of Sylvan Park" (153)—at a fraction of its value. Just as a previous generation of African Americans had been forced from Swede Hollow into "the brick-fields and swamps" that would become Five Points, another forced migration is underway. As Ash and Nora Davis depart to seek their future in New York City, Dr. Davis realizes, "He was leaving not only his friends but the one place—in America—where, for a time, the whites had permitted him to pretend that he was a scientist and a responsible citizen" (326). This reflection delivers a triple critique: the peculiar irony of African American soldiers and civilians accepted abroad while living under Jim Crow at home; the novel's leitmotif of the "job ceiling" that prevents Dr. Davis from realizing his intellectual and economic potential; and the shifting definition of citizenship and its relationship to residential geography in the postwar era.

In Sylvan Park, where properties are covered by restrictive covenants, the Kingsbloods' domestic security is also imperiled. Nevertheless, Neil clings to the house as their lone place of refuge and the "extreme symbol of dignity and independence" (308), a sentiment that echoes popular discourse pertaining to suburban homeownership and proper citizenship. When threatened with legal action, Neil refuses to sell and, anticipating *Shelley v. Kraemer*, vows to bring a countersuit against "the whole business of restrictive covenants. We'll make 'em illegal" (336). Yet Neil's flirtation with political activism is no match for the Neighborhood Association's harassment campaign, including "a full-dress Ku Klux Klan warning" (338), and the police prove hostile or, at best, indifferent to the family's concerns. In a last-ditch effort to save his house, Neil and his friends from Five Points gather an arsenal of weapons. As he selects "for his own firing-post one window of the living-room" (345), the house quite literally becomes the domestic front line in a war to preserve the racial purity of the neighborhood and "the equity of the innocent white property-holders in Sylvan Park" (335). While the opposing sides maintain a momentary standoff—long enough, in fact, for the Kingsbloods to notice a few neighbors protesting the mob—eventually they exchange gunfire, and several people are injured, including Vestal, who suffers a superficial arm wound.

Under arrest for instigating a riot and assaulting an officer, the Kingsbloods and their supporters are ushered toward a patrol wagon. As the officers urge the detainees along, Vestal delivers the novel's final line: "We're moving" (348).[43] Although apropos to the scene, the response portends a more ominous finality, as if Vestal has concluded that, in the end, the family has no place in "the Land of the Noble Free" (322). The Neighborhood Association, abetted by the legal system, has overcome their attempts to maintain the suburban haven that Neil had previously described as a "true home that was his love and Vestal's made visible" (80). Watts reads this eviction as a modern reenactment of colonial-era displacement, informed by the same "racist and imperialist forces which had impelled [the] disruption of the heterogeneous middle ground one hundred years before."[44] This assessment certainly underscores the stakes of this climactic residential battle and Vestal's resigned response, but the fraught violence of the eviction scene is also the culmination of the war rhetoric that characterizes *Kingsblood Royal* as a whole.

Earlier in the novel, at one of the "race-talks," Neil recounts his perception of insolence among Black G.I.s during the war. In response, Clem Brazenstar explains, "You white Iagos have built up a revolutionary army of thirteen million Othellos, male and female. Of course the colored boys are impolite to the white gemmuns, in a war they never wanted to fight. Their own war was closer" (140). Lewis later repurposes this war motif, portraying midcentury Jim Crow laws and the government's refusal to curtail racial discrimination as a continuation of the Civil War: "There was no Lincoln now to call for troops and, eighty-five years after it had started, the War Between the States was won by the South" (258). Pointedly, here, Lewis frames suburban nation building in explicitly sectional terms, signaling the triumph of a traitorous white nationalism. As a novel attuned to the residential and economic complexities of metro-regional segregation, *Kingsblood Royal* makes explicit what the pages of *House & Garden* and *House Beautiful* only implied: suburbia and, indeed, the individual suburban house will represent the new battleground in a war for democratic ideals and residential rights. The legal and extralegal pressures marshalled to evict Neil and Vestal from their Sylvan Park home represent just the latest tactics in an ongoing territorial battle, from the colonial era to the postwar period, to enshrine whiteness at the center of the country's forward-looking vision.

A Yard with a Little Patch of Dirt

Published a dozen years after Lewis's novel, *A Raisin in the Sun* reimagines this battle over property and domestic security in the midwestern city of Chicago, but the residential migration patterns are reversed. Lena "Mama" Younger is the maternal figure turned progressive activist who orchestrates the family's move from the South Side to the white, working-class neighborhood of Clybourne Park. The payout on her husband's $10,000 life insurance policy provides the occasion and the means to realize a dream she had nurtured for over thirty years, symbolized by her wilted, sunlight-deprived plant, to own a house and a garden. While this section of the chapter will center on Mama Younger's desire for "a yard with a little patch of dirt" (92), as well as the efforts of the Clybourne Park Improvement Association to dissuade her family, I begin with her son, Walter Lee Younger, whose initial resistance to buying a house makes him an unlikely source for what can only be described as a quintessentially suburban dream.

Having placed a down payment on the house, Mama entrusts the remaining funds to Walter who, in short order, will get fleeced by a partner in an ill-advised venture. For the moment, though, with his thoughts full of money, Walter talks to his son, Travis, about "a business transaction that's going to change [their] lives" for the better (108). He looks seven years into the future, to when Travis will be seventeen, and he pictures himself returning home from a typical day at a downtown office.

> And I'll pull the car up on the driveway . . . just a plain black Chrysler, I think, with white walls—no—black tires. More elegant. Rich people don't have to be flashy . . . though I'll have to get something a little sportier for Ruth—maybe a Cadillac convertible to do her shopping in. . . . And I'll come up the

steps to the house and the gardener will be clipping away at the hedges and he'll say, "Good evening, Mr. Younger." And I'll say, "Hello, Jefferson, how are you this evening?" And I'll go inside and Ruth will come downstairs and meet me at the door and we'll kiss each other and she'll take my arm and we'll go up to your room to see you sitting on the floor with the catalogues of all the great schools in America around you. . . . All the great schools in the world! (108–9, ellipses original)[45]

Hansberry makes no mention of a TV in the cramped kitchenette apartment, and it would be difficult to imagine the Younger family with the money, leisure, or inclination to huddle around the set in the evening, but Walter's vision seems cribbed straight from suburban sitcoms of the 1950s, like *Father Knows Best* (1954–60) and *Leave It to Beaver* (1957–63). The commute home from downtown, the hired help—"Jefferson," no less—the dutiful wife at the door, and generational prosperity are all recognizable signifiers of a white, male suburban fantasy that Walter reads as universal markers of success. Like Lutie Johnson in *The Street*, who reads herself into the advertisements and editorials for "Country Living," Walter envisions himself and his family within this white suburban vision.

Raisin in the Sun is set over the course of several weeks in an unspecified year "between World War II and the present" (24), but the play seems firmly rooted in the legal and extralegal residential battles of the mid- to late-1950s. To be certain, Hansberry had intimate knowledge of racial segregation and restrictive covenants prior to this period. In 1937, the Hansberrys purchased a home in the South Park community of Chicago, and almost immediately, the family was met with threats of violence and legal efforts to evict them. Her father, Carl Hansberry, was the plaintiff in the Supreme Court case *Hansberry v. Lee* (1940), in which the justices ruled that previous court decisions sustaining the authority of restrictive covenants did not prevent future plaintiffs from challenging those racial prohibitions.[46] As a result of such covenants, as Anita Hill writes, "85 percent of Chicago's communities were off-limits to blacks" in the decade preceding the *Hansberry* decision.[47] The case marked a key victory in the struggle to eliminate racial covenants in advance of the 1948 *Shelley* decision. Yet by the time the play premiered in

1959, the more consequential Supreme Court decision in *Brown v. The Board of Education of Topeka, Kansas* (1954) had begun to reshape legal and popular discussions pertaining to race in America, and it is the legacy of *Brown* that seems most germane to the conflicts staged in Hansberry's play. Although explicitly focused on racial segregation in public schools, the *Brown* decision resonated across the social and political landscapes of northern cities, like Chicago, and amplified concerns among white residents regarding control of their communities. During his research on racial integration and the ensuing riots in Chicago's Trumbull Park district, Arnold Hirsch discovered that "the barroom conversation in the wake of the *Brown* decision revolved not around school desegregation or the South's Jim Crow system, but around Black penetration of white neighborhoods."[48] Interracial hostilities initially peaked in 1954, which Hirsch describes as a "year of chronic violence," and while conflicts ebbed over the next two years, there was a "reescalation of racial tensions during the spring and summer of 1957."[49]

Mama's quest for a home and Walter's forward-looking, sitcom-suburban vision both unfold against this backdrop, and the prospect of violence hangs over the play from the outset. For the Younger family, the rights of equal citizenship, the freedom to choose one's place of residence, and a sense of domestic stability are all at stake. As Houston Baker writes, responding to Ellison's *Invisible Man* and Wright's *Native Son*, "For place to be recognized by one as actually PLACE, as a personally valued locale, one must set and maintain the boundaries. . . . Bereft of determinative control of boundaries, the occupant of authorized boundaries would not be secure in his or her own eulogized world but maximally secured by another, a prisoner of interlocking, institutional arrangements of power."[50] This is the "bounded," ghettoized system the Youngers find themselves living within and struggling against at the beginning of the play, and *Raisin* lays bare these "arrangements of power," from absentee landlords and pestilent slums to racist neighborhood associations and mob violence to ownership rights and private property. In the first conversation we witness between Walter and his wife, Ruth, Walter skims through the Chicago *Tribune* and reports, "Set off another bomb yesterday" (26). That subject-less sentence, evoking a faceless white "they," goes unremarked upon—according to stage directions, Ruth greets it with "*Maximum indifference*" (26)—but it lingers in the background, waiting to be triggered, as it were, in the next act when Ruth mentions "them bombs and things they keep setting off" shortly before Mama announces she has bought a house in Clybourne Park (82).

To say the very least, Hansberry's *Raisin* contains multitudes. What I am calling Walter's suburban reverie is an extension of his desire to make something of himself, to be a man instead of working for "the man," to own his own business and earn a decent living.[51] Beneatha offers a counterpoint to her brother's patriarchal, capitalist fixations, challenging gender expectations regarding education, career, and, at least before she entertains Joseph Asagai's proposal, the institution of marriage. Trapped in an economic landscape that limits her employment opportunities to domestic service, Ruth tries to hold the family together even as her initial inclination to terminate her pregnancy puts her at odds with traditional notions of motherhood and family, especially Mama's, and Walter's hesitancy to prevent the abortion renders him a mere shadow of a man in Mama's estimation.

This intra-family drama also speaks to the generational and regional conflicts in *Raisin*, the way Walter sees the world only through the prism of money and power, which blinds him to the struggles and sacrifice his mother had made. "In my time we was worried about not being lynched and getting to the North if we could and how to stay alive and still have a pinch of dignity too," Mama says. "You ain't satisfied or proud of nothing we done" (74). Beneatha's rejection of her mother's religious faith and her privileging of an African past over the family's southern roots is another facet of this conflict. Hansberry also stages an internecine division between the Black working class and the Black bourgeoisie, the latter represented by George Murchison, Beneatha's self-righteous suitor who refuses to disguise his distaste for her "atmosphere" (96) and his "boredom" with her family (84). The liquor store misadventure that costs the family the bulk of the insurance settlement exposes the tragic shortcomings of Walter's desire to become, in Beneatha's derisive phrase, "*Monsieur le petit bourgeois noir*" (138). At the end of the play, as she contemplates living as "a doctor in Africa" (150), Beneatha intimates that she might accept Asagai's proposal.

Whether or not she actually moves to Nigeria, Asagai's presence in the play points toward a kind of Black "internationalism," linking the struggles of midcentury African Americans to global imperialism and the hope of a postcolonial future. Such questions connect to an overarching concern in *Raisin* regarding assimilation and what Beneatha describes as the willingness of African Americans to "submerge [themselves] completely in the dominant, and in this case *oppressive* culture" (81). As Judith Smith aptly summarizes, the play offers "a critique of the materialistic and imperialist aspirations of the American Century, as well as of segregation, and an alternative vision of change drawing on the collective resources of black working-class women and families, African American labor, and worldwide anticolonial agitation."[52] Within this matrix of concerns, my interest lies in Mama's nostalgic conception of home and the ways Hansberry reinvents this familiar regionalist trope as a form of political activism, transforming the Younger family into "race pioneers" who challenge the midcentury consensus around whiteness and suburban citizenship.[53]

If we situate the Youngers' relocation from the South Side of Chicago within the context of other Black pioneers, then Mama's search for a home broadens our understanding of postwar suburbanization.[54] As Hill reminds us, "Despite the 1948 *Shelley v. Kraemer* decision barring racially restrictive covenants, blacks retained a limited suburban presence. Suburban neighborhoods where blacks resided were by and large segregated, and overall the suburbs were white."[55] The Younger family's move to Clybourne Park presents a direct challenge to this homogeneous vision of white suburbia, and in this way, the family reflects other postwar Black suburbanites who, according to Andrew Wiese, threatened "the dominant suburban ethos" of "white supremacy."[56] He counts *Raisin in the Sun* among the cultural works that draw on a "rustic suburban vision," in this case "to symbolize both the endurance and violation of African Americans' hopes for a better life in the urban North."[57] When Ruth asks Mama what she plans to do with the insurance money, she introduces the possibility that, if everyone pitched in, they "maybe could meet the notes on a little old two-story somewhere, with a yard where Travis could play in the summertime" (44). Mama's image of home evolves directly from the soil of the rural South: "I always wanted me a garden like I used to see sometimes at the back of the houses down home. This plant is close as I ever got to having one" (53). Mama "connects that garden to her Southern roots," and her plant, suffering from lack of sunlight, carries the weight of her thwarted aspirations.[58] As she reflects on the early weeks of her married life, when she and Walter Sr. first moved into the two-room apartment on the South Side, she confides to Ruth that they never intended to stay. The plan was to set aside enough money "to buy a little place out in Morgan Park," Mama says, continuing: "We had even picked out the house. [. . .] But Lord, child, you should know all the dreams I had 'bout buying that house and fixing it up and making me a little garden in the back—And didn't none of it happen" (44–45).

Morgan Park is an enlightened choice in terms of the play's historical context. Located south of the Loop, Morgan Park is a fringe suburb that dates to the 1870s, and its "winding streets, small parks, and roundabouts have evoked images of an English country town."[59] Given the setting of *Raisin* and the fact that Walter Jr. is described as a "young man in his middle thirties" (25), Mama and her husband would likely have been contemplating a move to Morgan Park in the late-1910s or early-1920s. Morgan Park was a predominantly white, Anglo-Saxon community at that time, but by 1920, 8.6 percent of its residents were African American; by 1960, that number had increased to 35.1 percent, though neighborhoods remained segregated along racial lines.[60] The persistence of segregation within ostensibly "integrated" suburban towns limited options for African Americans who sought to leave behind subdivided kitchenette apartments or blighted ghetto conditions. These limitations, in turn, relocated congested living conditions and decay to the fringes, as Mama notes when she remarks that the house she and Walter Sr. had selected "[l]ooks right dumpy today" (45). According to Will Cooley's research on Chicago's Black pioneers, suburbs like Morgan Park, Wabash, and South Park "gradually declined during the late 1910s and 1920s with overcrowding exacting an acute toll on the housing stock."[61] Of course, these patterns continued well into the 1950s, exacerbated by restrictive covenants, residential ordinances, and extralegal social pressure by neighborhood associations, including violence. In other words, from Mama's original plan to relocate to Morgan Park to the Younger family's eventual move to Clybourne Park, *Raisin in the Sun* encompasses nearly half a century, from the Great Migration to the postwar era, of domestic insecurity and contested residential rights for African Americans.

This historical context clarifies the material and symbolic value of the "offstage" single-family house and sharpens the play's focus on the implicit violence of urban decline and its inverse relationship to midcentury suburban plenitude. Mama's "rustic suburban vision" may be the thematic through line in the drama's conception of home, but the ghetto and the "indestructible contradictions" of domesticity are placed before the reader/viewer as a central preoccupation from the outset (23). The appearance of order and cleanliness suppresses the reality of a kitchenette apartment bursting at the seams, and when overcrowded by characters with strong personalities, the room adopts a kind of kinetic claustrophobia. Given the set design, Hansberry negotiates the play's various historical and thematic explorations not only vis-à-vis the Younger family, but also through the nonfamilial characters she allows to enter this space: George Murchison (Black middle-class pretensions); Asagai (colonialism, African heritage, assimilation); Bobo (intra-racial betrayal); and the neighbor, Mrs. Johnson, an accommodationist who quotes Booker T. Washington and predicts the headline she will read next month: "NEGROES INVADE CLYBOURNE PARK— BOMBED!" (102). Arguably the most consequential outsider to enter this domestic scene is Karl Lindner, Clybourne Park's emissary, but a less obvious, auditory intrusion also precedes Mama's purchase of the house. As the Younger women discuss Ruth's pregnancy, "*the shouts of children*" drift through the open window from the street below where Travis and his friends are "chasing a rat" (58). Although Travis describes the rat's demise with boyhood enthusiasm, the urban street spattered with "rat blood" provides the abject, anti-pastoral contrast to the yard and patch of dirt Mama imagines for her grandson (59). If the withered but dogged plant symbolizes Mama's "rustic suburban vision," the bloodied street is a metonym for the decline, blight, overcrowding, and disease that ensnares urban housing projects while money flows outward to the suburbs in the form of federally subsidized loans and new, single-family housing construction.[62]

Karl Lindner, a representative of the Clybourne Park Improvement Association, makes his appearance on moving day, and he reflects the advanced subtlety of the post-*Shelley*, post-*Brown* era to ensure the links among whiteness, residential rights, and property values. Although in *Kingsblood Royal* the neighborhood association began with less direct efforts to convince Neil and Vestal to relocate to a more "heterogeneous" neighborhood, it could in the end invoke a legally binding covenant and, with the support of the police, forcibly evict the Kingsbloods. Early in his conversation with the Younger family, Lindner alludes to "the incidents which have happened in various parts of the city when colored people have moved into certain areas" (116), but throughout the scene, he remains nonconfrontational and takes pains to couch his visit in terms of community and interracial conversation. He paints a portrait of a diligent, honest, working-class neighborhood, striving to maintain a particular vision of home, family, and community. In rhetoric that champions the rights of citizenship, Lindner tries to persuade the Younger family that their impending move threatens this domestic tranquility:

> But you've got to admit that a man, right or wrong, has the right to want to have the neighborhood he lives in a certain kind of way. And at the moment the overwhelming majority of our people out there feel that people get along better, take more of a common interest in the life of the community, when they share a common background. I want you to believe me when I tell you that race prejudice simply doesn't enter into it. It is a matter of the people of Clybourne Park believing, rightly or wrongly, as I say, that for the happiness of all concerned that our Negro families are happier when they live in their *own* communities. (117–18)

Hansberry has a keen ear for both the language of racist terror and the sanitized discourse of community control, especially the way the latter shifts the burden onto those denied the freedom to exercise their rights to domestic security. In the aforementioned exchange with the Youngers, Lindner's interpellative "you've got to admit" attempts to conscript Walter, Ruth, and Beneatha, inviting them to acquiesce to the notion that they are unfit for Clybourne Park. As GerShun Avilez gleans, "The 'certain kind of way' of living that Lindner obliquely references is 'White'; the Clybourne Park residents want their neighborhood to maintain this exclusive property."[63] Yet, in Lindner's contorted framing, racial segregation is an ancillary effect in the benign pursuit "of a common interest in the life of a community," exercised through the residential choices of white and Black families alike. Hansberry's script deftly captures the insidious nature of such rhetorically race-neutral "community control" arguments.[64]

Since Mama was out of the apartment, she asks whether Lindner had threatened or intimidated the family. Beneatha reassures her that "they don't do it like that any more. He talked Brotherhood. He said everybody ought to learn how to sit down and hate each other with good Christian fellowship" (121). *Kingsblood Royal* invokes the Ku Klux Klan and ends in a hail of gunfire; post-*Shelley*, post-*Brown*, *Raisin in the Sun* uses Lindner to expose the subtle adaptability of efforts to preserve the postwar suburban ideal—the synonymy of domestic security, democratic citizenship, and whiteness—after the *de jure* system upholding segregation has been dismantled.[65] At this historical juncture in the battle for residential rights, as Hana' Khalief Ghani suggests, "The character of Lindner symbolizes the mass of white people who are uncomfortable with their own prejudice and therefore deny it."[66] By adopting the rhetoric of communal interest, Lindner's plea registers an inflection point in the discursive history of race and suburbanization: a persistent desire for residential segregation now ill at ease with its own racist impulses. As a literary text, *Raisin* remains balanced on a fulcrum between historical terror and the future promise of universal civil rights. Travis, Beneatha, and, to a lesser extent, Ruth and Walter gesture toward that future, but the persistent threat of violence and Mama's vision of home ground the play in the rural South and the legacies of lynching and Jim Crow.

The decision not to put the Clybourne Park house on stage further contributes to this sense of historical and spatial limbo. While there were genuine financial and logistical reasons not to undertake such a set design, by keeping the house offstage, Hansberry underscores the still prohibited status of the suburban home for African

Americans.[67] The play ends poised between past and future, and Lindner's parting words loom over the scene: "I sure hope you people know what you're getting into" (149). As such, the conclusion cautions against an overly optimistic reading of the play, much less the possibility of ending residential segregation in the near term. A grim and alienating struggle likely awaits the Younger family in Clybourne Park. Since they do not purchase a house in an established Black neighborhood, their conception of home and neighborhood will reflect their fraught fate as midcentury pioneers. For these reasons, it is difficult to accept early critiques of the play as "assimilationist." Hansberry may have written with universal ideals of residential rights and social justice in mind, but *Raisin* appeals to an integrationist model in which Black Americans can participate as full citizens.[68]

Despite these impending difficulties and the lingering aura of menace, the Youngers do in fact break new ground, in ways Neil and Vestal Kingsblood cannot in the mid-1940s. While Lewis's novel ends with a forced eviction, *Raisin* concludes as the Youngers prepare to move into their new home. Walter reverses course on the debased minstrel performance he had planned for Lindner's return and rejects the Improvement Association's offer to buy out the contract on the house. Over the course of his second conversation with Lindner, Walter aligns himself with Mama's commitment to familial solidarity, and in doing so, according to Mary Esteve, he "tether[s] himself to the goals of developing familial wealth and stability over generations."[69] He comes to understand the house in Clybourne Park as a kind of patrimony: "we have decided to move into our house because my father—my father—he earned it for us brick by brick. We don't want to make no trouble for nobody or fight no causes, and we will try to be good neighbors" (148). Whether they want it or not, trouble will likely find the Youngers, but the assertion regarding the family's well "earned" residential rights and Walter's appeal to neighborliness suggest the possibility of a progressive residential politics.

This uplifting scene offers a moment of solace to a family whose individual aspirations have led to fractious discord, even if Hansberry suggests the détente may be brief: Walter and Beneatha promptly resume their squabble about her need to marry "a man with some loot" as they exit the scene (150). Significantly, though, Mama commands the stage as the lights dim, silently suppressing "*a great heaving thing ris[ing] in her*," perhaps contemplating what new hardships await when a dream deferred is at last realized.[70] But the focus on Mama reminds us that her "rustic suburban vision," the yard with the patch of dirt, has informed the play's idea of home from the start, a point reinforced by the gift the family presents to her. They give Mama a set of gardening tools and an oversized, humorously ornate hat, selected by Travis because it resembles the ones "ladies always have on in the magazines when they work in their gardens" (124). Despite its evocation of the antebellum South—Scarlett O'Hara and picking cotton are both mentioned—Mama declares the hat "beautiful" (124).[71] *Raisin* deconstructs a popular, media image and reappropriates this glossy nostalgia for the rural southern home—with its immanent racial violence and inequity—through a Black framework. Hansberry places an African American matriarch at the center of a battle for domestic security and residential rights, and in doing so, she offers a radically different version of a reclaimed southern-ness, an expression of a regional desire that longs to disrupt the totalizing material and ideological terrain of postwar racial containment.

As this analysis has shown, the initial decades of midcentury suburban nation building coalesced around a vision of residential rights, property values, and a prosperous white citizenry that would uphold the political and economic values American soldiers had fought to preserve. In Lewis's novel, the Kingsblood family must directly confront the forces who seek to defend "the equity of the innocent white property-holders" in Sylvan Park (335), and their efforts to protect their home expose the political interests and white supremacy of postwar home building. Yet, as this chapter has also argued, the cultural and racial exclusivity of the single-family home did not diminish its universal appeal as a transracial symbol of domestic stability and residential rights. The same "fat sleek magazines" that helped to conscript Lutie to the philosophy of "Country Living" in *The Street* also reproduce and perpetuate Mama's rustic vision for a home and a plot of land that would signal her family's claim to full citizenship. The tragic outcomes of novels like *The Street* and

Kingsblood Royal, and the uncertain fate that awaits the Younger family in *A Raisin in the Sun*, reveal the ways legal and extralegal racial prohibitions coexisted uneasily, at times fatally, with the cultural and residential reinvention of the country as a suburban nation in the 1940s and 1950s.

The texts discussed here, including *House & Garden* and *House Beautiful*, reveal a concerted effort throughout the early decades of the postwar era to depict the suburbs and the single-family home as a contested terrain—as the territory that was always at stake in World War II—and to enshrine white domestic security as central to national identity. The twelve years separating *Kingsblood Royal* and *Raisin in the Sun* witnessed new patterns of residential "pioneering," succession, and segregation, the evolution of pressure tactics, harassment, and mob violence, and the emergence of a rhetorically race-neutral discourse premised on shared communal interest, a rhetoric that seeks to cloak the pro-segregationist ideology that underwrites the postwar suburban nation. Fundamental to both works, I have argued, is a reconstructed regionalist critique of "whiteness" as immanent to the forward-looking nation at this critical juncture in U.S. residential history. The fact that African Americans were either excluded from or denied equitable access to this nation-building project has had lasting political and economic costs. Data collected in 2016 shows that 71.3 percent of whites owned homes compared to 41 percent of Black Americans, a vestige of redlining, restrictive covenants, and discriminatory lending practices.[72] From the postwar era to the lingering effects of the 2008 housing crisis, such disparities and inequities continue to haunt the literature that takes as its focus the political, economic, and cultural valence of the suburban home, the shifting battle lines of residential rights, and the uneven development of America's metropolitan regions.

2

Adjustment Culture

Compulsory Domesticity and Its Discontents

"For all the ambiguities and cross currents the dominant strain in
popular culture does seem to be adjustment to the system."
—WILLIAM H. WHYTE,
The Organization Man (1956)

"THAT WAS THE YEAR everybody in the United States was worried about homosexuality," writes John Cheever in a journal entry from 1959. "They were worried about other things, too, but their other anxieties were published, discussed, and ventilated while their anxieties about homosexuality remained in the dark: remained unspoken."[1] This account of the latent threat posed by homosexuality appears between entries that include notes for his second novel, *The Wapshot Scandal* (1964), and a childhood reminiscence about "a penis-measuring contest, followed by an orgy" that leaves him aching with remorse yet still "filled with terrible longings" (*J* 116–17). Guilt, shame, and self-incrimination are recurring motifs whenever Cheever's queer desires, past or present, appear in his posthumously published *Journals* (1991). "Is he? Was he? Did they? Am I? Could I?" (*J* 117), he writes, posing a series of questions that fittingly captures the widespread paranoia about homosexuality in the Cold War era. As the historian K. A. Cuordileone contends, "the increased awareness of the (invisible) male homosexual in every walk of American life added to the sense that a man was compelled to fulfill the life trajectory that experts deemed 'normal' and 'mature,' lest he be tainted by the stigma of homosexuality."[2] From his youthful days, Cheever suffered under the lash of an unsettling and "immature" same-sex desire, and he feared the disgrace that would attend his exposure as a bisexual. To compensate, he would appear as "normal" as possible, and with a deadening amount of alcohol, he adjusted to the heteronormative ideal of family life and a home in the suburbs.

From the mid-1950s to the mid-1960s, in the wake of McCarthyism and the "lavender scare," Cheever wrote some of his most memorable suburban fiction, including the stories collected in *The Housebreaker of Shady Hill* (1958) and, arguably, his best and most iconic short story, "The Swimmer" (1964). During that same period, his journals reflect a withering dread about his increasingly irrepressible homosexual desires. Some entries, like this one from 1957, express tempting curiosity and an empathic sense of agony: "In the public urinal I am solicited by the man on my right but I do not dare turn my head. But I wonder what he looks like. No better or no worse, I guess, than the rest of us in such throes" (J 86). Other accounts on the subject display a hyperawareness of effeminate mannerisms. "Over to *The New Yorker*, where there are mixed opinions about the suburbs," reads an entry from 1953. "Walked up Fifth Avenue. A fine procession; it is a procession. At the Fifty-seventh Street crossing the crowds seemed to group themselves for a second to form the features of a matriarchy. It was an ugly thought and it passed. A lot of homosexuals drifting around in mid-morning" (J 33–34). While the writing exhibits a casual stream-of-consciousness, the juxtaposition of suburban ambivalence and homosexuality—with a glancing shot at the "matriarchy"—strikes me as more than accidental. Although I have written elsewhere about trespass and transgression as modes of agency in his suburban fiction, *The Journals* bring into focus how Cheever interprets his own "transgressive" sexual desires against the normative force of the Cold War suburban ideal and "familial consensus."[3] Noting the prevalence of passages "filled with self-loathing," his biographer Blake Bailey suggests that Cheever's journals reflect the homosexual panic of the era, but they also register the implicit prohibitions within his suburban community: "Alleged 'sex perversion' was a bigger stigma than ever—the fifties were a time of rampant homophobia, of government witch hunts and random police raids—and there was a lot of heavy, nervous joking at suburban cocktail parties."[4] I would not be so bold as to suggest we read a repressed queer desire as the subtext for his 1950s and '60s suburban fiction—though perhaps a revaluation of his lecherous, drunken trespassers and occasional burglars is in order on that account—but in his journals, the sumptuary codes of suburban life converge with midcentury prohibitions, eclipsing his personal efforts to render an unabated desire legible.

Notably, suburban decorum shadows him even in his absence from Westchester County. During a family sojourn to Rome in 1956–57, Cheever remarks somewhat enviously on a nonchalant pair of "American homosexuals who have every reason to be pleased at finding themselves in Rome. Here . . . rough boys do not whistle at them as they go down the street, nor do respectable household-ers look on them with loathing and scorn" (*J* 76). Cheever's time abroad is marked with fretfulness as he awaits the publication of his first novel, *The Wapshot Chronicle* (1957). In that novel, Cheev-er's own dread finds a fictional surrogate in Coverly Wapshot, and conceivably part of his nervous tension about the book's reception can be traced to "the unsavory or homosexual part" of the story, which the "disinterested reader is encouraged to skip."[5] The previ-ous year, in 1956, as he was finalizing his draft of the novel, Cheever confided in his journal, "I would not like to be the kind of writer through whose work one sees the leakage of some noisome semise-cret" (*J* 61). Thus, even as he imagined himself fêted with "prizes, ribbons, and awards of all kinds" (*J* 63), perhaps he also feared he had exposed his "noisome semisecret" to the world. In the end, there was no need to worry about the critics—the novel was well received and went on to win the National Book Award—but while awaiting the initial reviews, he conceives his visit to Europe as an opportunity to free himself from a suburban parochialism and the punitive gaze of "respectable householders." Characterizing him-self as a refugee, he writes, "What I escape is the alcoholic life of a minor literary celebrity in Westchester; also the trying company of people I dislike; also perhaps a degree of sexual anxiety, based on some unhappiness in my youth and refreshed by the same scenes and types—scenery and people I don't see here" (*J* 77). Although he frames the nettlesome fact of his innate bisexuality as the conse-quence of an unhappy childhood, his enduring anxieties about sex are here specifically linked to the "scenery and people" he has left behind in the suburbs.

In the early 1960s, the journal entries speak more openly and explicitly about his homosexual encounters, and feelings of guilt and shame are manifest. "I spend the night with C.," Cheever writes in the fall of 1960, "and what do I make of this? I seem unashamed, and yet I feel or apprehend the weight of social strictures, the threat of punishment. But I have acted only on my own instincts, tried, discreetly, to relieve my drunken loneliness, my troublesome hunger for sexual tenderness. Perhaps sin has to do with the incident, and I have had this sort of intercourse only three times in my adult life" (*J* 143).[6] Although Cheever entertains the possibility of sinfulness, his references to "social strictures" and "punishment" more directly address his concerns about the stigma of being outed as one of the era's (invisible) homosexuals. In a particularly telling entry from 1962, Cheever reads his sexual desires as a betrayal of the familial consensus. "It is my wife's body that I most wish to gentle," he writes, "it is into her that I most wish to pour myself, but when she is away I seem to have no scruple about spilling it elsewhere. I first see X at the edge of the swimming pool. He is sunbathing, naked, his middle covered by a towel" (*J* 171). As their flirtation continues, Cheever calls upon "the spiritual facts," including his "passionate wish to honor the vows [he has] made to [his] wife and children," but in the end he worries these proofs will not be enough: "[his] itchy member is unconcerned with all of this" (*J* 171). His thoughts pivot between a commitment to marriage and family and an urge to explore the full compass of his sexuality. The journal discloses an increasingly unbearable duality: Cheever aspires to embrace his "instincts, to upset the petty canons of decency and cleanliness" (*J* 171), yet he remains beholden to the normative demands of the domestic realm and suburban decorum. "And, whatever the instinctual facts are," he concludes, "there is the fact that I find a double life loathsome, morbid, and anyhow impossible" (*J* 171–72).

In a 2009 piece for *Commentary*, marking the Library of America's publication of a two-volume edition of Cheever's complete works, Algis Valiunas poses the question: "Will the work of a once-lionized American writer endure?"[7] Although "The

Swimmer" may continue to find a place in the "post-1945" sections of American literature anthologies, and while his reputation as the "American Chekhov" or the "Dante of the cocktail hour" will likely endure, Cheever's fate among the canon of American letters seems understandably precarious.[8] Nevertheless, I would offer that the under-explored aspect of Cheever as a bisexual writer casts an oblique light on the cultural ideal of suburban domesticity as a central facet of postwar suburban nation building. As Valiunas persuasively notes, "Erotic release, [Cheever] believed, would bring his life's fulfillment, but the suburban householder's code of conduct strictly circumscribed his desires, and the commandments of respectability were etched in his bones."[9] As evidenced in his journals and his fiction, Cheever certainly apprehends the normative force of middle-class, suburban households and communities. To briefly return to *Wapshot Chronicle*, Coverly, plagued by unresolved homosexual desires, takes a job as a civil servant and moves with his wife to Remsen Park. The town is, for all practical purposes, a suburb of the military-industrial complex or a "government version of suburbia."[10] This bedroom community was hastily assembled "when the rocket program was accelerated; but the houses were dry in the rain and warm in the winter; they had well-equipped kitchens and fireplaces for domestic bliss and the healthy need for national self-preservation could more than excuse the fact that they were all alike" (*WC* 259). After an unconsummated flirtation with his supervisor, Coverly reunites with his wife, and though their future falls short of "domestic bliss," they have a child and adjust to suburban family life. The more compelling point, though, is the way Cheever so adeptly interweaves government programs, domesticity, and "national self-preservation" as a singular campaign. For, indeed, as discussed in the previous chapter, that is precisely how the suburbs were marketed to the forward-looking, postwar nation. As our closeted Chekhov, constantly weighing his private life against public prohibitions, perhaps Cheever was more apt than most ostensibly straight writers to identify the links between national security and heteronormative domesticity, as well as the way private suburban households secured and validated properly adjusted public citizens.

This chapter examines how works of fiction address the Cold War turn toward compulsory domesticity and its immanent demands pertaining to heterosexual desire, narrowly defined gender roles, and the clear separation of private and public realms. While this inquiry may seem orthogonal to the metro-regional patterns and implications of suburban development explored throughout this study, I show that institutionalizing the domestic realm as a regulatory domain is central to the postwar suburban nation-building project. If, as discussed in chapter one, the single-family house in the suburbs delineated a battle line for contested ideas about race, nation, and residential rights after World War II, then this chapter considers the geo-cultural ideal of the suburban home as a nexus within a social and political system that premises national security on narrowly defined gender and sexual identities during a contemporaneous period of American history. As a touchstone for the literary inquiry, I want to invoke William H. Whyte's assessment from the 1950s that "the dominant strain in popular culture does seem to be adjustment to the system."[11] I am interested in how the literature of the era challenges this adjustment and, as such, this chapter focuses on texts that attempt to queer, or at least trouble, heteronormative identity, the feminine mystique, the familial consensus, and organization life.

Although I will return to Cheever as a way to conclude this chapter, Richard Yates's *Revolutionary Road* (1961) and Patricia Highsmith's *The Price of Salt* (1952) will serve as the exemplary texts. In each literary context, I examine how these writers rework regional tropes evoking provincialism and domesticity to expose the formal and informal networks of surveillance intended to discipline queer desires and to compel "adjustment to the system." By reading these novels through a regionalist lens, I am also extending Fetterley and Pryse's notion of "queer regionalism" to Cold War suburbia. They write, "In its recognition that queer is not so much a fixed identity as it is a shifting signifier used to do the work of constructing the normal, regionalism both exposes and opposes that work, using the perspective of the so-called queer to suggest the oddity of the so-called normal and offering empathy as an alternative to terrorism in the approach to difference."[12] This approach also aligns my project with the scholarship of Nayan Shah who uses the term queer "to question the formation of exclusionary norms of respectable middle-class, heterosexual marriage.

The analytical category of queer upsets the strict gender roles, the firm divisions between public and private, and the implicit presumptions of self-sufficient economics and intimacy in the respectable domestic household."[13] Read as iterations of regional writing, I argue, *Revolutionary Road* and *Price of Salt* reveal suburban topography as a regulatory terrain defined by its adherence to strict gender roles and compulsory heterosexuality, ideologies that were inextricably bound to prevailing Cold War ideas about national security. Like Cheever's journals, both novels, though written from vastly different subject positions, raise important questions about what desires and identities can be accounted for, or rendered legible, within the framework of postwar domesticity and suburban nation building.

As part of this inquiry, I also unpack the fraught politics and the complicated power dynamics of domestic ideology in the 1950s and '60s, including its attendant anxieties related to gender and sexuality.[14] The suburbs as depicted by Yates and Highsmith offer the perfect site for such a study, not only because they are the locus for the Cold War–era's cult of domesticity, but also because, according to Whyte, they are "the dormitory of the new generation of organization men."[15] The suburbs "are not merely great conglomerations of mass housing," he continues. "They are a new social institution" that encourages the same commitment to communal belonging as that mandated by the corporation.[16] As a "social institution," the Cold War suburbs regulate and normalize procreative, heterosexual desire and the gendered division of labor. Within that system, I am particularly interested in outliers and their efforts, both failed and realized, to challenge the consensus regarding work, family, and sexual desire. As Robert Corber has shown, "Cold War political discourse tended to position Americans who protested the rise of the 'organization man' or who rejected the postwar American dream of owning a home in the suburbs as homosexuals and lesbians who threatened the nation's security."[17] In the novels under consideration, the suburbs and the nuclear family, as social organizations, discipline those who fail to conform, thus demonstrating the way suburban nation building delimits and restrains the identities of its forward-looking citizens. Although paths of genuine or fully realized resistance often end up foreclosed, I will argue that the writers discussed here attempt to disrupt the culture of adjustment and, in the process, queer our understanding of secure suburban domesticity.

Gender Trouble

American culture has cultivated a fraught and enduring fascination with the nuclear family and 1950s domestic ideology. Nostalgia for this particular era can be a toxic impulse, especially if it is called upon to underwrite regressive, anti-feminist policies or to promote an "America First" white nationalism. In the run-up to the 2016 election, when asked to expound upon his foreign policy, then-candidate Donald J. Trump pointed to the turn of the twentieth century as a time "when we were a great [*sic*], when we were really starting to go robust," adding that in "the late '40s and '50s we started getting, we were not pushed around, we were respected by everybody, we had just won a war, we were pretty much doing what we had to do, yeah around that period."[18] Although foreign policy might not rank first on the list for those who nurture a yen for the 1950s—after all, the United States and the Soviet Union were in the midst of a prolonged nuclear standoff—the decade was objectively not a bad time to be alive if you were white, straight, and gainfully employed, especially if you were a man. The postwar period of industrial and economic wealth, paired with a period of relative political consensus about the need to contain the spread of communism, created opportunities for personal prosperity and allowed for a new focus on the family. Rates of homeownership rose to unprecedented levels—from 43 percent to 62 percent between 1940 and 1960—and "[b]y the mid-1950s, nearly 60 percent of the population had what was labeled a middle-class income level."[19] Of course, as previously discussed, the federal government, real estate developers, realtors, and neighborhood organizations all colluded to exclude African Americans from access to this kind of domestic security, as well as the opportunity to build generational wealth through homeownership. For the majority of white Americans, though, a commitment to marriage, family, home, and clearly defined gender roles constituted the midcentury American dream.

The problems with this utopia are manifold. In addition to its racial exclusivity, the postwar suburban idyll perpetuates a kind of cultural amnesia, imagining the white nuclear family as the standard-bearer of the postwar era. According to Stephanie Coontz, though, the "nuclear family" was "a new invention . . . a historical fluke, based on a unique and temporary conjuncture of economic, social, and political factors," but made to seem inevitable by a sitcom-consensus regarding what "normal" middle-class life looked like during the Cold War.[20] Nevertheless, the now sacrosanct status of the nuclear family naturalizes the forced normalcy of suburban domesticity, and contemporary conservative appeals to the 1950s tend to obfuscate the tumultuous changes in gender roles taking place. As Elaine Tyler May has shown, "American superiority in the cold war rested not on weapons, but on the secure, abundant family life of modern suburban homes," and "female sexuality" played a central role in any conception of the domestic realm.[21] It did not matter that many women continued to work both inside and outside the home; what mattered was the domestic ideology of feminine beauty and ease made possible by the wonders of consumer capitalism.

In her analysis of the "kitchen debate" between Richard Nixon and Nikita Khrushchev, May glosses the pro-America argument as follows: "American women, unlike their 'purposeful' and unfeminine Russian counterparts, did not have to be 'hard working,' thanks to the wonders of American household appliances. Nor did they busy themselves with the affairs of men, such as politics. Rather, they cultivated their looks and their physical charms, to become sexually attractive housewives and consumers under the American capitalist system."[22] The conflation of consumerism, domesticity, sexual attraction, and national security contributed to Cold War–era gender trouble for both women and men. In 1963, in *The Feminine Mystique*, Betty Friedan identified "the problem that has no name"—that "nameless aching dissatisfaction" experienced by suburban housewives—and she excoriated the "vision of the happy modern housewife as she is described by the magazines and television, by the functional sociologists, [and] the sex-directed educators."[23] Friedan lamented the way a generation of women had been schooled to avoid careers in favor of the feminine ideal of housewife and mother. "A thousand expert voices applauded their femininity, their adjustment, their new maturity," she writes. "All they had to do was devote their lives from earliest girlhood to finding a husband and bearing children."[24] While Friedan's work has rightfully been critiqued for its racial, sexual, and economic blind spots, *The Feminine Mystique* was a groundbreaking text for its time, helping to redirect the discourse concerning the Cold War familial consensus by drawing attention toward the trials endured by women.[25]

During the 1940s and 1950s, when America was "great," both popular and expert assessments of compulsory domesticity tended to focus on men. To the extent that these publications did mention women, it was typically to vilify independent women, emasculating housewives, and suffocating mothers. In 1958, the editors of *Look* magazine published *The Decline of the American Male*, a slim collection of three essays that documented the prevailing grievances afflicting men. This list includes the "group think" of organization culture, the "rat race" that valorizes ambition and demands long hours of work to support patriotic consumer capitalism, and domineering wives who control the sexual and economic politics of the household and undermine their husbands' sense of virility.[26] On its face, the Cold War familial consensus would seem to shore up and reaffirm patriarchal authority, both in the private and public realms, but almost every popular and expert voice of the era tried to persuade their readers otherwise, arguing that the celebration of family life was creating a widespread crisis of masculinity and fueling the rise of homosexuality.

Women were left in an impossible bind amidst, on the one hand, the concurrent celebration of marriage and domesticity and, on the other, the cultural demonization of overbearing wives and mothers. In the 1940s, Philip Wylie gave voice to a particularly virulent, misogynistic and, unfortunately, popular perspective on the encroaching disease of "momism" devouring America. In his subtly titled *Generation of Vipers*, Wylie claims that "megaloid momworship has got completely out of hand. Our land, subjectively mapped, would have more silver cords and apron strings crisscrossing it than railroads and telephone wires."[27] This depiction, metaphorizing "apron strings" into competing "railroads and telephone wires," attributes to women, mothers in particular, a kind of economic and political power that even Wylie must have realized was a glaring exaggeration, but he was just getting warmed up. For him, the United States had devolved into a "gynecocracy" in which "every clattering prickamette in the republic survives for an incredible number of years, to stamp and jibber in the midst of man, a noisy neuter by natural default or a scientific gelding sustained by science, all tongue and teat and razzmatazz."[28]

Wylie may have been the most pernicious proponent of "momism," but he was hardly alone in his assessment of how wives and mothers had conspired to "neuter" their husbands and children. In his contribution to *The Decline of the American Male*, J. Robert Moskin writes, "A boy growing up today has little chance to observe his father in strictly masculine pursuits. . . . For years authorities have urged women to convert the father into a male version of the mother. Now they feel they have pushed him too far, that they have demasculinized him."[29] Moskin cites homosexuality, along with bachelorhood and "withdrawing from sex relations," as one of the three primary defenses against the destructive force of female dominance.[30] Even no less a feminist than Friedan entertained the threat posed by the disease of "momism," especially in regard to homosexuality. Tapping into the pervasive homophobia of the era, she viewed the "feminine mystique" and the rise of "overt male homosexuality" in midcentury America as intractably linked problems.[31] In the Cold War period, the familial consensus may have reduced American women to domesticated "sex creatures [and] sex-seekers," according to Friedan, but most writers at the time contended that the real victims were men: figurative castratos in the home and, in the public realm, corporate drones who must bankroll the consumerism that sustains the suburban domestic front.[32] Drawing on David Riesman's famous postulate about the midcentury shift to "other-directed" social character, Cuordileone contends, "Postwar prosperity provided the engine for a baby boom, and as the middle class expanded, so did consumption, suburban living, leisure, and narrow gender-role expectations, all of which appeared to destabilize male autonomy and inner-direction."[33] The ascendancy of "the organization," consumer capitalism, and the prioritizing of family life as a force of national security all coalesce in the suburban home, transforming domestic space into a crucible of gender instability and sexual anxieties during the initial decades of postwar suburban nation building.

This is the political, economic, and cultural backdrop to the literature explored in the following sections. Yates's *Revolutionary Road* is rife with the kind of gender trouble that characterized the postwar discourse discussed here, and much critical attention has been paid to Frank Wheeler and his "masculinity crisis." My reading touches on this topic, especially the way Frank's masculinity is scrutinized and monitored, but I also shift the focus to the novel's "maladjusted" characters: April Wheeler, who contests compulsory domesticity and the suburban dream, and John Givings, the mentally unstable son of the Wheelers' realtor, whom I suggest the novel positions as a "queer" figure. He is exiled from gainful employment, respectable middle-class marriage, and the suburban landscape, and thus he represents a threat to family and national security. In *The Price of Salt*, Highsmith portrays the love affair between Therese Belivet, a set designer and store clerk, and Carol Aird, an affluent suburban housewife, who meet by chance at the department store where Therese works. Among the works considered in this chapter, Highsmith's novel offers the most explicit example of how queer desires are surveilled and disciplined during the Cold War era, but the lovers' road trip, which occupies a crucial section of the narrative, also cleverly stages a queer reenactment of a familiar regionalist trope: the revolt from the village. In the end, the novel uses the road trip to expand the topography of queer desire and, as a result, provides the most successful rejection of compulsory domesticity. Collectively, Yates's and Highsmith's "queer" characters extend the work of regionalism to contest the construction of "the normal" and, in this instance, to contrast a compulsory adjustment to heteronormative, suburban citizenship.

Isn't It Queer?

Set in 1955 in a suburb of western Connecticut, *Revolutionary Road* tells the story of Frank and April Wheeler's doomed marriage, but Yates's first novel is also a clear-eyed assessment of organization culture, the way suburban domesticity sustains destructive gender norms, the widening gap between perceptions of the good life and its reality, and the performances demanded to cover this gap. Yates signals this disconnect between fantasy and reality from the beginning, most obviously with the Laurel Players, an uninspiring community acting troupe, and their abysmal performance of *The Petrified Forest*, but as the narrative progresses, Frank comes to embody most clearly the novel's performative tropes. The reader consistently finds Frank in front of mirrors or studying his reflection in a darkened window, cupping the flame from his Zippo to create an "intensely dramatic portrait," playing out idealized versions of scenes and conversations before they unfold, yet somehow the presumptive images never match the reality.[34] Frank's obsessive attention to the persona he attempts to project is merely an iteration of a more central strain in the novel, casting a sense of authentic personhood against "the larger absurdities of deadly dull jobs in the city and deadly dull homes in the suburbs" (20).[35] Frank positions himself against the perceived provincialism of suburbia, and though he reasons that financial situations or temporary setbacks, like April's first unexpected pregnancy, might necessitate concessions, "the important thing was to keep from being contaminated. The important thing, always, was to remember who you were" (20). As twin toxins, the corporation and the suburbs figure as the enemies of authenticity, and *Revolutionary Road* explores the sometimes fatal stakes of this battle.

Following that dreadful production by the Laurel Players, Yates stages one of the novel's more bravura scenes: a marital spat on the shoulder of Route Twelve. Weary of his incessant chattering about "these damn little suburban types," April pleads with Frank to "stop talking" (24). He pulls the car over and launches into a four-point defense—castigating her "imitation of Madame Bovary" and rejecting "the role of dumb, insensitive suburban husband" that she has "been trying to hang" on him since they moved from the West Village to western Connecticut (25)—but he only makes it through three of his arguments before April flees the car. The performative nature of the scene is predetermined, not just in Frank's reference to feeling typecast as the "suburban husband," but in the headlights that substitute for stage lights, in the audience of steady, oncoming traffic, and in the imagined onlookers behind "the friendly picture windows of the Revolutionary Hill Estates" on the hillside above the road (26).[36] In terms of its choreography, this *al fresco* quarrel draws the reader's attention to the non-spaces that sprawl creates, like the shoulder of Route Twelve. In ways that anticipate the function of the freeway overpass in DeLillo's *White Noise*, Yates mines the margins of suburban spatiality, in this instance to turn the Wheelers' dispute about domestic gender roles into roadside performance art. The novel adeptly recognizes how the automobile and suburban roadways could amplify or exacerbate household tensions since the lack of escape makes these spaces seem somehow more combustible.

That is, in fact, the case here: the argument escalates rapidly, and Frank and April trade barbs to exploit one another's vulnerabilities. The crux of the argument turns on who has ensnared whom in this marriage trap. "I've always known I had to be your conscience and your guts—*and* your punching bag," April says. "Just because you've got me safely in a trap you think you—" (27). In a fit of pique, Frank interrupts, "*You* in a trap! *You* in a trap! *Jesus*, don't make me laugh!" (27). April's revelation of past physical abuse should not be overlooked, especially as it prefaces her cutting remark about Frank's brittle masculinity: "'*Look* at you! *Look* at you, and tell me how by any *stretch*'—she tossed her head, and the grin of her teeth glistened white in the moonlight—'by any *stretch* of the imagination you can call yourself a man!'" (27–28). The accusation eviscerates Frank, laying bare deep-seated anxieties about his father and "man's work," and sends him into a frenzy of violence directed not at April, significantly enough, but at the automobile. He slams his fist repeatedly against the roof of the car, drawing attention to the vehicle that brought them to this spectacular roadside impasse. From a purely stylistic perspective, April's denunciation brilliantly captures how Frank's idealized, "portrait" of himself belies his gendered insecurity. Setting aside April's dramatic delivery—the toss of her head, the photographic detail of glistening teeth—the line underscores the importance of the "look," inviting Frank to scrutinize himself and his appearance, as he is always already doing, and his failure to envision a secure or stable masculine identity.

Yates pointedly connects this roadside fight to the day the couple first glimpsed their future home on Revolutionary Road. Frank and

April had followed the same route with their realtor, Helen Givings, as she guided them past the "little cinder-blocky, pickup-trucky places" and beyond the "perfectly dreadful new development called Revolutionary Hill Estates" to "a sweet little house and a sweet little setting," built just after the war (29). Although they were imagining something akin to *Mr. Blandings Builds His Dream House*, "a small remodeled barn or carriage house" (28), they admit the place has charm, despite "its outsized central window staring like a big black mirror" (29). The picture window, the maligned metonym of suburban culture, seems to be the only impediment, but notably it is Frank who downplays the garish "black mirror," noting that one window was unlikely "to destroy [their] personalities" (29).[37] And with that, Frank and April begin to visualize where the furniture will go and how they will decorate; they marvel at the perfection and "symmetry" of the house and determine that this could be a home. "The gathering disorder of their lives might still be sorted out and made to fit these rooms, among these trees," Yates writes, continuing: "Who could be frightened in as wide and bright, as clean and quiet a house as this?" (30). Following the failed performance and the roadside quarrel, though, the home now looms on its slope of lawn like a harbinger of regret and failed possibilities.

In these early chapters of the novel, Yates invites the reader to understand the antagonisms in Frank and April's marriage through the lens of suburban spatiality and Cold War domesticity. The initial description of the house underscores the regulatory power of the suburban home, adjusting any perceived instabilities or "disorder" into a balanced and secure refuge. Outside the domestic realm, the fight on the shoulder of Route Twelve marks a less obvious way that the novel draws attention to the non-domestic, equivocal spaces created by suburban development. A similar dynamic will occur late in the novel when Frank pursues April, now pregnant with their third child, as she tries to find some privacy in the remaining stretch of woods behind their house: "But they couldn't fight up here—they were well within sight and earshot of houses down on the road" (293). In these scenes, Yates deliberately links the domestic "trap" both to the peripheral spaces created by metro-regional sprawl and to the interior space of that "sweet little house." The suburban home that they had invested with the impossible desire to arrange the "disorder of their lives" had perhaps done so too well. They had "another child to prove that the first one hadn't been a mistake" (51), Frank has settled into a mundane office job at the same corporation where his father had worked, and April has reluctantly adjusted to the feminine ideal of housewife and mother. This is the fraught starting point from which the novel begins to explore compulsive domesticity and adjustment culture alongside the non-normative identities they proscribe.

As previously noted, the character of Frank Wheeler embodies the Cold War–era "organization man" and his endangered masculinity. His pervasive concerns about "emasculated" men and his diatribes against the suburbs, "sentimentality," and "'adjustment' and 'security' and 'togetherness'" all coordinate as cover for his own gendered insecurities and the belief that he has failed to live up to his father's manly ideal (128–29). A former G.I., Frank now feels adrift in a postwar world of meaningless office work that undermines his conception of productive labor. He embodies what C. Wright Mills dubbed the corporate "hero as victim," an individual completely alienated from the products of his labor and defined by his docile nature and lack of agency.[38] Locating this ennui in consumerism and mass culture, Michael Moreno contends that "the political and economic discourses of Cold War America transformed the identity of the (predominantly Anglo-) American male by manufacturing and containing his identity within the consumptive topography of suburbia."[39] These critical accounts locate the crisis of masculinity in the feminization of the white-collar worker and the diminution of male identity on the consumerist domestic front.

In a scene overdetermined by gendered signifiers, a hungover Frank belatedly wakes to the sound of the lawn mower and sees April "wearing a man's shirt" and cutting the grass (35). Worse yet, as he putters around the house in his bathrobe, Mrs. Givings arrives to witness this gender-bending scene that, according to Claudia Falk, "completes the impression of male inadequacy."[40] The incident also conjures humiliating childhood memories for Frank and underscores a number of issues concerning the relations of power between men and women in the novel. To compensate, Frank dons "an old pair of army pants and a torn shirt" and recommences work on a stone path: "At least it was a man's work. . . . [H]e could take pleasure in the sight of his own flexed thigh, . . . the heavily veined forearm that lay across it and the dirty hand that hung there—not to be compared with his father's hand, maybe, but a serviceable, good-enough hand all the same" (45). Frank tries to reinhabit both the garb and the mindset of the G.I. in order to reclaim the sense of virility that April's cross-dressing yardwork has appropriated, though as Moreno notes, this "wartime image of himself as hero and fighter fuels his fantasy of a world to which he no longer can return," an impossibility designated by the incomplete path.[41]

As the narrative progresses, April becomes more assertive, formalizing their plans to relocate to Paris where she will support the family and, thus, save them all from "the great sentimental lie of the suburbs" (112). Although initially intrigued by the freedom to discover his authentic self, "an intense, nicotine-stained, Jean-Paul-Sartre sort of man" (23), eventually the lure of Paris wanes for Frank. He probably realizes what April has suspected all along: he is no philosopher manqué, and there was never an inner-directed self for him to discover, either at home or abroad. Gradually, cracks begin to show in his façade of dissatisfaction with both organization life and the suburbs. Although, initially, Frank delights in perceiving the suburbs as a provincial, backward locale, a regional foil to his purportedly cosmopolitan ethos, he eventually views their "very neat and white" house as a place "where everything, in the final analysis, was going to be all right" (274). Yet, before the blush fades on their European adventure, both Frank and April delight in sharing the news with friends, neighbors, and coworkers. This draws an array of secondary characters into action, allowing Yates to explore the organization and suburban neighborhoods as social institutions that monitor narrowly defined gender expectations and guard against deviance.

At the office, once word gets around about "this noble experiment" (169), Frank's coworkers pose insinuating questions about how he plans to spend his time in Paris while April supports the family financially. Although Frank has a glib retort at the ready, such questions will prove nettlesome when an opportunity arises to advance further within the Knox corporation than his father ever had. After learning about the proposed move, Shep and Milly

Campbell, neighborhood friends of the Wheelers, privately question Frank's manhood. A befuddled Shep asks his wife, "I mean what kind of a man is going to be able to take a thing like that?" (150). Notably, besides nurturing an unrequited love for April, Shep also bears his own repressed crisis of masculinity, a haunting sense of scarcely averted queerness cultivated by his "wealthily divorced mother" who dressed him in "tartan kilts" until the age of eleven. Echoing midcentury indictments of neutering "momism," Shep will still occasionally complain to friends, "She woulda made a God damn *lollypop* outa me!" (137). In other words, Shep may be more attuned than other characters in the novel to schemes that smack of gendered or sexual "inversions."

Although dismayed about the Wheelers' proposed relocation for personal reasons, Mrs. Givings, the busybody realtor, also labels the Paris plan "unsavory," a loaded term suggesting a kind of deviant sexual arrangement. She confides to her indifferent husband that "people don't *do* things like that. . . . Unless they're—well, running away from something, or something? . . . And they always seemed such a steady, settled sort of couple. Isn't it queer?" (163). In proposing to opt out of the heteronormative division of labor, April and Frank threaten to unsettle or, to borrow from Mrs. Givings, to "queer" the Cold War social institution of suburban domesticity. Moreover, taking up residence in Paris so that Frank can pursue his writing would further imply a retreat from the superiority of U.S. consumer capitalism for the effete life of a dilettante in Europe. Collectively, these suspicions expressed by coworkers, friends, and neighbors radiate in both directions. Talk of unsavory arrangements impugns April's femininity and Frank's masculinity alike, but they also redound on the current arrangement of the accusers' own lives—their dead-end jobs, their unfulfilling marriages, their fractured families—and for no one is this more true than Shep, who cannot separate his critique of Frank from his aching desire for April.

The most interesting figure within this network of secondary characters is also the novel's preeminent outsider. John Givings, Mrs. Givings's institutionalized son, articulates the most strident critique of the gender trouble in the Wheelers' marriage. Part Shakespearean "fool," as Kate Charlton-Jones notes, and part prophet of doom, John Givings exists outside the heteronormative demands of the nuclear family, and his clinical madness exiles him from the social conventions of middle-class suburbia and the financial demands of organization labor.[42] Read within the Cold War context of homophobia and the "lavender scare," the novel also positions John as a "queer" figure with an overbearing mother. While his mental state most clearly marks him as an outsider—he was committed after breaking a coffee table and threatening his mother (229)—his former life as a single man and mathematician would have already rendered him suspicious. In the postwar era, men faced pressure to marry, raise a family, and climb the corporate ladder, and thus the life of a bachelor became suspect, perhaps even indicative of "'deviant' sexuality."[43] Corber finds a similar dynamic at work in Cold War film noir: "The men who were most likely to become objects of suspicion in the intensely homophobic climate of the postwar period were not those who participated actively in the domestic sphere or who submitted passively to corporate structures . . . but those who refused to settle down and raise a family."[44]

In the initial meeting between the Wheelers and John Givings, these are precisely the fault lines that emerge during their conversation: job, marriage, family, and home. John asks what Frank does for a living, and when Frank replies that he has a "stupid job," nothing "interesting about it," John seizes the opportunity to question his manhood, suggesting only "[w]omen and boys" care about such matters (186). John corrects course, though, and offers an apology that redirects attention to the Wheelers' home. "You want to play house, you got to have a job," he says. "You want to play very *nice* house, very *sweet* house, then you got to have a job you don't like" (187). He perceptively identifies both the cost of the Cold War consensus and the implicit deviance of those, like himself, who do not conform. "This is the way ninety-eight-point-nine per cent of the people work things out," John surmises, noting the near-universal adjustment to organization culture and family life in the 1950s—not to mention its attendant sorrows—while simultaneously classifying himself an outlier to this consensus: only someone "on a four-hour pass from the State funny-farm" would question such arrangements (187).

As a queer and disruptive presence in the novel, John Givings stands in direct contrast to the constructed nature of "normal," reproductive, suburban domesticity. He refuses to echo the familiar objections to the Wheelers' proposed disavowal of the corporate grind, the gendered division of power, and the suburban dream, and he endorses their move to Europe in order to escape "the hopeless emptiness of everything in this country" (189). Moreover, he expresses his approval of the Wheelers in explicitly gendered terms. April strikes him as a real "female," not a dainty "feminine woman" like his mother, and he suspects that, beneath the gray flannel suit, Frank is a real "male" (190). Given this gendered rhetoric, it is unsurprising that when he later learns April is pregnant and the plans for Paris have fallen through, John's scathing response turns pointedly sexual. Now, April appears as a domineering wife and emasculating shrew, and Frank's manhood is once again suspect: "I wouldn't be surprised if you knocked her up on purpose, just so you could spend the rest of your life hiding behind that maternity dress" (287). He also intuitively discerns what has, in fact, taken place, namely Frank's adjustment to corporate life. "You decide you like it here after all?" John asks. "You figure it's more comfy here in the old Hopeless Emptiness after all, or—Wow, that did it!" (286–87). Citing his freedom to speak "uncomfortable truths," Charlton-Jones contends that John's "behavior is de-stabilizing, and deliberately so."[45] I would add that his ability to destabilize is directly linked to the Cold War familial consensus and to his status as an outsider to the era's compulsory domesticity. As an institutionalized bachelor, removed from the marketplace of the organization and the modern suburban home, John seems preternaturally aware of the political currents that construct citizenship in terms of the heteronormative family. "Big man you got here, April. . . . Big family man, solid citizen" (287), he adds before his father escorts him away. In his brief appearances in *Revolutionary Road*, John gives voice to the predominant midcentury anxieties about "momism" and emasculated men, but he also embodies the pathologized figure of the sexual deviant: the man who rejects, or who is unable to fulfill, the "normal" obligations of (re)productive, heteronormative, middle-class suburban citizenship.

April Wheeler's decision to induce a miscarriage and terminate her third pregnancy similarly stigmatizes her as a defector from the familial consensus and as hostile to the Cold War belief in the suburban American Dream. In the case of April, the novel offers an exaggerated, almost parodic version of the discourse used to denounce women who reject child-rearing as the established norm. After weeks working the angles on abortion and psychological dysfunction to scuttle their Paris plans, Frank can barely suppress his enthusiasm when April finally asks about "[t]he psychological thing behind this abortion business. Is that what women are supposed to be expressing when they don't want to have children? That they're not really women, or don't want to be women, or something?" (231). In response, Frank references Freud and the lingering effects of "infantile penis-envy" as the impetus for abortion (231). Citing "common sense," he counsels April "that if most little girls do have this thing about wanting to be boys, they probably get over it in time by observing and admiring and wanting to emulate their mothers—I mean *you* know, attract a man, establish a home, have children and so on" (232). In these exchanges, the novel echoes popular sentiments about maladjusted women, but the reference to "penis envy" would seem purposefully intended to highlight how regressive Frank's ideas are, even for the 1950s.[46] His remarks about how psychologically healthy girls eventually seek "to emulate their mothers" strike me as more consequential. He tries to diagnose April's doubts about the enforced cultural ideal of child-rearing as the closeted expression of an immature or queer wish to be a man. In a flailing effort to reinforce his threatened masculinity, Frank attempts to re-conscript April into compulsory domesticity and its mandatory adjustment to the suburban home and the feminine ideals of marriage and motherhood.

April's account of the inevitable and tragic momentum of the feminine mystique proves edifying in this context. Yates had previously rehearsed the couple's courtship and early married life in a flashback focalized from Frank's perspective, but toward the end of the novel we revisit this formidable period through April's memory. For her, marriage and motherhood have turned out to be a "subtle, treacherous" web: "And all because, in a sentimentally lonely time long ago, she had found it easy and agreeable to believe whatever this one particular boy felt like saying, and to repay him for that pleasure by telling easy, agreeable lies of her own, until each was saying what the other most wanted to hear—until he was saying 'I love you' and she was saying 'Really, I mean it; you're the most interesting person I've ever met'" (304). The time lapse from flirtation to ill-advised marriage, all premised on insecurities and falsehoods, highlights the tangled nature of a feminine ideal that, as Friedan has outlined, requires submission to marriage, child-rearing, and sexual passivity. Frank's pop psychology cannot free April from this sense of fatalism or the apparent inevitability of her current predicament. As Jill Anderson writes, "April cannot be cured on the couch in a psychoanalyst's office. Instead, she is a casualty of the systemic wrongs of the way suburbia disciplines women's bodies into seeming ill or out of place for wanting something outside of its normalizing expectations."[47] In *Revolutionary Road* and other works, despite his dismissive views of feminism, Yates consistently draws attention to the standardizing, controlling, and confining nature of suburban spaces, especially for women.[48] If, as Yates famously noted, anyone in the novel exemplifies the country's "best and bravest revolutionary spirit" (xx), it is April Wheeler, but despite her plans for Paris and efforts to break free from the confines of compulsory domesticity, the novel cannot imagine an alternative to those prescriptive roles that does not prove fatal.

On the surface, at least as it pertains to a character like Frank Wheeler, *Revolutionary Road* would seem to support Whyte's assessment about "adjustment to the system." After April's tragic death from a self-induced miscarriage, the reader learns through the neighborhood gossip network that Frank seems to be getting on with his life. A new neighbor inquires, "I mean did he seem to've made a—a fairly good adjustment?" (329). Shep and Milly Campbell share that the children are now living with Frank's brother's family in Massachusetts, but Frank has a job on Madison Avenue and has become the kind of "mild" and "boring" guy who talks about the breakthroughs he is making with his analyst (330–31). For much of the novel, "deadly dull homes in the suburbs" (20) and the "disease" of "sentimentality," and "'adjustment' and 'security' and 'togetherness'" (128–29) have signaled Frank's visceral rejection of a regional provincialism at odds with his own imagined existential urbanity. In the end, Yates subverts these facile stereotypes about suburban living, and Frank's meek revolt from the village is rendered as a simple readjustment to organization life.

This clears the way, though, for a more detailed and comprehensive account of suburban topography as a regulatory terrain, a landscape that surveils and disciplines queer desires in the name of national security, with its most dire consequences falling on those unable to adjust to prevailing gender and sexual ideologies. Unfortunately, alternatives to adjustment culture in *Revolutionary Road* seem foreclosed or destined to failure. John Givings may give voice to inconvenient truths, but he is repaid for his trouble with electroshock therapy and the stigma of institutionalization. Insofar as he has been exiled from the reproductive, heteronormative suburban dream, John poses a literal threat to his family and a figurative threat to the security of the nation's postwar familial consensus. As the novel's sacrificial heroine, April dies in an attempt to fashion a life beyond the prescriptive, reproductive demands of the suburban ideal and its prohibitions pertaining to the gendered division of labor.[49] While her ambivalence about marriage and motherhood would seem to contest the feminine mystique, the fictional world of *Revolutionary Road* cannot imagine a secure space from which to enact such a direct challenge. The novel's "queer" figures are effectively expunged, pushed offstage, condemned to the madhouse or the morgue.

Do You Like the Country?

Corporate culture and adjustment figure prominently in the opening pages of Highsmith's *The Price of Salt*. The novel begins inside the throng of organization life at "lunch hour in the co-workers' cafeteria," and before even meeting one of the principal characters, we perceive the threat of being devoured inside "a single huge machine."[50] While anxiously dining on the unappetizing fare, nineteen-year-old Therese Belivet grapples with a version of communal recruitment. She peruses "the 'Welcome to Frankenberg' booklet," making note of how "vacation benefits" accrue over time (3), but she finds it impossible to picture herself existing within this Frankenbergean future of multi-week vacations on company-sponsored campgrounds. Instead, her thoughts drift toward a totalizing, dystopian corporate system that would account for all aspects of life: "They should have a church, too, she thought, and a hospital for the birth of babies. The store was organized so much like a prison, it frightened her now and then to realize she was a part of it" (3-4). Highsmith foregrounds the interpellative demands of the organization—"Are *You* Frankenberg Material?" (4—to establish from the outset a critique of corporate culture, and she routes Therese's refusal to adjust to the system through aesthetics. Turning her attention away from the booklet, she notes that "[t]he great square window across the room looked like a painting by—who was it? Mondrian. The little square section of window in the corner open to a white sky. And no bird to fly in or out. What kind of a set would one make for a play that took place in a department store? She was back again" (4). But not for long. Therese is a temporary worker, hired on as a clerk for the Christmas rush, and soon she will focus all her attention on the only two things in her life that matter: set design and Carol Aird, the elegant suburban housewife who wanders into the department store and with whom Therese, *coup de foudre*, falls in love upon gazing into her "calm grey eyes" (28).

The Price of Salt has received extensive critical attention in recent years, augmented by a pair of Highsmith biographies and the release of Todd Haynes's film adaptation, *Carol* (2015).[51] Arguably, within the context of this study, the novel should count as only obliquely "suburban." It begins as a New York City novel—with formative visits to Carol's "country" home in the New Jersey suburbs—transforms into a road novel, and then evolves into a kind of epistolary tale in which letters, both delivered and unsent, play an outsized role in the fate of its characters. Yet, as I have argued in this chapter, if we understand the suburbs as a social institution and a regulatory framework for the postwar nation, then I would offer that the suburban house here serves as a unique instance of organization life. In fact, I would contend that heteronormative domesticity exists as part of that "single huge machine" threatening to destroy Therese at the beginning of the story. In this light, the organization, the nuclear family, and the suburbs serve as nodal points within a system that disciplines individuals, normalizes heterosexual desire, and adjusts expectations to the demands of domesticity, the gendered division of labor, and the separation of private and public realms. It is impossible to disarticulate corporate capitalism and, as previously quoted from May, the "abundant family life of modern suburban homes" from the postwar suburban nation-building project. Even if the Airds' house exists at the margins of the narrative, it remains the central metonym for the domestic ideology that judges Therese and Carol's love deviant.[52] Just as the offstage, suburban house in *Raisin in the Sun* represents the invisible but real ideological center of the play, demarcating the national battle lines pertaining to race and residential rights, the "country" home in *Price of Salt* marks the contested terrain of sex, security, and citizenship in Cold War America.

Over the course of the novel, Highsmith uses the Aird household to connote multiple possibilities. Readers can infer that, prior to the narrative present, Carol perceived the house as a trap, characterized by the marital strife that precipitated her divorce from her husband, Harge. As she later confides to Therese, speaking of Harge and his family, "One's just supposed to conform. I know what they'd like, they'd like a blank slate they could fill in. A person already filled in disturbs them terribly. . . . I think [Harge] wants to control me" (113). As described here, the family sounds not unlike a corporation trying to recruit and inscribe a proper wife and mother: Are *You* Aird Material? At the present, before their road trip, the house offers a more capacious space that Carol can share, intermittently, with Therese as their relationship develops. Although Carol's husband and her best friend, Abby Gerhard, both disrupt this idyll on different occasions, the house nevertheless facilitates an awakening in Therese that transforms every other space she occupies, including the family home of her spurious boyfriend: "This morning she had awakened in Carol's house. Carol was like a secret spreading through her, spreading through this house, too, like a light invisible to everyone but her" (78). Eventually, though, the house becomes a site of domestic surveillance, abetted by the Airds' housekeeper, Florence, who discovers an undelivered letter that exposes Therese's feelings for Carol. In this way, Highsmith integrates the suburban home into a Cold War system of spying and wiretapping to expose transgressive sexuality, a system that extends to the coercive power of the state in an effort both to discipline Carol's queer desires and to restrict her role as a mother to her daughter, Rindy.

As bleak as all that sounds, the novel ends happily, if indecisively, with the promise that Therese and Carol will reunite.[53] Perhaps because the novel does not turn toward the extremes of asexual misogyny that one finds, for example, in Highsmith's *Deep Water* (1957), a macabre story of sociopathic suburbanites, *The Price of Salt* offers a more nuanced imagining of desires and human relationships beyond the nuclear family. Therese's refusal to adapt herself to organization life at Frankenberg's anticipates her dismissal of heterosexual norms and traditional domesticity. She does maintain a threadbare relationship with Richard Semco, her would-be fiancé, and entertains a flirtation with Dannie McElroy, a graduate student in physics, but after her first encounter with Carol, all her desires are measured against the ineffable, often unnameable, feelings that Therese harbors for her. When Richard suggests they spend an evening with their friends, Sam and Joan, she reluctantly agrees, but inside she roils at this blunt attempt to recruit her to married life. "She hated it," Highsmith writes. "Two of the most boring people she had ever met, a shoe clerk and a secretary, happily married on West Twentieth Street, and she knew Richard meant to show her an ideal life in theirs, to remind her that they might live together the same way one day" (127). Therese's rejection of an imprisoning corporate life is of a piece with her rejection of tedious, obligatory domesticity, but these refusals initially leave her searching for a language in which to think and name her own desires.

Indeed, her fleeting interest in Dannie seems entirely premised on the assumed certainty granted by his field of study that "[l]ife is an exact science on its own terms" (104). Highsmith writes, "Therese looked down at the opened books on his desk, the pages and pages covered with symbols that she could not understand, but that she liked to look at. Everything the symbols stood for was true and proven. The symbols were stronger and more definite than words" (103). This desire for the "true and proven" contrasts with her recurrent inability to define her attraction to Carol. As Victoria Hesford observes, the conversation with Dannie "offers Therese a way of thinking about her relationship with Carol free of moral judgment or, indeed, 'undercurrents.'"[54] Therese also tries to draw Richard into conversation about the possibility of men falling in love with men, or women with women, but he is too dense an interlocutor to offer any perspective. She wonders, "Was it love or wasn't it that she felt for Carol? And how absurd it was that she didn't even know. She had heard about girls falling in love, and she knew what kind of people they were and what they looked like. Neither she nor Carol looked like that" (83). Even as she struggles to account for emotions that fall outside default heterosexuality, she must also reconcile her own desiring body with Cold War stereotypes about "dykes" and "lesbians." Initially, her only recourse is to the language of individual "perversities" (104), and she polices herself by deliberately averting her gaze from women who have the "look," women "in slacks" or who "had hair cut like a boy's" (128). It is only after they are on the road and, in truth, after she and Carol have consummated their sexual relationship that Therese finds something "more definite than words" that would, at least in part, quiet this quest for certainty: "she did not have to ask if this was right, no one had to tell her, because this could not have been more right or perfect" (168).

As metaphor, the open road certainly creates the space for such revelations, and Carol says as much after they have sex—"My angel. . . . Flung out of space" (168)—but Highsmith had previously intimated the car as a potentially liberating and transgressive space. During one of their early outings, Carol picks up Therese at Frankenberg's and drives her back to her house in the New Jersey suburbs. "'Do you like driving?'" Carol asks. "She had a cigarette in her mouth. She drove with her hands resting lightly on the wheel, as if it were nothing to her, as if she sat relaxed in a chair somewhere, smoking" (48). Looking on from the passenger seat, Therese reads the dangling cigarette and Carol's deft touch on the wheel as indicative of her insouciant power and the control she has at her disposal as the more mature, settled, and wealthier partner. Nearing their destination, Carol asks, "Do you like the country?" (48). As they turn off the main road and into the driveway, the Airds' "white two-storey house" and its "projecting side wings like the paws of a resting lion" (49) reiterate a sense of latent power, as if the automobile and the home were extensions of Carol.

The question about "the country" is also provocative insofar as it both conflates the suburban dream with "country" living, as discussed in the introduction to this study, and slyly expands the query to the nation as a whole. This becomes evident once Carol and Therese hit the road. As they drive west as far as Utah, the spaces of the road—the car, the cafés, restaurants, bars, and hotels—allow their relationship to flourish away from the determinative, gendered realms of postwar domesticity. Addressing both the Airds' country house and the rural countryside, Derrick King argues, "It is the country that unlocks the possibility of queer sexuality for Carol and Therese, . . . deepening further the association of the country with the possibility of a queer utopia."[55] Yet, even as they enjoy a certain freedom of movement, they remain conscious of public proscriptions against homosexuality and McCarthy-era suspicions about subversive same-sex desire, and in that way, the sexual prohibitions embodied in the suburban home trail them. As Hesford observes, invoking May's arguments about domestic containment, "When Carol and Therese 'escape' from the New Jersey house, they reveal in the process the threat posed by its normative claims. . . . Highsmith links the regulatory role of the home quite explicitly to the Cold War rhetoric of patriotism, but in a way that inverts the ideology of 'homeward-bound' nationness."[56] The detective hired by Harge to track the women and the legal threat to deny Carol custody of her daughter offer the clearest examples of the regulatory regime within which compulsory domesticity operates. Yet because she has so much at stake, Carol also curbs the couple's public behavior. After they have sex for the first time, Therese considers how this newfound intimacy might ripple through their everyday encounters, but "when she simply took Carol's arm as they stood choosing a box of candy in a shop, Carol murmured, 'Don't'" (171). Later, discussing Carol's brief but intense love affair with Abby, Therese asks:

> "Does [Harge] still talk about it?"
> "No. Is it anything to talk about? Is it anything to be proud of?"
> "Is it anything to be ashamed of?"
> "Yes. You know that, don't you?" Carol asked in her even, distinct voice. "In the eyes of the world it's an abomination."
> (175–76)

At this point in the novel, Carol cannot reconcile her queer desire with motherhood, and since she wishes to remain a central figure in Rindy's life, she gives voice to the disciplinary system of suburban family life and the stigma of homosexuality, in effect reinscribing the boundaries as they transgress them.

The deeper implications of Carol's provocative question, "Do you like the country?" come into focus during an intriguing sequence as the couple continues their westward journey. While on the road, Therese receives a patronizing letter from Richard that belittles her feelings for her "whimsical friend." The sense of shame and "abomination" that Carol describes pervades the letter's implicit accusation: "one day you'll blush," Richard assures her. He nevertheless concludes by professing his love for Therese and promises to meet her on the road: "I'll come out to you—and show you what America's really like" (177). Richard promises a kind of sexual reorientation through tourism, positioning himself as a phallic guide to an authentic America. Having found the letter insulting, Therese destroyed it, but when Carol asks about the latest news from Richard, she can recall its contents, privately, in photographic detail. The next day, back on the road, "taking an indirect highway on a whim," the couple drive through a bucolic countryside of barns and farmhouses, and the scene inspires in Therese "a fervid burst of patriotism—*America*" (178). She connects the emotion welling up within her to the enchanted landscape, which she compares to a "magic carpet" (178), but these are also the moments right before they discover a detective has been tracking them and their journey begins to unravel.

The juxtaposition of these two "Americas" at such a critical juncture in the novel seems charged with significance. There is the "real" America, or what America is "really like," that Richard invokes to stigmatize Therese's relationship with Carol, implying that, in the car and the hotel rooms and the roadside cafés, they have been indulging some queer simulacrum. The America that Richard promises (or threatens) to show Therese would seem entangled with what Hesford calls "the America of the private detective, the regulatory space of heterosexual norms and middle-class hegemony."[57] Highsmith contrasts that America with the impassioned, orgasmic, "fervent burst" of "America" that surges through Therese. Since that overflow of emotion precedes the realization about the detective, Hesford reads this as an instance of "sentimental misrecognition," but I think that minimizes the effect Highsmith creates by casting these two "Americas" against one another.[58] The juxtaposition reveals the complexity of place in the novel, a complexity that invites overlapping readings. For example, even after they realize they are being tracked, the couple remains devotees of the road for a time, seeking out minor adventures, coursing "aimlessly over the zigzagging roads" through the mountains and climbing hills as Highsmith continues to frame their affair in these non-domestic spaces (191). And they continue to have sex, despite the dangers posed by surveillance notes and Dictaphone tapes. "That night," she writes, "talking over the road map about their route tomorrow, talking as matter of factly as a couple of strangers, Therese thought surely tonight would not be like last night. But when they kissed goodnight in bed, Therese felt their sudden release, that leap of response in both of them, as if their bodies were of some materials which put together inevitably created desire" (195). The couple discovers a most improbable kink, the aphrodisia of road maps, as travel and desire intersect in mutually reinforcing currents.

This crucial sequence in Carol and Therese's westward journey sustains the tension between both the normative, regulatory force of "the country"—embodied in the Airds' suburban home, the detective, and the legal realm of parental custody rights—and, as cited earlier, the possibility of a "queer utopia" beyond the reach of that disciplinary regime. Eventually Carol must return to New York, and her fight to retain custody of her daughter will subject her sexuality to the full regulatory power of the state, leaving the two lovers estranged until they reunite in New York City. But the normative domestic, social, and legal institutions are not the only America that the novel makes space for. Read as a critical response to the contradictory yet intersecting constructions of place, as a novel engaged with the regional complexities and differential spaces of the postwar nation, *The Price of Salt* reveals these contested realities, so that "the country" is both an extension of suburban hegemony and the possibility of escape into a differently configured queer future. In this way, the road trip functions as a subtly deployed, reconfigured regionalist aesthetic within the novel. Highsmith troubles a familiar trope from seminal works of regional fiction written by men, such as Twain's *The Adventures of Huckleberry Finn* (1885) or Sherwood Anderson's *Winesburg, Ohio* (1919), and offers a radical reenactment of an escape from the confines of the provincial "country." Read as "queer regionalism," *The Price of Salt* contests the ways suburban topography and compulsory domesticity construct the postwar heteronormative ideal.

Earlier I suggested that, once the road trip ends, the novel becomes a kind of epistolary tale, and I want to close by considering the role of letters and the idea of the ineffable. Right before Carol posed the question, "Do you like the country?" Therese had been thinking about "the unmailed letter" she had written to Carol (48). Like the return of the repressed, the words of unmailed letters surface at different moments in the novel. "*I feel I am in love with you, . . . and it should be spring. I want the sun throbbing on my head like chords of music*" (108). Therese recalls these words during an edgy conversation with Carol about Abby, and later, when Richard asks why she is so infatuated with Carol, lines from "some letter she had written to Carol and never mailed drifted across her mind. . . . *I feel I stand in a desert with my hands outstretched, and you are raining down upon me*" (134). Of course, the letter concealed between the pages of the *Oxford Book of English Verse* proves the most consequential artifact. This is the evidence that the Airds' housekeeper discovers and sells to Harge, and the disclosure of Therese's feelings for Carol precipitates the hiring of the detective. This betrayal allows Highsmith to integrate the domestic realm within the Cold War regulatory network of surveillance and wiretaps, but this undelivered letter is also a stand-in for Therese's recurrent inability to find a language to name her desires. Just moments before she realizes that she had left the book on a bedroom nightstand, Therese "felt there were thousands of words choking her throat, and perhaps only distance, thousands of miles, could straighten them out. Perhaps it was freedom itself that choked her" (153). The unmailed letters, the chronic sensation that Therese "could never say exactly what she wanted to say" (163), and the bartered note that betrays their affair all suggest the illegible nature of queer desire in suburbia. The "country" opens up contested spaces, albeit always in proximity to the pressures of enforced domesticity, where prohibited desires vie for expression within a regime meant to stifle queer identities; but in the end, it is the city that offers refuge to Carol and Therese as the place to configure a possible future together.[59]

Thus it is only by abandoning the suburban home that Highsmith can, at least tentatively, envision progressive alternatives to adjustment culture and the regulatory demands of marriage and motherhood. Whereas *Revolutionary Road* leaves its "queer" figures either institutionalized or dead, *The Price of Salt* offers the promise of a happy ending, even if it is laden with sacrifice. As Sashi Nair writes, "In imagining a 'happy' ending that entails the queer mother's loss of her child, *The Price of Salt* shifts the ground upon which queer romance is possible."[60] Earlier in the novel, after her split with Harge, Carol laments her shrinking network of friends: "Everything's supposed to be done in pairs" (88). Through Carol and Therese, Highsmith renders a positive and powerful reimagining of this "coupling" imperative within a queer framework, outside the normative institution of the nuclear family. In this way, *The Price of Salt* would seem to counter Whyte's assessment about Cold War literature: "Fiction heroes and heroines . . . have been remarkably passive for some time. It is not enough, however, to show that they are not masters of their own destiny; there now seems to be a growing disposition on the part of writers to go out of their way to show that they *cannot* be."[61] The novel offers a corrective to that impulse, one that does not lead to death or madness. In the final analysis, Highsmith confers a sense of agency upon her characters while also keeping her readers keenly aware of the intractable demands of regulatory institutions, including both the costs of opting out of the suburban ideal and the pleasure of contesting its prohibitions.

Cheever's journal entry about the silent threat of homosexuality found its way into his second novel, *The Wapshot Scandal*. "Now that was the year when the squirrels were such a pest and everybody worried about cancer and homosexuality," Cheever writes, adding carcinomas to the list of invisible threats terrorizing the nation.[62] Melissa Wapshot, married to Moses, the elder scion of the Wapshot family, lives in the affluent suburb of Proxmire Manor, a "handsome and comfortable" enclave that "seemed to have eliminated, through adroit social pressures, the thorny side of human nature" (*WS* 38). One evening at a neighbor's cocktail party, Melissa stumbles into a dark bedroom where she is promptly "embraced" by a woman who enfolds her, "groaning with ardor" (*WS* 40). As soon as the woman realizes her mistake, she apologizes and leaves, but Melissa is left to puzzle over this chance homosexual encounter. She assumes that "two of her neighbors, two housewives, had fallen in love and had planned a rendezvous," but she quickly dismisses the idea: "It must have been someone from out of town; someone from the wicked world beyond Proxmire Manor" (*WS* 40). Later, when Melissa falls ill and the ailment persists, the doctor orders her to the hospital where she spends several nights, plagued with fever and a "cutting pain in her breast," before convalescing (*WS* 74). Yet even after she is discharged, Melissa remains convinced that she has cancer and, distrustful of the doctors, she invites a nurse out for a drink. "I wanted to ask you about my x-rays," she says (*WS* 77). As it turns out, Melissa is just fine, and soon thereafter, she runs off with a nineteen-year-old grocery boy. The decision by Cheever, though, between his journal entry and the novel, to link the perils of homosexuality and cancer speaks not only to his own lingering anxieties about the "pathology" of queer desire, but also to the Cold War compulsion to expose subversive homosexuals. In *Wapshot Scandal*, Cheever presents cancer and homosexuality as asymmetrical threats: one can be revealed by x-rays, diagnosed, and subjected to medical treatment; the other, despite the "adroit social pressures" of upscale suburbs, proliferates in furtive chambers, but "remained in the dark[,] remained unspoken" (*J* 117).

In varying ways, the three writers considered in this chapter explore Cold War–era discriminatory systems at the convergent geo-cultural scales of the single-family household, the suburban neighborhood, and the nation more broadly conceived. Cheever's rare but telling accounts of homosexuality in his suburban fiction most clearly reflect the "noisome semisecret" he disclosed—and bemoaned—in his private journals, while Yates, as his title suggests, has his sights set on loftier ideas about how the nation's "revolutionary spirit" has hit a dead end in the repressive social institutions of postwar America. Only Highsmith offers something more positive and liberating in her heroines' flight from the stifling confines of the heteronormative nuclear family, but it requires Carol and Therese to reject rather than remodel a queer suburban domesticity. Taken together, their work raises important questions about how mid-century literature accounts for, and makes legible, desires that do not square with the procreative and consumerist demands of the suburban dream and the familial consensus. Moreover, as texts that "queer" the postwar suburban region, these works expose and contest the disciplinary forces of heteronormativity and "question the formation of exclusionary norms."[63] Postwar domestic nation building depended upon the social institutions of the suburbs and the nuclear family, alongside the shift to organization culture, to provide a framework for the consumer capitalism that was central to the vision of a forward-looking America. The idealization of the suburban home as a regulatory domain will prove essential to the development of the country's metropolitan regions in the decades to come. As I will take up in the next chapter, the secure, private, suburban household will provide a material foundation for the neo-liberal ideologies that propel the country into the next era of suburban development and a new era of domestic containment.

PART II

Neoliberalism and the Post–Cold War Era

(1970s–1990s)

3

Serious Fiction

*Consumer-Citizenship, Market Logic,
and the Postmetropolis*

"The privatization of public space can only be understood as occurring at the
nexus of global, national, urban, and neighborhood scales."
—NEIL SMITH AND SETHA LOW,
The Politics of Public Space (2006)

ON JUNE 12, 1995, Jonathan Franzen initiated a correspondence with Don DeLillo in a letter that, he admitted, might
seem "intrusively introspective," especially considering they had
never met. Over the course of three singled-spaced paragraphs,
Franzen describes a project he had agreed to write for the *New York
Times* magazine on "the decline of the novel's cultural authority in
the U.S.," and he concludes by asking DeLillo if he would like to "talk
about audience and authority" over coffee.[1] In this and subsequent
letters, Franzen sounds every bit the ardent young writer appealing
to a literary giant whom he deeply admires, acknowledging that
"[b]ack when I was learning how to write, working on 27th City,
I took your novels like purgatives, cobweb-clearers, possibility-
expanders."[2] Collectively, these early letters show Franzen piecing
together a definition of literary value, what he comes to call "serious
fiction," but they also reveal a writer who is both acutely concerned
with the recognition of his peers and skeptical of a "larger audience
of unserious readers," even as he worries that no one "will be making

a living selling books ten years from now."[3] In a fretful letter dated July 29, 1995, he cites a reawakening to "the substantiality of words," but also acknowledges "the free market/technological erosion of literary culture," and struggles to align his own sense of unease about the future of the novel with the apparent lack of anxiety "the closer [he gets] to the actual site of literary production."[4]

Read in context, the "site of literary production" refers simply to novelists who produce literature, but given Franzen's concerns about cultural authority, unserious readers, and the free market, the phrase also evokes Pierre Bourdieu's distinction between "the field of large-scale cultural production," in which works of art circulate and accrue value (or fail to) among "the public at large," and "the field of restricted production," which assigns value based upon the judgments of a "peer group whose members are both privileged clients and competitors."[5] Franzen's appeal to DeLillo and his suspicions about unserious readers suggest his interests hew more closely to "the field of restricted production" and the respect of "privileged clients and competitors." Yet, in this same letter, he also expresses a more common concern for any young writer. He asks: "How do I square the idea of the writer-alone-in-the-shadows with the imperative that so many of us feel nonetheless to address matters of central importance to the culture? . . . What if you're in the shadows and nobody <u>cares</u> that you're in the shadows?"[6] The question suggests an aspiration for cultural relevance and, perhaps, popular recognition, but more tellingly, this line of thinking about readership and literary culture suggests a type of market sensibility. In other words, Franzen seems to be asking how a novelist should position himself and hone his craft so that he might get noticed out there "in the shadows" of an eroding literary marketplace.[7]

For the purposes of this inquiry into suburban literature, I am most struck by the way Franzen ultimately maps these nascent concerns about the "decline of the novel's cultural authority" onto the nation's transforming metropolitan regions. In the end, his essay was declined by the editorial board at the *New York Times* magazine, but *Harper's* picked it up and published the piece in April 1996 under the title "Perchance to Dream," and Franzen subsequently reprinted the essay under the title "Why Bother? (The *Harper's* Essay)" in *How to Be Alone* (2003). The essay reflects on the attenuated literary culture he discovered in the wake of his first novel: "The literary America in which I found myself after I published *The Twenty-Seventh City* bore a strange resemblance to the St. Louis I'd grown up in: a once-great city that had been gutted and drained by white flight and super highways. Ringing the depressed urban core of serious fiction were prosperous new suburbs of mass entertainments."[8] Later, lamenting what he sees as a trend toward solipsism, Franzen proclaims, "I mourn the retreat into the Self and the decline of the broad-canvas novel for the same reason I mourn the rise of suburbs . . . I still like a novel that's alive and multivalent like a city" (*HTBA* 80). Most provocatively, as Franzen expounds upon the engagement between author and reader, the transformation from an urban to a suburban nation figures as central to his conception of the novel and its loss of cultural authority. He writes, "In the past, when the life of letters was synonymous with culture, solitude was possible the way it was in cities where you could always, day and night, find the comfort of crowds outside your door. In a suburban age, when the rising waters of electronic culture have made each reader and each writer an island, it may be that we need to be more active in assuring ourselves that a community still exists" (88).

The analogies rely on familiar critiques of suburbia—its perceived shallowness, crass consumerism, homogeneous populations, and lack of communal spaces—but an undercurrent of market logic persists. "Mass entertainments" and "electronic culture" have conspired to narrow the audience share for "serious fiction," but as Franzen figures it, suburban sprawl itself acts as an accomplice, aiding and abetting the erosion of the novel's authority and influence. While the first two passages metaphorize the metro-region (urban = serious, alive, complex; suburban = unserious, inert, frivolous), the third passage indicts the "suburban age" writ large as complicit in the destruction of literary America. The essay insists that we view literature and exurban sprawl as interwoven, and it does so by interpolating metropolitan topography into vexed discussions about authorship, audience, and the literary marketplace. In short, Franzen's informing question about the contemporary (market) value of "serious fiction" implicitly situates today's "serious reader" as inevitably entangled in the geopolitics of the suburban nation.

This chapter explores the contested terrain of exurban sprawl and notions of literary value in DeLillo's *White Noise* (1985) and Franzen's *The Twenty-Seventh City* (1988). More specifically, I argue that DeLillo and Franzen present two distinct responses to the coinciding exigencies of neoliberalism and the emergent postmetropolis in the 1980s. Given their importance to their authors' respective careers, these novels offer interesting case studies for such an evaluation. Certainly, DeLillo was already well-known and respected among writers and critics when he published *White Noise*, but the novel, which garnered the National Book Award, undoubtedly moved him into "the field of large-scale cultural production." Over the next twelve years, he would publish *Libra* (1988), *Mao II* (1991), and *Underworld* (1997), the latter earning the prestigious William Dean Howells Medal in 2000. Taken alongside *White Noise*, this enviable run reinforced his reputation as a leading figure in American letters. For Franzen, who in the 1980s was reading DeLillo's novels like "purgatives," *The Twenty-Seventh City* was an initial foray into the literary marketplace and onto the national scene. By the time he wrote to DeLillo in 1995, he had published a second novel, *Strong Motion* (1992), but "the broad-canvas novel" that would liberate him from the shadows as yet eluded him. Still, one can detect in Franzen's first novel the geopolitical stakes that would come to inform his notion of "serious fiction" and his concerns about a dwindling audience of serious readers.

Beyond these career trajectories, however, *White Noise* and *Twenty-Seventh City* also appear on the scene during a pivotal moment in the history of postmodern literature, as the experimental literature associated with the period of "high postmodernism" gives way to "late" or "exhausted" postmodernism and the resurgence of the realist novel.[9] As such, these two very different novels offer a chance to think broadly about definitions of "serious fiction" and the ways writers represent the regional complexities of the built environment during this fraught period of metropolitan development. My reading will suggest that there is a submerged regional aesthetic at work in these "serious" novels, specifically evident in their critical response to an interconnected pattern of place constructions. In the end, this chapter shows that *White Noise* traffics more easily amidst the disorienting patterns of the postmodern landscape and more effectively situates the suburban home as a nexus for national and international concerns—including global capitalism and exposure to industrial hazards—whereas *The Twenty-Seventh City* evinces a commitment to realism and the mappable boundaries of the modern metropolis, with its clearly discernible urban center and suburban periphery. Nevertheless, and in ways DeLillo does not, Franzen adeptly formulates the apparent inevitability of neoliberalism, its commitment to hierarchies of race, and its deleterious effects on the public realm and democratic life.

Neoliberalism and the Postmetropolis

Before delving into these two novels, I want to clarify the intersections among neoliberalism, suburban nation building, and the rise of the postmetropolis. Neoliberalism is itself a contested term in literary studies, no doubt because it is notoriously capacious. "Depending on your critical viewpoint," write Mitchum Huehls and Rachel Greenwald Smith, "the expansiveness of the term makes it either absolutely vital or totally useless for critical work on contemporary culture."[10] The attempts by philosophers and scholars to describe the economic policies, political ideologies, and the social and cultural saturation of neoliberalism register the term's sprawling nature. In his lectures at the Collège de France, Michel Foucault portrays American neoliberalism as a response to the New Deal programs of the 1930s and "the growth of the federal administration through economic and social programs" from the 1940s to the 1960s that were intended to combat poverty and racial segregation.[11] In perhaps his most succinct articulation, he defines neoliberalism as "the inversion of the relationships of the social to the economic" or, more intricately, as a systematic effort by its adherents to apply the "analyses of the market economy to decipher non-market relationships and phenomena which are not strictly and specifically economic but what we call social phenomena."[12] In short, all aspects of society—from marriage, to the household, to education, to criminal justice, to governmental programs—are subjected to or delimited by the logic of the market.[13]

Lisa Duggan also traces the rise of neoliberalism to a backlash against New Deal policies, arguing that the nation's temporary commitment to "a very limited form of welfare state liberalism" yielded, in the 1970s and 1980s, to "the creation of a new vision of national and world order, a vision of competition, inequality, market 'discipline,' public austerity, and 'law and order' known as *neoliberalism*."[14] By design, neoliberal policies redistribute wealth upward to a class of corporate and economic elites but—and this is key—they do so in ways that make this redistribution seem both a natural occurrence and a universal good. As Duggan continues, "This 'neo' liberalism is usually presented not as a particular set of interests and political interventions, but as a kind of nonpolitics—a way of being reasonable, and of promoting universally desirable forms of economic expansion and democratic government around the globe."[15] David Harvey arrives at similar conclusions regarding neoliberalism's adherence to the marketplace as the arbiter of personal interest and human welfare. He writes, "Neoliberalism is in the first instance a theory of political economic practices that proposes that human well-being can best be advanced by liberating individual entrepreneurial freedoms and skills within an institutional framework characterized by strong private property rights, free markets, and free trade."[16] As a political and economic framework, neoliberalism has proven so durable because, according to Bourdieu, it is also a "programme for destroying collective structures which may impede pure market logic."[17] In his formulation, neoliberalism functions as a utopian discourse that effectively creates its own material reality. This discourse "is so strong and so hard to combat only because it has on its side all of the forces of a world of relations of forces, a world that it contributes to making what it is."[18]

This snapshot of the sober and diverse conversations surrounding neoliberalism highlights a number of the ideology's central elements: an emphasis on the individual as entrepreneur and agent of self-interest; the free market as the primary measure of human desire, social well-being, and cultural value; a predilection for lower taxes, deregulation, and the upward redistribution of resources; an animosity toward social welfare programs or government intervention, especially to address income inequality or racial injustice; and an apolitical façade intended to make corrosive policies appear benign and natural. This provides a useful political and economic context for what I see as the fraught historical confluence that occurred in the mid-1980s, one that interlaces the ascendency of neoliberalism, the emergence and eventual crystallization of the postmetropolis across the metropolitan regions of the U.S., and the literary shift noted from late postmodernism toward realism. Arguably, the entire process of postwar suburbanization in America, with its focus on private property and property values, laid the groundwork and provided a domestic front for "the grim reach of US imperial power" and "the rapid proliferation of neoliberal state forms throughout the world from the mid-1970s onwards."[19] Suburban isolationism and privatism—defined as an increased emphasis on the private realm and the pursuit of individual and family interests—complement and abet a neoliberal ideology that privileges "individualism, private property, personal responsibility, and family values" over the public realm or the state.[20] Under the Reagan administration in the mid-1980s, these ideas coalesced around a set of proposals and policies that had become essential to "a political conservatism motivated by anticommunism, Christian morality, and a generalized fear of minorities and immigrants."[21]

Admittedly, the initial decades of suburban nation building may seem far removed from the "neoliberalism" discussed here. As described in the introduction to this study, suburbanization was premised on economic practices and policies that favored labor and depended upon the government to subsidize the development of, and insure the mortgages on, these new single-family houses. Yet, given the beneficiaries of these programs—predominantly white, working- and middle-class families—we can quite easily recast this federal largesse as a kind of down payment, an investment in the private realm, self-interest, and "the favored form of family life": white, patriarchal, heterosexual.[22] Moreover, the ideology of privatism that helped to underwrite suburban nation building created, in turn, a social foundation for neoliberalism in America's suburban and exurban settlements. Roger Keil offers a similar line of reasoning: "Neoliberalism values the privatization of economic decision making and responsibilities over collective solutions, and suburbanization has proved to be an ideal field for a comprehensive restructuring of social and spatial relationships."[23] Neoliberalism has flourished by promoting the universal virtue of private interest and the infallibility of the market, even—or especially—to those who have no hope of benefitting from an economic and political agenda to restore class power to an economic elite, power that had been temporarily curtailed during the initial postwar era.[24]

In the United States, the rise of neoliberalism coincides with and, I would contend, facilitates a pivotal era in the history of urban restructuring, bridging what Joel Garreau identifies as the second and third waves of moving into "new frontiers." Postwar suburbanization constitutes the first wave; the second wave encompasses the "malling of America" in the 1960s and 1970s; and the third wave is distinguished by the movement of jobs out of urban centers.[25] This third wave leads to the creation of "edge cities" that, according to Garreau, constitute the latest contested site in the battle between "utilitarian" and "pastoral" impulses, what Leo Marx regarded as the tension between "rural myth" and the "counterforce" to that myth in the form of industrialization: "The history of America is an endless repetition of this battle."[26] The neoliberal emphasis on the dictates of the market—the interests of economic and corporate powerbrokers, deregulation and maximizing profits, and the privatization of public services and spaces—provided an ideological underpinning for these sprawling landscapes, as well as a veneer of naturalness and inevitability.

Edward Soja offers a more global perspective on this restructuring process—dating back 11,000 years to the origins of "urban agglomeration"—and he identifies the postmodern metropolis, or "postmetropolis," as "the latest stage in the geohistory of city-space."[27] Soja underscores the "postmodern" of postmetropolis, despite its disfavor among certain scholars, to suggest both an expansion of the modern city and a profound break from familiar patterns of urban development. The postmetropolis designates the "selective deconstruction and still evolving reconstitution of the modern metropolis," the emergence of the globalized city during the post-Fordist era.[28] "The postmetropolis can be represented as a product of intensified globalization," according to Soja, a process that rescales the metropolis and our conceptions of urban and suburban spaces: "What was once central is becoming peripheral and what was the periphery is becoming increasingly central, an observation that pertains to cityspace, with the intensive urbanization of the suburbs into Outer Cities or Edge Cities while the Central Cities or Inner Cities become edgily filled with diasporic migrants from the world's poorest regions."[29] During this pivotal era of urban history, deindustrialization and decentralization collapse the rigid distinction between the urban core and its commuter suburbs, giving way to the "regional scale" of the postmetropolis.[30]

These concurrent political, economic, and geographic transformations also coincide with the transitionary period of late postmodernism in American literature, and my interest in *White Noise* and *Twenty-Seventh City* lies in the tension between the modern and postmodern metropolis and, more specifically, the ways DeLillo and Franzen attempt to limn the reconstruction of the metro-region in the early neoliberal era. As Fredric Jameson remarks, a perception "tend[s] to emerge in the most energetic postmodernist texts, and this is the sense that beyond all thematics or content the work seems somehow to tap the networks of the reproductive process and thereby to afford us some glimpse into a postmodern or technological sublime, whose power or authenticity is documented by the success of such works in evoking a whole new postmodern space in emergence around us."[31] The ensuing sections of this chapter will, in a sense, hold *White Noise* and *Twenty-Seventh City* to account by examining how each novel evokes this new space. Moreover, I want to suggest that their evocation of the postmetropolis aligns these two works of "serious fiction" with the tenets of regional writing as defined throughout this project. Written during a pivotal moment in the history of urbanization, these novels expand our understanding of region as a geographical and ideological site of nation building, as well as our understanding of suburban fiction as a critical response to the sprawling dimensions of the built environment and the changing structures of American society.

White Noise situates the Gladney family within an elusive, often disorienting cognitive map in which public spaces have been transformed by expressways, strip malls, and mega shopping centers as the novel interrogates the perceived liberty of consumer choice and the role of the private household in the processes of consumption and production. The "airborne toxic event" further exposes the permeability of the domestic sphere, but it also attunes the reader to the deeper sense of environmental precarity that transgresses the borders of this edge city. *The Twenty-Seventh City*, on the other hand, offers a hyper-realistic portrait of the St. Louis metro-region as the narrative explores the corruptibility of state agencies and the ways a free-market ideology reshapes corporate and residential geographies. The novel depicts, at a local level, how neoliberalism undermines collective action and promotes uneven geographic development, a process that tends "to increase social inequality and to expose the least fortunate elements in any society . . . to the chill winds of austerity and the dull fate of increasing marginalization."[32] Jameson's observation about postmodern space provides a criterion, of sorts, for assessing those literary narratives that take aim at the postmetropolis. As works of late and "exhausted" postmodernism, respectively, *White Noise* and *Twenty-Seventh City* elucidate the reconstitution of metropolitan regions under neoliberalism and clarify the stakes of U.S. suburban literature as regional writing in the twilight years of the Cold War era.

The Recesses of the American Home

White Noise famously begins on "the day of the station wagons," as well-heeled parents chauffeur their children to the College-on-the-Hill for the fall term.[33] The vehicles disgorge a Whitmanesque catalog of consumer goods: "the stereo sets, radios, personal computers; small refrigerators and table ranges; the cartons of phonograph records and cassettes; the hairdryers and styling irons; the tennis rackets, soccer balls, hockey and lacrosse sticks, bows and arrows; the controlled substances, the birth control pills and devices; the junk food still in shopping bags" (3). Jack Gladney observes this annual ritual from his office window, delighting in the overloaded stations wagons, the frenetic reunions among students, the detached but self-assured parents, and the aura of "massive insurance coverage" (4). The scene depicts a social order premised on class privilege, consumer power, and the ability to secure (or insure) the private interests of the family, but DeLillo also presumes a broader, naturalized system that validates and reflects back a common identity: "This assembly of station wagons . . . tells the parents they are a collection of the like-minded and the spiritually akin, a people, a nation" (4). The scene resonates with Foucault's argument that, under neoliberalism, "the individual's life itself—with his relationships to his private property, . . . his family, household, insurance, and retirement—must make him into a sort of permanent and multiple enterprise," an entrepreneur of self-interest linked to "a multiplicity of diverse enterprises connected up to and entangled with each other."[34] This is the quotidian nature of neoliberal ideology, coupling the concerns of a "like-minded" economic elite to those of the nation. As one of the most celebrated works of late postmodernism, *White Noise* has garnered significant critical attention over the past thirty-five years. Although fewer scholars have read the novel specifically for its insights into neoliberalism and suburban studies, the critical focus on advertising, consumerism, mass media, and exurban sprawl clearly indicates the significance of late capitalism to our understanding DeLillo's work.

To cite one prominent example in the novel, the pharmaceutical corporation that produces Dylar, the intricately designed, off-market pill Babette takes to eliminate her fear of death, suggests the way multinational corporations intervene in everyday life and configure contemporary anxieties. Babette's ability to barter sex in exchange for the drug from the nebulous Mr. Gray/Willie Mink transforms an existential fear into "a capitalist transaction" (185). Later, when her daughter, Denise, implores her to apply sunscreen before running, Babette concludes, "It's all a corporate tie-in. . . . The sunscreen, the marketing, the fear, the disease. You can't have one without the other" (252). In his reading of *White Noise*, Ralph Clare notes that "the dead and the living are completely separated not because of the imposition of any subjective belief system about death but because of the structures of late capitalist society itself. The scientific, technological, and economic principles that mediate lives also mediate deaths."[35] References to state-of-the-art pharmaceuticals, international credit card companies, and automobiles manufactured by Toyota and Nissan—foreign corporations that both established plants in the United States in the 1980s—situate the narrative within a framework of multinational capital.[36] Referring to DeLillo's original title for the novel, "Panasonic," Martina Sciolino writes that the company name "would have asked readers to put the domestic fiction of the Gladney family in global terms. [Nevertheless,] the title we do have suggests the whitewashing of cultural difference to create standardized markets here and abroad,

. . . [A] kind of white noise everywhere, a complacent chaos of entrepreneurial aggression that now belongs to no nation."[37]

I would propose that the global stakes of this domestic novel remain intact, regardless of the title, and it is precisely this local-global intersection that makes *White Noise* a valuable artifact for suburban studies and, more specifically, for suburban literature in this early neoliberal, postmetropolitan era.[38] Jack Gladney and his family live in Blacksmith, a midwestern town and home to the College-on-the-Hill, where Jack chairs a self-designed program in Hitler studies. The town is located nearby, but unconnected to, the depressed urban core of Iron City. While Blacksmith may not square with the traditional postwar suburban settlements depicted in *Kingsblood Royal* or *Revolutionary Road*, it does resemble the evolving regional patterns of the postmetropolis. "Babette and I and our children by previous marriages live at the end of a quiet street in what was once a wooded area with deep ravines," Jack says. "There is an expressway beyond the backyard now, well below us, and at night as we settle into our brass bed the sparse traffic washes past, a remote and steady murmur around our sleep, as of dead souls babbling at the edge of a dream" (4). Whether we call it a suburb, an exurb, or an edge city, Blacksmith is a once-pastoral setting now enmeshed in a landscape of expressways and residential sprawl created, like many suburban communities across the nation, through "[e]xpansive metropolitanization" and "the selective abandonment of the inner urban core" by industry and retail, as well as working- and middle-class populations, beginning in the 1960s and 1970s.[39]

The Gladney home and the broader postmetropolis in which *White Noise* unfolds serve as the domestic and regional fronts for the omnipresent media culture of "late, consumer or multinational capitalism."[40] In Laura Barrett's assessment, "*White Noise* is a comic appraisal of the rise of mediation in the twentieth century, a clear-eyed assessment of the postmodern condition that is simultaneously hilarious and unnerving."[41] The novel's unsettling nature derives, in part, from the way DeLillo alters our understanding of the places we inhabit. To develop this line of thinking, I want to focus on two critical ways that *White Noise* challenges our understanding of suburban domesticity and the emergent postmodern metropolis. First, DeLillo fragments the trope of the postwar nuclear family and subverts the security of the single-family house, two of the original endowments of postwar suburban nation building. While the close-knit Gladney family appears to embrace a sense of privatism, the traditional nuclear family has been replaced by a collective of children from Jack's and Babette's multiple marriages. Indeed, at times, the family seems more like a cooperative of individuals, each pursuing her or his own self-interest, though united in their admiration and concern for the youngest child, Wilder.[42] The private realm the family shares is exposed to the relentless bleed-through of corporate advertising—"Kleenex Softique, Kleenex Softique" (39), "*Coke is it, Coke is it, Coke is it*"(51), "Toyota Corolla, Toyota Celica, Toyota Cressida" (149)—and rendered vulnerable to the deleterious effects of environmental disaster.[43] Second, *White Noise* evokes the privatized, consumerist built environment of the postmetropolis. This is most evident when the airborne toxic event forces residents to evacuate their homes, but one also detects these evolving spaces in the novel's gathering sites: the supermarket, the mall, and the repurposed non-space of the freeway overpass, where the citizens of Blacksmith gaze at the dazzling "postmodern sunset[s]" (216).

At the geo-cultural scale of the single-family home, *White Noise* highlights the extent to which the nuclear family and the suburban idyll were, from the beginning, a consumerist construction. As examined in the first chapter of this study, postwar suburbanization was underwritten by popular advertising campaigns that relied upon the marketability of democratic values—such as freedom, property, and self-reliance—to promote new residential construction and the purchasing of household goods. *White Noise* provides a forty-year update on how these patterns have reshaped and reframed the domestic realm. The single-family house serves as a nexus within an imperceptible network of market forces. As part of this network, the home is susceptible to the harmful effects of macrolevel dynamics, whether through the insidious reach of mass media and advertising or through the long-term consequences of industrial deregulation and environmental degradation. Yet the private household, as a "unit of production," remains essential to the perpetuation of these macrolevel patterns, most notably through the semi-transcendent process of consumption.[44] In *White Noise*, post-nuclear family domesticity participates in a cyclical movement of consumerism and eradication, from the stockpiling of consumer goods to the ceremonial, cathartic purge. Jack plays a particularly critical role in this dynamic as the would-be patriarchal figure in the family. DeLillo has replaced the traditional suburban "organization man" or "the man in the gray flannel suit" with an entrepreneurial figure in an academic robe, one who has invented his own discipline of study at the College-on-the-Hill and whose sense of status is validated and reinforced through consumerism.

The spiritual nature of the consumer-citizen under late capitalism takes shape early in the novel. After a trip to the supermarket with Babette, Jack notes "the mass and variety of [their] purchases," and he describes "the sense of well-being, the security and contentment these products brought to some snug home in [their] souls" (20). A short time later, following a successful ATM transaction, Jack integrates his sense of personal validation within a weblike arrangement that evokes the currents of global capital. "The system had blessed my life," he says. "I sensed that something of deep personal value, but not money, not that at all, had been authenticated and confirmed. . . . The system was invisible, which made it all the more impressive, all the more disquieting to deal with. But we were in accord, at least for now. The networks, the circuits, the streams, the harmonies" (46). Jack experiences a sense of ecstatic validation, one that surpasses the momentary frisson of a singular purchase or mere currency.[45] This encounter initiates an obsessive desire to remain in sync with the "system." Money on its own may be crass, but these capitalist interfaces—the supermarket, the ATM, and, ultimately, the material abundance of the suburban home—connect him to this hidden network that, in turn, authenticates his value.

In the novel, television plays an obvious role in linking the Gladney household to this invisible system and to the external world where "the outer torment lurks, causing fears and secret desires" (85). At its most basic level, the TV facilitates the media saturation of the domestic realm, but Jack's colleague, Murray J. Siskind, also considers it "a primal force in the American home" (51). Murray, a visiting lecturer on media and popular culture, sees television as a pathway into a different mode of perception: "It's like a myth being born right there in our living room, like something we know in a dreamlike and preconscious way. . . . It opens ancient memories of world birth, it welcomes us into the grid, the network of little buzzing dots that make up the picture pattern" (51). In the Gladney household, Babette rations the children's time with the television so as to mitigate "[i]ts narcotic undertow and eerie diseased brain-sucking power" (16), but the results seem uncertain. During the toxic event evacuation, Jack overhears his daughter Steffie murmuring *Toyota Celica* in her sleep (148), and he realizes she is "repeating some TV voice" bartering "[s]upranational names" (149). Yet, like his encounter with the ATM, Jack senses something ecstatic in the refrain: "Whatever its source, the utterance struck me with the impact of a moment of splendid transcendence" (149). Certainly, it is no coincidence that DeLillo often pairs scenes around the television with the literal consumption of take-out Chinese food (16, 64) and the figurative consumption of news reports covering disaster, death, or the promise of mass graves in backyards (64, 211). The novel stages these set pieces around the TV, so redolent of postwar advertisements for suburban family togetherness, in order to replicate the habitual and pernicious logic of consumerism: "Every disaster made us wish for more, for something bigger, grander, more sweeping" (64).

This compulsive consumerism is nowhere more evident than in Jack's shopping spree at the Mid-Village Mall. For many readers, this episode proves critical to an understanding of the novel's dissection of consumer culture and the way it creates "an aura of connectedness among individuals."[46] Yet for my purposes, the most compelling aspect of this scene is the way Jack's voracious appetite for consumer goods seems fueled by the capacious interior of the mall itself.

> We moved from store to store, rejecting not only items in certain departments, not only entire departments but whole stores, mammoth corporations that did not strike our fancy for one reason or another. There was always another store, three floors, eight floors .... I shopped with reckless abandon. I shopped for immediate needs and distant contingencies. I shopped for its own sake, looking and touching, inspecting merchandise I had no intention of buying, then buying it. . . . I began to grow in value and self-regard. I filled myself out,

found new aspects of myself, located a person I'd forgotten existed. Brightness settled around me. We crossed from furniture to men's wear, walking through cosmetics. Our images appeared on mirrored columns, in glassware and chrome, on TV monitors in security rooms. . . . Voices rose ten stories from the gardens and promenades, a roar that echoed and swirled through the vast gallery, mixing with noises from the tiers, with shuffling feet and chiming bells, the hum of escalators, the sound of people eating, the human buzz of some vivid and happy transaction. (83–84)

I have quoted the scene at length because it brings together two key facets of this inquiry. On the one hand, this bender at the mall displays the raw power of rash consumerism and its ability to restore existential value. As such, Jack does not operate in the mall as a mere consumer, but rather as an agent of production, an "entrepreneur of himself," as Foucault would say: "And we should think of consumption as an enterprise activity by which the individual, precisely on the basis of the capital he has at his disposal, will produce something that will be his own satisfaction."[47] The logic of the marketplace recasts consumer transactions as the production of value and self-worth. The noncommitted, "reckless abandon" that characterizes Jack's consumption further reflects the relentless constraints under neoliberalism to delimit and discern agency as an extension of the market. As Huehls and Greenwald Smith note, "The market does not require specific economic pursuits, political commitments, or ideological beliefs; it only requires our presence, our being in and of it."[48] On the other hand, White Noise also adeptly accounts for the way that space itself embodies and underwrites these imperatives. The dizzying, postmodern architecture that propels Jack forward both connects him to the invisible ebb and flow of the market and epitomizes how the private interests of "mammoth corporations" shape suburban and exurban environments. Here, at the mall, we encounter the intersection of two patterns in the novel: the private consumer-citizen as agent of self-interest and the privatized built environment of the postmetropolis.

The Mid-Village Mall, cited earlier in the novel as "a vast shopping center out on the interstate" (59), succinctly symbolizes the second wave of postwar suburbanization, what Garreau sardonically designated the "malling of America." These evolving patterns of regional development provided the materiality for 1980s "mall culture," offering residents young and old a corporatized public realm, a pseudo-urb where they could stroll, shop, gather, and intermingle with their fellow citizen-consumers.[49] The monopolizing of the environment—via vast networks of superhighways, privatized industrial "parks," strip malls, and megalithic shopping centers—distinguishes this period of urban restructuring. In *White Noise*, the interior design of the Mid-Village Mall disorients Jack but also holds him in thrall; like a windowless casino, the mall conspires to maintain its captive clientele. This canny portrayal of the mall anticipates Soja's depiction of the labyrinthine interior of the Los Angeles Bonaventure Hotel in ways that prove edifying to this discussion. Soja describes the Bonaventure as "fragmented and fragmenting, homogeneous and homogenizing, divertingly packaged yet curiously incomprehensible, seemingly open in presenting itself to view but constantly pressing to enclose, to compartmentalize, to circumscribe, to incarcerate."[50] The carceral effect of the mall comes into focus when, a few days after his shopping spree, Jack remarks that Gladys Treadwell had "died of lingering dread, a result of the four days and nights she and her brother had spent in the Mid-Village Mall, lost and confused" (98). The aged siblings had wandered aimlessly "for two days, lost, confused and frightened, before taking refuge in [a] littered kiosk" (59). How they got to the mall or why they refused to seek help remains unknown, but Jack speculates that "the vastness and strangeness of the place . . . made them feel helpless and adrift in a landscape of remote and menacing figures" (59–60). Jack's orgiastic shopping spree may produce a sense of value and satisfaction, but this absurdist turn exposes the fatal underside of these alluring postmodern spaces. As Soja explains of the Bonaventure, "Everything imaginable appears to be available in the micro-urb but real places are difficult to find, its spaces confuse an effective cognitive mapping, its pastiche of superficial reflections bewilder co-ordination and encourage submission instead."[51]

The domestic realm would seem the logical antidote to these unreal spaces that defy "cognitive mapping," but consumerism, like media saturation, muddles the interior of the home as well.

Although for his step-daughter, Denise, possessions provide "an archaeology of childhood" and retain "their value as remembering objects, a way of fastening herself to a life" (102), for Jack, the clutter of consumer goods and old mementos has transformed the home into a labyrinth. After an ambivalent doctor's visit, one promising only more tests to track the effects of Nyodene D, Jack returns home and, as if to undo the earlier binge, expels the accumulated mass of things: "fishing lures" and "torn luggage," "old furniture" and "bent curtain rods," "picture frames" and "TV trays" and "broken turn-tables," "manuscripts" and "galley proofs" (249). As the discarding process continues, he discovers a different kind of endless pattern, a reduplicative process that complements the compulsive buying at the mall. "The more things I threw away, the more I found," Jack says. "The house was a sepia maze of old and tired things. There was an immensity of things, an overburdening weight, a connection, a mortality. . . . I just wanted to get the stuff out of the house" (249–50). Days later, he reprises the effort, disposing of even more detri-tus, this time with a greater sense of urgency: "I was in a vengeful and near savage state. I bore a personal grudge against these things. Somehow they put me in this fix. They'd dragged me down, made escape impossible" (280). Cynthia Deitering reads these scenes, and *White Noise* more broadly, as emblematic of a "toxic conscious-ness" in 1980s American fiction, "a shift from a culture defined by its production to a culture defined by its waste."[52] Jack's cathartic purge suggests a revision to the consumer-subject: the individual who "find[s] one's identity not in the commodities themselves but in their configuration as waste products."[53] This is a sharp obser-vation, to which I would add that DeLillo uses this shift to a cul-ture of waste to again alter our understanding of space. Perhaps counterintuitively, the purge creates a sense of symmetry between the Mid-Village Mall and the Gladney household, aligning the processes of consumption and waste. Just as the seemingly lim-itless and "menacing" nature of the mall temporarily interns the Treadwells, here Jack describes the domestic realm as its own kind of commodified prison, a "sepia maze" that "made escape impos-sible." Television, mass media, advertising, and consumer goods convert the suburban home into its own version of a carceral-consumerist matrix.

This conflation of domestic and corporate space offers an opportunity to explore further the ways *White Noise* evokes the privatized, built environments of the postmetropolis. In the novel, the supermarket reigns supreme as the ersatz public gathering site. According to Murray, it is akin to the bardo of Tibetan Buddhism, a liminal plane of existence between death and rebirth, a place that "recharges us spiritually, it prepares us, it's a gateway or a pathway. . . . Here we don't die, we shop. But the difference is less marked than you think" (37–38). The natural world remains at a distance in *White Noise*, as neighborhoods, expressways, malls, and supermarkets have displaced the formerly wooded areas. Yet as detailed in Murray's encomium to spiritual regeneration, and in "the sense of well-being" Jack and Babette experience in the "snug home in [their] souls" (20), the supermarket and its standardized, generic offerings facilitate a kind of transcendent experience.[54]

In many ways, though, the airborne toxic event provides the novel's clearest example of late capitalism's impact on this era of suburban development and the contested transition from the modern to the postmodern metropolis. The onset of the toxic event ironically invokes the uneven geographic development under neoliberalism. In reaction to the disaster, Jack says, "These things happen to poor people who live in exposed areas. Society is set up in such a way that it's the poor and the uneducated who suffer the main impact of natural and man-made disasters" (112). Even as the threat arising from the toxic event escalates, he reiterates the safety of his status and location: "I'm not just a college professor. I'm the head of a department. I don't see myself fleeing an airborne toxic event. That's for people who live in mobile homes out in the scrubby parts of the country, where the fish hatcheries are" (115). Jack engages in a version of identity politics, aligning himself with an elite class who, like the parents on the day of the station wagons, consider themselves insulated from calamity and deprivation. Yet, as Ursula K. Heise observes, Jack "bases his argument on natural disasters such as floods and hurricanes, not on human-made crises like the one in which he is already immersed. . . . DeLillo is concerned with the way in which new kinds of risk have invaded the lives of even those citizens that might earlier have had reason to believe themselves safe from their most dire consequences."[55] Policies consistent with

neoliberalism—the supremacy of the free market, corporate imperialism, and widespread deregulation to maximize profits—create
the possibility for these new forms of environmental risk, including
hazards that threaten to nullify the upward redistribution of personal security. Because it crosses all natural and man-made boundaries, from "the scrubby parts of the country" to exurban enclaves,
the airborne toxic event reflects a more lethal version of postmodern, postmetropolitan sprawl.

Perhaps better than any other facet of the novel, the toxic event
generates an environmental awakening to the new exigencies of
the postmetropolis. *White Noise* offers a prescient look at how the
combination of market logic, deregulation, and unlimited sprawl
will continue to threaten the places we inhabit. The disaster turns
the residents of Blacksmith into exurban exiles and temporary ref-
ugees, forced out of their homes, into their automobiles, and, eventually, into makeshift shelters. A "tragic army of the dispossessed"
makes its way along congested roadways lined by "a sordid gantlet
of used cars, fast food, discount drugs and quad cinemas" (124,
117). If earlier Blacksmith had seemed detached from "the path
of history and its contaminations" (85), the airborne toxic event
serves as a reintroduction into the flow of history and geopolitics.
Driven from the presumed security of the domestic realm, these
transient exiles now "seemed to be part of some ancient destiny,
connected in doom and ruin to a whole history of people trekking
across wasted landscapes. There was an epic quality about them
that made [Jack] wonder for the first time at the scope of [their]
predicament" (119).

Jack's dawning awareness exhibits an attention to environment
and to scale. Just as the domestic realm has been rendered permeable to the streams of capital, media, consumerism, and waste, the
airborne disaster repositions "the recesses of the American home"
within regional patterns of environmental degradation and the
toxic currents of man-made, chemical catastrophes (235).[56] Interest-
ingly, the environmental disaster also precipitates an ad hoc, simu-
lated sense of community: "We'd become part of the public stuff of
media disaster. . . . Out of some persistent sense of large-scale ruin,
we kept inventing hope" (141). In his essay "Toxic Discourse," Lawrence Buell writes, "More and more it may become second nature

to everyone's environmental imagination to visualize humanity in relation to environment, not as solitary escapees or consumers, but as collectivities with no alternative but to cooperate in acknowledgement of their necessary, like-it-or-not inter-dependence."[57] While it may be too generous to apply this sense of *esprit de corps* to the "public stuff of media disaster" taking shape among these displaced exurbanites, *White Noise* does serve as a catalyst for imagining the interdependence of humanity and environment. In terms of suburban studies, DeLillo's most brilliant turn is to force everyone out of the house and into the postmodern metropolis. In its temporarily abandoned state, the post-nuclear family home unsettles our expectations about suburban domesticity and, like Jack, we are obliged to reframe the household and our understanding of an exurban community within a grid of metro-regional, national, and multinational entanglements.

Real-Estate Terrorism

To give Franzen his due, he has dedicated a not insignificant amount of time and thought to America's metropolitan regions and the indirect costs of exurban sprawl. In *How to Be Alone*, alongside questions of literary culture, conurbation appears often enough to be considered a leitmotif. "First City," an essay originally written for *The New Yorker*, is an encomium to urban centers, and Franzen laces the text with references to such canonical works as Jackson's *Crabgrass Frontier*, Witold Rybczynski's *City Life*, and Jane Jacobs's *The Death and Life of Great American Cities* (*HTBA* 179–94). "Lost in the Mail" links the woes of Chicago's Post Office to the demands created by sprawl (98–138), and "Imperial Bedroom" implicates America's edgeless metropolitan regions in the demise of the public sphere (39–54). In "Meet Me in St. Louis," when Franzen arrives at his childhood home to shoot B-roll footage for Oprah's Book Club, he discovers, almost inadvertently, that he cannot identify anything distinctive about his old suburban neighborhood (286–302). Thus, in "Why Bother?" when he indicts the "suburban age" for undermining literary culture, that sentiment is of a piece with his anti-suburban stance. It is tempting to read Franzen's *The*

Twenty-Seventh City as the repressed subtext of that semi-infamous *Harper's* essay. The critical response to the novel would seem, in part, the impetus behind the piece. He writes that "the biggest surprise—the true measure of how little I'd heeded my own warning in *The Twenty-Seventh City*—was the failure of my culturally engaged novel to engage with the culture. I'd intended to provoke; what I got instead was sixty reviews in a vacuum" (60–61). That unobserved "warning" is a reference to Franzen's own reading of the novel, which for him is "about the innocence of a Midwestern city—about the poignancy of St. Louis's municipal ambitions in an age of apathy and distraction" (60). Naturally, he seems to say, his "serious fiction" would inevitably founder amidst the same sea of indifference, fall prey to the disengaged suburban age.

"[S]et in a year somewhat like 1984 and in a place very much like St. Louis," Franzen's first novel imagines a moment of crisis in the ongoing conflict between the prosperous county and the financially depressed city.[58] This counterfactual St. Louis is under attack by the Osage Warriors, a local terrorist group with vague connections to Native American tribes displaced from the Missouri territory, whose public statements invoke the country's history of "imperialist" conquest (*TSC* 150). Bombs explode outside a downtown stadium and beneath a highway overpass, subdivisions are strafed with gunfire, a suburban house is burned to the ground, and a housewife is kidnapped at gunpoint. At one end of this crisis is the newly instated police chief, S. (Susan) Jammu, a woman from Bombay, India who supports a plan for city-county reunification that would bring high-tech industry, corporate offices, fashionable townhouses, and other residential developments into the city. At the other end of the crisis is Martin Probst, a contractor famous for building the Gateway Arch and the chairman of Municipal Growth, a group that oversees new development and that opposes the merger. Key investors and prominent citizens vie for position, compete for contracts, double-cross and spy on one another, engage in real-estate speculation and adulterous affairs, and generally try to avoid the terror.

The reader learns early on, however, that the police chief and a cohort of family members and associates are the masterminds behind the violence and that the overt tactics of the Osage Warriors are meant to distract from a subtle, Machiavellian campaign.

Jammu's support for reunification and the renewal syndicate Urban Hope disguises a clandestine real-estate scheme intended to displace Black residents from city neighborhoods, consolidate corporate power in downtown St. Louis, deplete property values in the county, and drain investment funds from suburban developments—like Martin Probst's Westhaven project, a "comprehensive work and lifestyle environment" (*TSC* 37)—all while accumulating political capital for herself and actual capital for her family and associates. Written in the 1980s, amidst edge-city sprawl and, as Soja notes, an era when "diasporic migrants" populated central cities, Franzen's novel uses a transnational, postcolonial figure to re-enact the racial displacements and dispossessions central to St. Louis's metro-regional history.[59]

As this description suggests, there is a whiff of the postmodern "Systems" novel in these conspiratorial networks and the intricate plots and counterplots; a minor character even name-checks Thomas Pynchon when asked if he is "paranoid or something" (*TSC* 55). Yet, in the final analysis, *Twenty-Seventh City* seems more representative of what Mathias Nilges has labeled "exhausted" postmodernism. Nilges contends that "[p]ostmodernism disappears from literature once it becomes the new structural reality of our present. . . . But postmodernism did not exactly die. It transitioned from a fictional life to a real existence."[60] *Twenty-Seventh City* offers an incipient example of a text trying to account for this new structural reality, and in effect, Franzen surrenders his first novel to the economic and political realities of the emerging neoliberal era. While *White Noise* better acclimates readers to the evolving, vertiginous spaces of the corporatized and commodified postmodern metropolis, Franzen's novel attempts to circumscribe the modern metropolis and to create a stable snapshot in time. The result is a hyper-realistic novel dedicated to urban history and the residential politics of the St. Louis metro-region.[61] In lieu of homogeneous expressways, supermarkets, strip malls, and megalithic shopping centers, Franzen depicts downtown St. Louis and its surrounding suburbs with a granular, cartographic precision. In fact, the novel begins with a map entitled "St. Louis and Vicinity." The narrative pays such careful attention to municipalities, street names, coordinates, and local monuments that it seems Franzen wants to ward off disorientation and to reassure his readers, and perhaps himself, that "you are here."

To advance this line of thinking I will focus on two interrelated concepts. The first concerns the novel's preoccupation with history, real estate, and terror; the second involves the failure of the city-county referendum. Franzen takes pains to situate the novel's fictional real-estate conspiracy within the authentic and contentious history of St. Louis metropolitan development. The conspirators even cite the historical consistency of municipal policies and a century's-long commitment to the "*romantic vision of westward progress*" as central to their selection of the city (*TSC* 310). A geographically constrained city and a cabal of westward expansionists create an opening for Jammu and her associates to exploit, a vulnerability premised on an idyllic (but historically accurate) commitment in St. Louis to limitless sprawl as manifest destiny. As the police chief explains to one of her operatives, "Real-estate speculation is a formalism. . . . Once it gets going—once we set it in motion—it works by itself and drags politics and economics along after it. Terror works the same way" (76–77). In the novel, both real-estate speculation and terror render space "abstract" in the Lefebvrean sense. Shaped by capitalism's demands for standardization, abstract space "serves those forces which make a *tabula rasa* of whatever stands in their way, of whatever threatens them—in short, of differences."[62] The real-estate conspiracy that underlies the referendum for reunification corporatizes urban space at the expense of vulnerable minority populations who are effectively rendered invisible in the process of metropolitan reconstruction.

The map, "St. Louis and Vicinity," ironically participates in this process of abstraction. Building on Lefebvre's theory of spatiality, Nicholas Blomley explains that maps play a pivotal role in projects of displacement and dispossession. He writes that maps "offer an enframing of space . . . that helps make possible the very idea of 'space' as an external category"; as dominant depictions of space, maps "conceptually empty[] a space of its native occupants" and clear the way for reoccupation.[63] In *Twenty-Seventh City*, the map that precedes the narrative and the real-estate terror campaign cooperate, at different registers, to transform metro-regional geography into an abstract category, a dominant "idea of space," subject

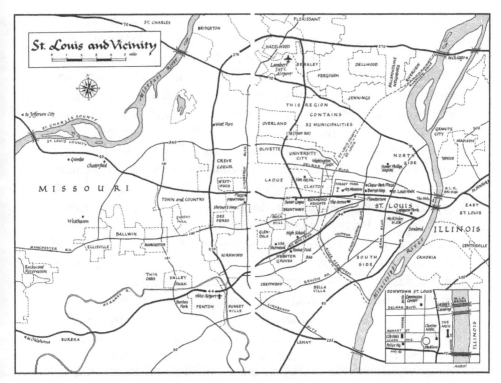

An idea of space: "St. Louis and Vicinity." Courtesy of Farrar, Straus and Giroux.

to private interests and the logic of the market. The ultimate failure of the referendum reflects the civic "apathy and distraction" that Franzen reads as the novel's central theme, but I would contend this failure is necessitated by Franzen's commitment to hyper-realism. In other words, the indifference of the electorate—"little better than one eligible adult in seven had bothered to go to the polls" (*TSC* 502)—restores the novel to the flow of history and the actual topography of St. Louis city and its satellite municipalities. Arguably, this is an inherently conservative turn on Franzen's part, but in doing so, *The Twenty-Seventh City* forecasts the triumph of neoliberalism as the dominant political and economic reality in the 1990s and early 2000s.

From the outset, the novel intertwines factual and counterfactual aspects of St. Louis. The second chapter begins with a condensed version of the city's precipitous decline in the census rankings from the fourth city in 1870 to the twenty-seventh city in 1980. The narrator offers the reader a thumbnail sketch of urban history: the secession of the city from the county in 1876; the failed attempts by the city in the early 1900s to annex county land; the in-migration of Black families and the out-migration of white families in the 1930s; the city's population decline and contracting tax base in the 1940s; the celebration of the Pruitt-Igoe public housing project in the 1950s and its infamous failure in the 1960s; and concluding in the 1970s with "the Era of the Parking Lot, as acres of asphalt replaced half-vacant office buildings downtown" (*TSC* 25–26).[64] Trapped between the Mississippi River and the county it willingly seceded from, the city had few options to alleviate the devastating economic crises of the twentieth century. Later attempts at annexation met unwavering opposition from fiercely autonomous municipalities.[65] This autonomy contributes to a legal and political neoliberal bind. As Gerald Frug notes, "Current law not only has fragmented the metropolitan area but is perpetuated by the kind of person this fragmentation has nurtured," the kind of citizen who bases every decision on the primacy of individual interest.[66] This is the geopolitical history the novel enters into, and the real-estate conspiracy and the failed bid to reunify St. Louis city and county essentially extend this narrative of decline.[67]

Yet Franzen tempers this focus on the bare facts of metropolitan history by suggesting that the city, any city, is just as equally an "idea." After recounting rumors about the 1870 census and the suspiciously inflated numbers that had earned St Louis the rank of "America's Fourth City," the narrator concludes, "But all cities are ideas, ultimately. They create themselves, and the rest of the world apprehends them or ignores them as it chooses" (*TSC* 24). The observation serves as more of an aside than an assertion, and though it is repeated a few paragraphs later, the remark intends to put St. Louis in its parochial place. "What becomes of a city no living person can remember . . . ?" the narrator inquires. "Only St. Louis knew. Its fate was sealed within it, its special tragedy special nowhere else" (26). Fair enough, local tragedy always resonates more keenly for locals, but this impulse to diminish the "fate" of St. Louis distracts from the way the city as "idea" vibrates across the thematic threads of the novel and its depictions of the metropolitan region. This notion anticipates the dialectic that Carlo Rotella envisions between the city of feeling and the city of fact. "Cities of feeling, then," Rotella writes, "are shaped by the flow of language, images, and ideas; cities of fact by the flow of capital, materials, and people. And each, of course, is shaped by the other."[68] For a time, Jammu and her co-conspirators adeptly manipulate this dialectic, creating a counter-discourse to offset a half-century marketing campaign for westward, exurban expansion that, in turn, disrupts residential patterns and reroutes the stream of capital to the city. The very idea of reunification begins to reshape the physical topography of the metro-region.

In the long game of metropolitan reunification, Jammu is careful to maintain an emphasis on renewal and financial opportunity to distract from her manipulation tactics and to cover over the devastating material changes wrought by her land-grab campaign. In the first place, she convinces powerful heads of corporations, politicians, and investors to buy into her plans for the city, not through physical intimidation and force, but by placing them in "the State." Alternately described as an "absorbing parallel world," a condition of "suspended animation," or "an exhaustive sense of fate" (*TSC* 77, 197, 495), the "State" subtly directs these agents of self-interest toward the inevitable acceptance of a path that had already been chosen for them. As the narrator says, "The State had two advantages over more conventional forms of coercion. First, it was oblique. It arose in a quarter of the subject's life unrelated to Jammu, to the police, and, often, to the public sphere in general. Second, it was flexible. Any situation could be developed, any weakness on the subject's part" (30). In short, these key figures, unaware they have been stage-managed, imagine themselves as pioneers in the real-estate market. There is something wickedly sardonic about using "the State" to orchestrate this corporatized takeover of city space. The ascendant brand of 1980s neoliberalism—with the debt it owes to Ayn Randean "objectivism," rapacious self-interest, and the erosion of the social safety net—would insist on keeping the State as much out of private life as possible. As Bourdieu writes, "All direct and conscious intervention of whatever kind, at least when it comes from the state, is discredited in advance and thus condemned to efface itself for the benefit of a pure and anonymous mechanism, the market, whose nature as a site where interests are exercised is forgotten."[69] Jammu hopes to achieve something else through her "State": a remodeling of civil society in the image of private capitalist interest.[70]

Another approach taken by the conspirators is a bit more traditional: leveraging and reversing the discourse of decline. Commenting on the latest attack by the Osage Warriors, a reporter standing at the city-county line notes, "In my second report we saw how borders such as this one enable lawbreakers to enter and leave suburban neighborhoods with relative impunity, and how difficult it is to trace these lawbreakers in a county which is currently a hodgepodge of more than fifty independent police forces. The burglary rate in St. Louis County stands at an all-time high. However, for the last four months the city rate has been dropping steadily" (*TSC* 262). The scene replicates a popular media focus on "urban crime," but with a difference. The report maintains the threatening specter of criminals slipping through the porous borders of suburban counties, but the reporter concludes by noting the reversal in crime statistics. Such media coverage aids the conspiratorial effort by redirecting the familiar discourse of crime and decline toward the suburbs. The intended effect is to make the city-county merger more urgent in the minds of voters. Jammu realizes that in St. Louis the idea of the suburbs as a collage of sheltered and secure enclosures depends upon a circumscribed notion of urban iniquity. As she tells Martin Probst, "A bankrupt, crime-ridden inner city is fundamental to your outlook as an old St. Louisan, and you don't *want* it to change" (382). Jammu knows she must not only reduce urban crime rates in the city but counter this deep-seated viewpoint about the inner-city. The media abets the process by sending an oblique but clear message to constituents: if the city and county were reunited, police forces could mobilize more efficiently to prevent the incursion of crime into the suburbs.

Positive reports about the city's economic opportunities supplement this more familiar media discourse on criminal activity. In fact, at times, the novel describes the material transformations orchestrated by Jammu and her co-conspirators as all but undetectable except as discourse and data. "To look at [the suburbs of] Webster Groves or Ladue or Brentwood you would never guess what was going on. But the poor performance of the economic indicators was creating self-fulfilling prophecies. A front-page article in the *Wall Street Journal* had glowingly described the city's efforts to attract new business, darkly delineated the county's consequent problems, and forecast more of the same, only better, only worse" (*TSC* 288). The St. Louis metro-region seems predisposed to accommodate discursive representations of itself. As Robert Beauregard would have it, the discourse of decline "precedes" its actual reality, only in *Twenty-Seventh City* the discourse is directed against the suburbs, not the urban center.[71] There is the promise of a wry reversal here, but the St. Louis metro-region is locked in a zero-sum game. As reported during a Municipal Growth meeting, "The city's rise and the county's fall were the same event, and it was occurring now for two simple reasons: the altered investment policies of a handful of executives, and the drastic drop in the city's crime rate" (286). The potential to revitalize the city center and to create a downtown that is "alive and multivalent," as Franzen would have it, must come at the expense of county "blight."

The tangible and more menacing consequences of Jammu's real-estate conspiracy speak directly to the history and culture of race in St. Louis. In short, Black people seem to be disappearing. During the conversation with Jammu about the centrality of a "crime-ridden inner city" to the suburban imaginary, Martin reflects on a significant displacement unaccounted for in recent media reports: he "didn't see where all the frightening black young men of North St. Louis had vanished to. He'd seen their faces. He knew that none of them had ended up in Webster Groves or in any of the other nice county towns. Where were they? Somehow the reality had gone underground" (*TSC* 381). Readers encounter some of the most memorable images of dispossessed Black residents through the eyes of Clarence Davis, an African American owner of a demolition business. As his crew prepares to raze a stripped-down and supposedly vacant building on the north side, they realize they had failed to inspect the basement. A family of three, a woman and her two children, had taken up residence in the cellar. They had come to St. Louis from Mississippi in search of the children's father. "One thing leads to another," Clarence says, "and come December she's living in a coal cellar and eating soup-line, too dumb or too shy to do any better. . . . Now, not that people *should* be living in coal cellars. It's that I was tearing down to make room for office space. It's people like this exist, and there's a winter coming on" (206). Clarence serves as a voice of conscience in the novel, but he senses his own complicity in this corporatization of formerly residential space. Driving around on Christmas Eve "with his back seat full of gifts," he knows he cannot complain, but he also recognizes the double-bind Jammu has placed everyone in: "Only those with no voice have much to complain of" (256).

Taken together, Martin Probst and Clarence Davis, the developer and the demolition man, clarify both the "idea of space" as capitalist abstraction and its insidious, material implications for those populations without a voice. Reflecting on his opposition to the city-county merger, Martin observes, "The North Side boom was built on paper, on being in the middle, on buying low and hoping, later, to sell high. The spirit of the renaissance was the spirit of the eighties: office *space*, luxury *space*, parking *space*, planned not by master builders but by financial analysts" (*TSC* 333). Premised on speculation and market logic, the real-estate conspiracy is an exercise in the production of an idea of space, an idea based on the desire to maximize profitability that will, in turn, systematically displace "dispensable" populations. As Jammu assures an associate, if all goes according to plan, St. Louis "will be an all-white city in another ten years" (308). In the meantime, as Clarence observes while cruising through demolished neighborhoods, "the scope of the transformation" has been vast: "square *miles* fenced and boarded, not *one* man visible, not *one* family left" (256). The overtly racist agenda of Jammu's conspiracy exposes the links between her neoliberalist project and identity politics. According to Duggan, "*The goal of raising corporate profits has never been pursued separately from the rearticulation of hierarchies of race, gender, and sexuality in the United States and around the globe.*"[72] The fact that Jammu, a postcolonial Indian woman, orchestrates the plot only underscores the global nature of this hierarchical agenda. For, as Franzen writes, although "she'd had perhaps the only opportunity ever to arise in latter-day St. Louis to bring a small revolution to its black residents, she'd subverted subversion instead. She was on the wrong side of the law. Poverty, poor education, discrimination and institutionalized criminality were not modern. They were Indian problems, sustaining an ideology of separateness, of meaningful suffering, of despairing pride" (399). As with all exploitative schemes, the vulnerable have no access to levers of power and no ability to contest their displacement. They lack access to the speculative practices that produce space as profit but also a right to their own domestic security. They exist on the nether side of the city; as Martin suspects, they "had gone underground."

As the novel draws to a close, these displaced persons end up in two locations—one predictable, one surprising. The former is East St. Louis, Illinois, sarcastically dubbed "Jammuville" by a prostitute working the streets (*TSC* 492). As it turns out, Jammu has reduced the urban crime rate in St. Louis by relocating criminal activity three miles east of the Mississippi River. While the specter of crime infiltrating suburban communities had worked in her favor, as an argument on behalf of the merger, the increased crime, prostitution, and violence across the river hardly make news. From the Missouri side of the river, East St. Louis is a world apart, an underworld that affords crime its proper invisibility. As such, it provides a convenient wasteland for Franzen's novel because it remains an essentially unknown, conceptual space for readers. Yet, when contextualized within the novel's attention to metro-regional development, East St. Louis takes on greater significance as a city that has "been devastated by suburbanization, deindustrialization, and globalization in the postwar period."[73] Setbacks in industrial and economic sectors led to drastic changes in demographics, exacerbated by white flight and the outmigration of the Black working- and middle-class residents. This demographic vacuum led to a sharp rise in poverty, high crime rates, and a ravaged and unequal educational system.[74]

The Twenty-Seventh City relies on this historical reality, but Franzen's real interest seems to be in the *idea* of East St. Louis. Although barely visible on the map "St. Louis and Vicinity," the city ends up playing an outsized role in the "idea of space" at the center of the real-estate terror campaign. In an effort to intensify the strategy against Martin Probst, Jammu's associate kidnaps his wife, Barbara. While Martin believes his wife has left him to live with her lover in New York City, Barbara is being held inside an apartment in an abandoned warehouse in East St. Louis. She, too, is led by her captor to believe she is in New York, so when she is set free on the night of the referendum and stumbles out of the warehouse, she is surprised to find herself in "a Hiroshima neighborhood in the spring of '46, so flat and lifeless that it seemed almost to promise safe passage" (*TSC* 490). After Barbara sees the Arch in the distance and realizes where she is, fear takes over. "She was lost in the place of her nightmares," Franzen writes, "of the nightmares of every citizen of Webster Groves, in a skeletal maze where every kid had a gun and every woman a knife, and a white female face was a ticket to gang rape after she'd been bludgeoned if she'd let them know she was afraid" (497). As the menacing idea of itself, East St. Louis exists as the ultimate other, the antipode to the city west of the river, and unfortunately, Franzen's "serious fiction" about St. Louis and its contentious history of racial segregation does nothing to complicate this idea. The novel's facile treatment of East St. Louis enacts its own kind of environmental repression, unwilling to challenge the city's status as the ultimate "nightmare" of the suburban imaginary.

The other, unexpected locale for dispossessed city dwellers offers readers something far more provocative. In one of the novel's clever turns, the pressing lack of housing created by Jammu's urban renewal project results in an ironic reversal. Summarily displaced from their North Side homes, nine Black families take up residence in two spacious, though unfinished, houses in a secluded subdivision in the upscale suburb of Chesterfield. The homes were left incomplete after the builder declared bankruptcy, leaving the subdivision in a state of boarded-up disrepair typically associated with a blighted inner-city neighborhood. Despite the efforts of armed state troopers and the promise of "first-class housing in a public project, immunity from prosecution, and a sizable cash damages award" (*TSC* 443), the displaced families refuse to vacate the homes. Are these nine families suburban or urban? What happens when suburban-style tactics of racial exclusion and real-estate speculation are turned back on the urban center? The novel is most enticing when it challenges such "settled" identities and territories. The diversity and multivalence Franzen associates with serious fiction take root in a more expansive conception of the metropolitan region, one that accounts for the currents and patterns that produce these differential spaces.

Of course, the final success of the real-estate conspiracy depends upon residents voting to approve the referendum. When voters fail to deliver, Jammu and her stakeholders are left only with a ballooning budget deficit and the collateral damage wrought by their machinations, including the death of Barbara Probst, accidentally shot by a police officer in the midst of a bungled car chase. Reasoning that *"[p]ublic life required that popular figures sometimes play the sacrificial victim"* (*TSC* 509), the police chief takes her own life rather than live with a tarnished reputation or face the consequences of her actions. The failure of the electorate to deliver on metroregional reunification reflects the "apathy" Franzen associates with the suburban age, but the novel shrewdly links this singular referendum to broader political and economic trends at work in the nation. "America was outgrowing the age of action," Franzen writes (503). Applied to this specific counterfactual case study, that means leaving intact a metropolitan region forged by decades of discriminatory federal housing policies, residential segregation, and racial animus. "No matter how a region was structured, well-to-do white people were never going to permit their children to attend schools with dangerous black children. . . . [T]axes were bound to hit the unprivileged harder than the privileged, . . . All political platforms were identical in their inadequacy, their inability to alter the cosmic order" (503–4). As sinister as that reality is, *The Twenty-Seventh City* suggests something more pervasive and insidious is also at work.

In the mid-1980s, as neoliberal ideology plays a more determinative role in American political and economic policies, Franzen recognizes how self-interest, the status-quo, the logic of the market, and a resistance to political action have been recast as forms of benign "enlightenment." The novel is set in 1984, and that means it is Reagan's "Morning in America." Citizens can openly declare their "devotion to arbitrage and tax-free bonds and leveraged buyouts, to profits devolving from mathematics itself, the music of the spheres" (*TSC* 504). The indirect costs of this economic free-for-all—"the toxic wastes and consumer complaints and labor unrest and bankruptcies"—could be offshored, allocated to the developing nations of the world (504). If, as Bourdieu suggests, neoliberalism targets any collective that would check the logic of the free market, then the novel conveys how this agenda trickles down to the local level of the "economically and racially differentiated" consumer-citizen, "expecting the best return for the price paid in taxes."[75] Franzen writes, "The path to enlightenment led through the perception that all communal difficulties are illusions born of caring and desire. It led through non-action, non-involvement, and individual retirement accounts. The new generation had renounced the world in return for simplicity and self-sufficiency" (504). The novel concludes with a scathing portrait of this "new America" coming into being in the mid-1980s, to the country's "passive and defeated acceptance of the movements of capital."[76] While this ending, and the novel more generally, have been read as a failure by Franzen to imagine a progressive alternative to this dismal America, I rather see it as an incisive portrait of how neoliberal ideology is being leveraged across the United States to transform metropolitan regions and dispossess unwanted residential populations.[77] More broadly, the novel is a prescient if inchoate attempt to formulate the problem in real time and to draw attention to the economic and political policies that, from Reagan through Bush II, would shape our normative social and cultural realities, as all aspects of daily life, from education to entertainment, from art to technology, from healthcare to the legal system, conform to the mandates of "profit maximization."[78]

For all the unreal circumstances and conspiratorial turns that differentiate this counterfactual St. Louis, the novel ultimately creates a hyper-realistic portrait of St. Louis, nearly indistinguishable from its historical counterpart. Nevertheless, the failure of Jammu to achieve her racist, corporatized Utopia should, quite obviously, prompt readers to imagine what genuine progressive change might look like. What if, to paraphrase Franzen's narrative, the subversion had not been subverted? What if public officials and private investors had acted in good faith to revitalize the city, to create a mixed-use downtown, and to offer affordable housing and a degree of domestic stability to underserved minority populations?[79] In this regard, *The Twenty-Seventh City* is "serious fiction," or a fiction we should take seriously. The novel demonstrates the insidious nature of neoliberal thinking, the way it exploits existing demographic fissures, facilitates corporate gentrification and residential displacement, and exacerbates domestic insecurity during this contested period of metro-regional development.

Taken together, *White Noise* and *The Twenty-Seventh City* offer divergent but unexpectedly complementary efforts to account for the transformations of the postmodern metropolis in the 1980s. As Soja contends, "The boundaries of the city are becoming more porous, confusing our ability to draw neat lines separating what is inside as opposed to outside the city; between the city and the countryside, suburbia, the non-city; between one metropolitan city-region and another; between the natural and the artificial."[80] DeLillo's novel seems at home in the kind of metropolitan fluidity Soja describes, as well as under the pressures exerted by late-capitalism on the built environment and by neoliberal self-interest on the consumer-citizen. The airborne toxic event masterfully reinforces the blurred and "porous" boundaries of this new "city-region": as a chemical disaster, it epitomizes efforts to draw down environmental regulations and relax safety precautions, while its deleterious effects recognize neither geographic boundaries nor hierarchies of class. Of singular importance, however, is the way DeLillo reimagines the nuclear family and recalibrates the real and imagined borders of the domestic realm, locating the suburban home as a vector within the evolving patterns of the postmetropolis, including the currents of consumer capitalism and toxic waste.

In contrast, *Twenty-Seventh City* evinces a nostalgia for the modern metropolis, a desire to forestall the effacement of space and the universal standardization immanent to the postmodern metropolis.[81] The map, "St. Louis and Vicinity," signals this desire at the outset. In his faithful adherence to cartographic detail, Franzen effectively becomes a painter of St. Louis city and its satellite municipalities, securing the city and the suburbs within their historical boundaries. Yet the map also foregrounds an idea of metropolitan space, seemingly dispossessed of inhabitants, a blank slate open to conspiratorial renewal projects that exploit racial animus and advance corporate interests, private investors, and the logic of the market. In the twilight years of the Cold War era, Franzen's "new America" appears both predatory and apathetic, and the novel's commitment to the historical realism of decline points toward the foreseeable permanence of structural realities that increase domestic insecurity for vulnerable populations, reinscribe hierarchies of race, exacerbate residential segregation, and undermine democratic engagement.

In 2001, Franzen published "the broad-canvas novel" that would finally, permanently elevate him from the shadows. *The Corrections*, winner of the National Book Award, garnered both critical and popular attention, though not entirely in the way its author had hoped. The public kerfuffle surrounding the selection of the novel for Oprah's Book Club offered, as Franzen described it at the time, "blood sport entertainment for the literary community," a distraction from the horror of 9/11.[82] As is well known, his disparaging remarks about the "schmaltzy, one-dimensional [books]" Oprah had chosen in the past eventually led to his dis-invitation from the on-air book club.[83] Critics and authors from across the literary world, including heavyweights like Toni Morrison and Janice Radway, lined up to condemn his "dismissal of women's engagement with literature," and the consensus opinion portrayed Franzen as the latest gatekeeper of literary value premised on an equivalence between women readers and mass-market trash.[84]

Although the Franzen-Oprah skirmish has amounted to nothing more than a blip on the radar of literary history, the subject and the terms of the conflict were long-standing and pervasive. One of the more compelling aspects of this literary spat, however, and the reason I cite it here in conclusion, is the regional subtext of Franzen's response. In December 2001, he published an essay in *The New Yorker* that attempted to set the record straight. Entitled "Meet Me in St. Louis," the piece recounts a September visit to his former hometown and the suburb of Webster Groves to shoot B-roll footage for the book club. Part *mea culpa*, part "Aw, shucks," the piece showcases Franzen's efforts to resist his construction as a suburban writer for Oprah's audience while preserving his cosmopolitan literary sensibilities for his *New Yorker* audience. In short, the real issue for Franzen is geography. His initial description of the film crew sets in motion the essay's central conflict. "The cameraman, Chris, is a barrel-chested, red-faced local with a local accent," he writes. "The producer, Gregg, is a tall, good-looking cosmopolitan with fashion-model locks" (*HTBA* 286). Franzen uses the production staff to construct a tension between the local and the cosmopolitan, a tension he himself feels most acutely: "I'm a Midwesterner who's been living in the East for twenty-four years. I'm a grumpy Manhattanite who, with what feels like a Midwestern eagerness to cooperate, has agreed to pretend to arrive in the Midwestern city of his childhood and reexamine his roots" (287). Before agreeing to film this local footage, he tried to convince one of the producers that "St. Louis doesn't really have anything to do with [his] life now" and, instead, "volunteered that between [his] apartment and [his] studio in Harlem . . . there was quite a lot of visual interest in New York!" (289). Franzen's earnest plea evokes the sacred tenet of real estate: location, location, location. When he references the Midwest, he does not mean farms and factories; he means suburbia. And in this instance, he suspects that Oprah's film crew is trying to frame a cosmopolitan New Yorker, with a Harlem studio no less, as a midwestern suburbanite.

The most illuminating aspect of "Meet Me in St. Louis" is the way the essay updates concerns about the provincial and pejorative associations of regional writing in the context of contemporary suburban fiction. Throughout the piece, Franzen tries to maintain an outsider's, touristic view of his former hometown for *New Yorker* readers, and as a result, the suburb emerges as the site for an ideological battle over region and literary value. As Judith Fetterley and Marjorie Pryse suggest, there is a discursive tradition in U.S. literary history that "locates regionalism as inevitably representing 'narrow interests'; it also locates aesthetic value . . . in a text's capacity to be de-localized, stripped of its 'geography,' and removed from any sense of 'situatedness.'"[85] Franzen's response shares the same repressive impulse: he wants to tell us, once and for all, that his midwestern, suburban past no longer figures in his life as a writer, never mind he can't stop writing about it (see *Freedom* [2010], see *Crossroads* [2021]). As an author, his interest in the novel as a form remains bound to the relationship between city and suburb, nation and region, but his notion of literary stature seems incompatible with such geographic "situatedness."

Yet Franzen's defensive response to his construction as a regionally located, suburban writer should, on its face, prove an invitation for his "serious readers" to reimagine the suburbs as a contested terrain for enduring debates about regionalism and literary value.

As I have suggested throughout this project, "serious fiction" that attends to the overlapping geographic scales of the built environment is engaged in the critical work of regional writing. Such literary works expand our understanding of the work regionalism performs in the contemporary era, the way it can awaken readers to their embeddedness in complex spatial patterns of coexistence, from suburban homes and neighborhoods to sprawling exurban territories shaped by national (neoliberal) politics and multinational capital. Perhaps despite the cosmopolitan ambitions of their white male authors, *White Noise* and *The Twenty-Seventh City* exhibit a submerged regional aesthetic that updates and expands our understanding of regionalism as a critical response to the structural transformations of the residential landscape and the uneven and unequal geographic development of the U.S. postmetropolis.

4

Containment Culture

Suburban Domesticity and Nation as Home

WITH FEW EXCEPTIONS, previous readings of Jeffrey Eugenides's *The Virgin Suicides* (1993) have focused on some unique intersection among the following thematic concerns: adolescence and coming-of-age narratives; misogyny, voyeurism, and eroticism; death and desire; point of view and the narrative's "impossible" voice.[1] The novel clearly lends itself to such readings. Briefly stated, *The Virgin Suicides* recounts the obsession of a group of teenage boys with the enigmatic Lisbon sisters: Cecilia, Lux, Bonnie, Mary, and Therese. Set in 1970s suburban Detroit, the story is told in retrospect by the young boys who, now "approaching middle age," with "thinning hair and soft bellies," still fret over the girls who "hadn't heard [them] calling" all those years ago.[2] Through recollection, speculation, and surreptitiously gathered "exhibits," the narrators attempt to piece together the events that transpired over the course of roughly "thirteen months" (*VS* 1), between Cecilia's first suicide attempt and the suicides of her sisters. In one of the more astute approaches to the novel, Debra Shostak argues that *The Virgin Suicides* "offers an allegory of reading," and that all the conflicting elements of narrative voice "converge on the main subject matter of the novel: the erotic and its relationship to death."[3] Although Shostak crafts a persuasive analysis, I want to suggest that the implications of this "allegory" extend beyond a psychoanalysis of eroticism and death to a fuller account of suburban nation building and domesticity, increased residential inequality, and the threat to environmental sustainability across the long Cold War era. This chapter argues for the novel's geopolitical significance, drawing out the national discourses of privatism, isolation, and containment that take shape around the narrators' monomaniacal account of the Lisbon girls.

Admittedly, Eugenides plays fast and loose with historical detail, and as Shostak contends, his narrators demonstrate a "resistance to composing a history" in favor of mythologizing the Lisbon girls.[4] Yet as I will show, despite this penchant for mythology and its attendant nostalgic residue, history continually intrudes upon *The Virgin Suicides*. In their account of the novel, Kenneth Womack and Amy Mallory-Kani go so far as to date Cecilia's first suicide attempt to "Tuesday, June 13th, 1972," the week of the "break-in at the Watergate Complex," reading the decline of the Lisbon family as a parallel to "the demise of the Nixon administration."[5] While such bold claims for historical specificity ultimately prove problematic, we can safely locate the main narrative in the mid-1970s.[6] The "contrapuntal exchange" of songs between the narrators and the Lisbon girls a few nights before the mass suicides provides a rudimentary historical framework, with song selections ranging from The Beatles' "Dear Prudence" (1968) to Janis Ian's "At Seventeen" (1975), and including several additional tracks recorded and released between 1970 and 1973 (*VS* 190–91). This era may represent, as Womack and Mallory-Kani assert, a "signal moment in twentieth-century American history,"[7] but what most intrigues me about *The Virgin Suicides* is the way historical markers and oblique allusions continually expand the novel's historical frame. The novel pushes us back in time and pulls us into the contemporary moment of its production in the early 1990s, thus transforming the 1970s into a crossroad for the novel's retrospective analysis of residential sprawl and the geo-cultural scale of the suburban domestic realm.[8]

In brief, this chapter examines the shards of history that collect at the margins of the narrative: the social and cultural conditions that gave rise to the postwar suburban nation in the 1940s and '50s; the racial violence, the enduring anxieties about privacy and security, and the economic and political crises of the 1960s and '70s (contemporaneous with the lives of the Lisbon girls); and finally, the manifest unsustainability of suburban living that comes to the foreground at the point of narration in the early 1990s. To develop this line of thinking, I read *The Virgin Suicides* as a late–Cold War iteration of the redefined suburban regionalism this book has explored, as a work that takes on the complex "place constructions" and the "various scales and motives" that have shaped national politics and residential geography across the second half of the twentieth century.[9] As Lutz claims, "The hallmark of local color and later regionalist writing . . . is its attention to both local and more global concerns, most often achieved through a careful balancing of different groups' perspectives."[10] In Eugenides's novel, a communal illusion of the suburban ideal mediates these local and global interests. Through the eyes of the neighborhood, the Lisbon home poses an increasing threat to the perceived sanctity of the domestic realm, a threat that must be contained. According to Alan Nadel, "Although technically referring to U.S. foreign policy from 1948 until at least the mid-1960s, [containment] also describes American life in numerous venues and under sundry rubrics during that period," including "the cult of domesticity and the fetishizing of domestic security."[11] The ersatz community in *The Virgin Suicides* remains enthralled to this vision of "American life," but I would argue the narrators' obsession with the Lisbon daughters also participates in this containment project. Indeed, their narrative devolves into its own warped "cult of domesticity" as these now-mature men—who confess themselves "happier with dreams [of the Lisbon girls] than wives" (*VS* 164)—recreate an attenuated version of the domestic realm in a decrepit tree house, adorned with their decaying photographs and exhibits.

But the novel, I argue, invites us to read against the grain of the narrators' nostalgic, fetishistic project and instead to understand the Lisbon family home and their suburban neighborhood as nodal points for regional, national, and even transnational concerns. Read as regional writing, *The Virgin Suicides* offers one of the most capacious treatments of the suburb as *national region*—both as a geographical and ideological site of postwar nation building and as "a location for critique and resistance."[12] In other words, Eugenides makes available to readers a compelling critique of the suburb and its ideological privileging of privacy and domestic security as the twentieth century draws to a close. As Amy Kaplan claims,

"'Domestic' has a double meaning that links the space of the familial household to that of the nation, by imagining both in opposition to everything outside the geographic and conceptual border
of the home."[13] The Lisbon "familial household" embodies a similar
oppositional dynamic, giving us a portrait of the nation as suburban home during a "second moment" of empire in U.S. history, the
era of "American globalism that flowered after 1945."[14] During this
era of "American globalism," as I have discussed, residential development in the U.S. extended patterns of fractal, imperialist sprawl,
creating a topography of suburban privatism. Reading *The Virgin
Suicides* and, more specifically, the Lisbon household against the
fraught, contradictory impulses of this era—isolationism, globalism—clarifies the ways in which the borders of the suburban home
recast our understanding of the domestic and the foreign, as well
as the nature of internal and external threats. In the end, the narrators may not offer any genuine insight into the Lisbon suicides, but
the novel does successfully offset our suburban nation's entrenched
geopolitical amnesia.

A Comfortable Suburban Home

This "double meaning" of the domestic emerges in the novel with
the retelling of the first suicide. Cecilia, the youngest of the ill-fated
Lisbon sisters, is the first to go, and she exits in spectacular form.
Just a few weeks after a failed suicide attempt—a private affair with
a razor in the upstairs bathroom—she jumps from a second-story
bedroom window and impales herself on the fence below. Moments
before, she had been lazing around the Lisbon rec room in a tat-
tered wedding dress, indifferently attending a party with her four
sisters and some neighborhood boys. The party was staged at the
recommendation of Cecilia's psychiatrist, who had previously
urged the Lisbon parents to "relax their rules" and provide a "social
outlet" for their daughters (*VS* 19). As Mrs. Lisbon ladles punch
and Mr. Lisbon rhapsodizes about his tools for the boys—providing
a temporary resurgence of masculinity for this otherwise ineffec-
tual patriarch—Cecilia retreats to her room. The narrators recount,
"First came the sound of wind, a rushing we decided later must

have been caused by her wedding dress filling with air. . . . The wind sound huffed, once, and then the moist thud jolted us, the sound of a watermelon breaking open" (27). Mr. Lisbon dashes upstairs and, one by one, the boys and the Lisbon girls emerge from the depths of the basement into the summer night.

After taking refuge across the street, the narrators consider the horrific tableau: "Mr. Lisbon was still sunk in bushes up to his waist, his back jerking as though he were trying to pull Cecilia up and off, or as though he were sobbing. On the porch Mrs. Lisbon made the other girls face the house. The sprinkler system, timed to go on at 8:15 P.M., spurted into life just as the EMS truck appeared at the end of the block" (*VS* 30). Cecilia's dramatic escape from this world leaves her body transfixed upon a familiar suburban symbol, the fence that typically delineates the borders between domestic properties or between private lawns and public sidewalks. Still among the living, the rest of the family cannot escape the programmed rituals of lawn care, and as if to redirect the focal point of the scene, the remaining Lisbon women "face the house."

This turn toward the house opens onto a scene that announces the novel's dialectic tension between geographic scales of the domestic and the foreign. While the EMS workers try to resuscitate Cecilia, the narrators climb onto the rooftop across from the Lisbon home, providing a wider vantage point onto the metropolitan region:

> [W]e could see, over the heaps of trees throwing themselves into the air, the abrupt demarcation where the trees ended and the city began. The sun was falling in the haze of distant factories, and in the adjoining slums the scatter of glass picked up the raw glow of the smoggy sunset. Sounds we usually couldn't hear reached us now that we were up high, . . . sounds of the impoverished city we never visited, all mixed and muted, without sense, carried on a wind from that place. Then: darkness. . . . Up close, yellow house lights coming on, revealing families around televisions. (*VS* 31–32)

Their postmortem account moves metonymically from the fence upon which Cecilia has impaled herself to the "abrupt demarcation" between the suburb and the city, tacitly linking the domestic and regional drawing of borders. Yet the unfamiliar sounds, "mixed and muted, without sense," that waft over from the city challenge such delineations, and in the impending "darkness" the narrators' perspective contracts, telescoping back to familiar images of domestic isolation and mass-mediated family togetherness.

The Lisbon suicides—which the narrators divulge in the first sentence—immediately undermine any notion of a suburban idyll, but this rooftop perspective extends beyond an ironic portrait of suburbia as a safe haven. The scene reveals what at ground level the trees conveniently disguise: the realities of socioeconomic inequality and racial segregation that exist on the other side of the tree line. This is the promise of the suburbs, as Laura Miller suggests: they "hold out the possibility of escape from a messy and chaotic social world into pure and tranquil nature—to a place where socioeconomic differences are hidden away, not just in the next neighborhood, but often in the next town."[15] With this scene, Eugenides repositions the supposedly remote domestic realm within an expansive and seemingly "foreign" metro-regional map of urban poverty, factory pollution, ecological crisis, and death. In addition to the Lisbon tragedy, neighborhood trees infected with Dutch-elm disease are being cut down, "the cemetery workers' strike" has "bodies piling up" across the city (VS 12), and houses and cars are covered in the annual "scum" of fish flies "[r]ising in clouds from the algae in the polluted lake" (2). Although through a glass darkly, *The Virgin Suicides* confronts readers with the complex interconnectedness among the suburban home, the neighborhood, the metropolitan region, and the nation at a moment of political and environmental precarity in the 1970s.

While Mrs. Lisbon and her daughters "face the house," this totalizing perspective positions the reader to recognize the tension between the protective and political functions of domestic borders. According to Jessica Blaustein, "To be a good citizen of a stable nation, it was assumed (and arguably still is) across large sections of built, textual, and visual worlds, one must inhabit an autonomous, detached unit with identifiable boundaries that at once announce its contents to the social world and seal, stabilize, and defend them from it."[16] Cecilia's suicide may be the first indicator that something is unstable in the Lisbon house, but as the novel continues, the concentric circles around this family tragedy continue to expand. The Lisbon suicides provide the occasion for a comprehensive examination of the fragile insularity of the domestic sphere and the geographic containment of a perceived "foreign" menace.

In the weeks and months following Cecilia's suicide, Mr. and Mrs. Lisbon experiment with varying degrees of incarceration to secure their remaining daughters and, with few exceptions, the reader is kept outside looking in, exiled along with the narrators to read for evidence of the girls in the structure of the house itself. The narrators forecast this focus with their first exhibit, a photograph of the house:

> Exhibit #1 shows the Lisbon house shortly before Cecilia's suicide attempt. It was taken by a real estate agent . . . whom Mr. Lisbon had hired to sell the house his large family had long outgrown. As the snapshot shows, the slate roof had not yet begun to shed its shingles, the porch was still visible above the bushes, and the windows were not yet held together with strips of masking tape. A comfortable suburban home. (*VS* 3)

The artifact offers readers two representations at once: a pristine home prepped for sale and the image of its eventual decay. This palimpsest evokes the essential nature of all photographic images. "To take a photograph is to participate in another person's (or thing's) mortality, vulnerability, mutability," writes Susan Sontag. "Precisely by slicing out this moment and freezing it, all photographs testify to time's relentless melt."[17] The narrators did not "take" the photograph in the sense Sontag implies, but they did take (as in steal) all the family photographs they could scavenge precisely to "participate in"—or forestall—this "relentless melt."

Yet Exhibit #1 also produces a more provocative effect on our reading of the novel. The narrators' layered description of the "comfortable suburban home" mimics the belief that the exterior of the house should reflect the family it contains, and their inverse reading of the forthcoming ruin marks an effort to create this alignment. In other words, the narrators read this image of the house so that it will conjure the decay the photograph predates, and in this way, they anticipate how the Lisbon home will serve as a fixture for the neighbors' perception of a menace in their midst. In her study of confessional poetry and legal decisions related to privacy from the 1960s to the 1980s, Deborah Nelson suggests that "[t]he cold war seems to have coincided with—and exaggerated—a widely experienced topological crisis in which bounded spaces of all kinds seemed to exhibit a frightening permeability. All sorts of entities were imagined as bounded spaces: nations, bodies, homes, and minds."[18] While *The Virgin Suicides* includes traditional instances of domestic spaces poised against an external threat, the Lisbon family tragedy seems to ignite a "topological crisis" internal to this community. If only obliquely, Eugenides positions the suburban home as a central coordinate within a pervasive discourse concerning border anxieties and the expanding topology of domestic peril.

Cecilia's suicide overlaps with several iterations of death and decay across the metropolitan region. The bodies left unburied by the cemetery workers' strike, the diseased elm trees, the miasma from the polluted lake, and the seasonal dying-off of fish-flies would seem to confront this suburb with death on all sides, and yet it takes Cecilia's demise to jar the neighborhood into a kind of dawning awareness of mortality. The narrators note:

> There had never been a funeral in our town before, at least not during our lifetimes. The majority of dying had happened during the Second World War when we didn't exist and our fathers were impossibly skinny young men in black-and-white photographs—dads on jungle airstrips, dads with pimples and tattoos, dads with pinups, dads who wrote love letters to the girls who would become our mothers, dads inspired by K rations, loneliness and glandular riot in malarial air into poetic reveries that ceased entirely once they got back home. (*VS* 32)

This depiction relegates violence and death to a distant realm, the "jungle airstrips" that now exist only as a collage of photographic images—a clever detail linking the history of World War II to the narrators' exhibits of the Lisbon girls, both rendered as a catalog of visual artifacts.

The juxtaposition of war with the placid image of a deathless town underscores the historical reality that, at least until September 11, 2001, acts of war and terrorism had taken place far from America's civilian neighborhoods. Eugenides is more explicit about this in his second novel, *Middlesex* (2002). The narrator Cal Stephanides reflects, "To live in America, until recently, meant to be far from war. Wars happened in Southeast Asian jungles. They happened in Middle Eastern deserts. They happened, as the old song has it, *over there*. But then why, peeking out the dormer window, did I see, on the morning after our second night in the attic, a tank rolling by our front lawn?"[19] The then seven-year-old Callie hops on her bicycle and follows the tank into the city where her father is trying to guard the family diner during the 1967 riots. As she peddles across the suburban neighborhoods, Callie thinks, "I have looked through my father's World War II scrapbook many times; I have seen Vietnam on television; . . . But none of it has prepared me for warfare in my own hometown. The street we are moving down is lined with leafy elms" (*M* 249). Unlike the dying elms in *The Virgin Suicides*, these trees thrive, contributing to the uncanny experience.

Although *Middlesex* has the edge in terms of historical specificity, this notion of wars happening "over there," intruding upon the domestic realm only through visual relics, echoes the war references in Eugenides's first novel. I would argue, however, that the narrators' allusion to "the Second World War" also evokes the connection between the war effort abroad and the suburban nation-building project at home. With the support of the Federal Housing Administration (FHA), the Home Owner's Loan Corporation (HOLC), the G.I. Bill, and the Veterans Administration, developers created the expectation among white Americans that owning a suburban home was synonymous with the social mores of middle-class life.[20] In the decade after World War II, during the early years of American globalism, federal policies created the conditions for suburban isolation and detachment on the domestic front. As detailed in the introduction to this study, returning war veterans, like the narrators' fathers, found federal programs in place to help them settle into their newfound suburban life. All of these policies favored new construction, often depleting funding for any urban renewal. As Dolores Hayden explains, thanks to this federal largesse, "banks gave loans for the construction of ten million new homes between 1946 and 1953, creating a gigantic private housing industry."[21] In other words, international warfare gave way to a tacit and protracted domestic war against America's urban centers, creating the residential segregation and social inequality we see in a novel like *The Virgin Suicides* or, as previously discussed, in such literary works as *Kingsblood Royal*, *A Raisin in the Sun*, or *The Twenty-Seventh City*. The narrators' passing reference to "dads on jungle airstrips"—the same fathers who returned from the warfront and bought homes in a town secluded from the violence and poverty of urban Detroit—glosses a charged period in U.S. history, linking the military outposts of American empire to what had become by the 1970s, as a result of these postwar policies, an imperialist expansion of suburbia at the expense of the country's urban centers.

While the narrators may be monomaniacal when it comes to the Lisbon girls, such historical allusions within *The Virgin Suicides* should expand the reader's frame of reference. In short, the narrators provide the foreshortened, nostalgic vision that we read against as the novel arcs toward a geopolitical reading that destabilizes the illusion of suburban detachment, inviting us to see the broader regional interconnectedness of the domestic realm within a thoroughly historicized context. "Occasionally we heard gunshots coming from the ghetto," the narrators reflect, "but our fathers insisted it was only cars backfiring. Therefore, when the newspapers reported that burials in the city had completely stopped, we didn't think it affected us" (*VS* 32–33). The novel presents a series of these moments that signal the real but repressed connections between Detroit and its suburban neighborhoods, as well as the macrolevel, historical trajectories that link the "jungle airstrips" of World War II to postwar domestic policies and, eventually, the "dying empire" of the 1970s (226).

At the microlevel, the effort to find a burial site for Cecilia brings the local scale back into focus. Since the only suburban cemetery "had filled up long ago in the time of the last deaths," the funeral director and Mr. Lisbon set out to consider their options in the city (*VS* 33). "On the West Side they visited a quiet cemetery in the Palestinian section," the narrators explain, "but Mr. Lisbon didn't like the foreign sound of the muezzin calling the people to prayer, and had heard that the neighbors still ritually slaughtered goats in their bathtubs" (34). Unable to reconcile his personal loss with such "foreign" elements, he considers a "Catholic cemetery that looked perfect, until, coming to the back, Mr. Lisbon saw two miles of leveled land that reminded him of photographs of Hiroshima" (34). This reference to photographs, World War II, and the somber memory of U.S.-inflicted terror segues into a miniature history lesson in urban renewal by way of industrial destruction. According to the funeral director, "GM bought out like twenty-five thousand Polacks to build this huge automotive plant. They knocked down twenty-four city blocks, then ran out of money. So the place was all rubble and weeds" (34).[22] The Lisbons' decision to bury Cecilia in "a public nondenominational cemetery located between two freeways" serves as a further reckoning with the demands of residential geography and the disappearance of public commons (34)—especially the way postwar planning models have made the American landscape conform to the "voracious needs" of the automobile and the "space-grabbing, free-for-all highway."[23]

Yet another ground-level link between domestic tragedy and international warfare figures prominently when the men in the neighborhood gather to remove "the murdering fence" upon which Cecilia had died (*VS* 51). The narrators note that their fathers "struggled with the fence, bent over like Marines hoisting the flag on Iwo Jima" (50). As a physical act, the fence removal offers an opportunity for these veterans turned organization men to reassert their masculinity, but more significantly, it reframes the tragedy as an architectural issue that can be remedied through a tactical (if parodic) military-style assault. Later in the novel, on the night they hope to rescue the girls from their house incarceration, the narrators will echo this language: "In single file, like paratroopers, we dropped from the tree. . . . We advanced on the house from different directions" (199). Some of the boys even resort to "crawling army-style" (200). The fence removal scene is another rescue fantasy of sorts. The neighbors eradicate what they view as a chink in the domestic armor and a broader threat to the security of the neighborhood. In her examination of political subjectivity and "suburban privatized domesticity," Blaustein contends that "[t]he outward appearance of the home . . . was required to designate, express, *authenticate* that which it contained—the private life of an American family of free citizens."[24] In this instance, tearing out the fence is meant to shore up domestic borders while reestablishing the Lisbon house's proper "outward appearance," thus re-authenticating the nationalizing function of this single-family home.

Having finally uprooted the fence with the aid of a pickup truck, the men "leaned on shovels, mopping brows, even though they hadn't done anything. Everyone felt a lot better, as though the lake had been cleaned up, or the air, or the other side's bombs destroyed" (VS 52). Here the fence substitutes for a range of global, systemic concerns: the dangers posed by pollution, environmental decay, and the lingering threat of Soviet warheads. Indeed, the scene not only parodies a military assault but also allegorizes Cold War–era anxieties about national security. According to Campbell Craig and Fredrik Logevall, "between 1945 and the early 1980s," political debates among politicians and U.S. policy makers made it seem "that America was in a life-and-death struggle with an implacable, ruthless, and fundamentally evil foe and that it was on the verge of losing this epic struggle. . . .Talking up the threat, perpetuating the politics of insecurity, became the mission."[25] The catharsis provided by the fence removal suggests a widespread concern linking the threat posed by the Lisbon house to the security and sanctity of the neighborhood and the nation. Later efforts to rake the Lisbons' leaves, clean their windows, and tidy the exterior of the house extend this line of thinking, as if containing the disrepair might prevent a "domino effect" across their suburban community.[26]

Ultimately, the failure of the house's outward appearance to disguise a sense of "creeping desolation" draws the ire of the neighborhood and the attention of the media (VS 85). The local paper had refused to report Cecilia's suicide because it was a matter of "personal tragedy," and the city newspapers saw nothing noteworthy in its "sheer prosaicness" to compete with the cemetery workers' strike and the layoffs at the automotive plant (89). Not until a neighbor writes a letter about the pressures facing teenagers does a circumspect reference to the suicide make it into print. The narrators report that "the rest of the town had forgotten about Cecilia's suicide by that point, whereas the growing disrepair of the Lisbon house constantly reminded us of the trouble within" (90). The

Lisbon house makes visible the infelicities of violence, death, and decay that the private realms of suburbia have been built to keep out or, at the very least, to repress as a matter of decorum. "Years later," the author of the letter confesses to the narrators: "'You can't just stand by and let your neighborhood go down the toilet. . . . We're good people around here'" (90). The open wound of the Lisbon household erodes the foundational geographic scale of the neighborhood's suburban ideal and, along with it, the cult of suburban domesticity.

After both direct and indirect efforts on the part of the community fail to make the Lisbon house perform its ideological function, a new narrative takes hold that locates the threat within the collective body of the Lisbon girls. Shaped by the media and local psychologists, this version of events casts Cecilia as "the crazy one" (*VS* 220), the patient zero of a viral self-annihilation, "infecting those close at hand" (152) and culminating in "an esoteric ritual of self-sacrifice" (217). This shift in focus from the home to the body is in keeping with Nelson's observation about the "topological crisis" of "bounded spaces," reproducing anxieties about the individual, the private realm, and their violations across the long Cold War era. The surveillance efforts on the part of the narrators, as well as Mrs. Lisbon's sense that she was caught in the gaze of "a hundred eyes" (132), also remind us that the suburbs and "the suburban home, while marketed as a source of privacy and upheld in cold war political rhetoric as the acme of American democratic self-governance, was in fact defined by surveillance, especially though not exclusively for women."[27] Within the community, Cecilia now provides a convenient fall girl in a narrative of internal menace: "In the bathtub, cooking in the broth of her own blood, [she] had released an airborne virus which the other girls, even in coming to save her, had contracted. No one had cared how Cecilia had caught the virus in the first place. Transmission became explanation" (152–53).

The rhetoric of contagion reaches its apex when a neighbor, Mr. Eugene, excited by the prospect "that scientists were on the verge of finding the 'bad genes' that caused cancer, depression, and other diseases, offered his hope that they would soon 'be able to find a gene for suicide, too'" (*VS* 241). In *Middlesex*, Eugenides turns this preoccupation with genetic-level mutation and transmission into an epic, intergenerational narrative, providing a sort of through line across his first two novels. "Sing now, O Muse, of the recessive mutation on my fifth chromosome!" Cal, the novel's intersex narrator, intones. "And sing how Providence, in the guise of a massacre, sent the gene flying again; how it blew like a seed across the sea to America, where it drifted through our industrial rains until it fell to earth in the fertile soil of my mother's own midwestern womb" (*M* 4). Cal's genetic odyssey takes place within international, national, and regional conflicts in which race, ethnicity, war, a threatening and dehumanizing urban center, and an increasingly friable sense of suburban security all shape his sense of self. In *The Virgin Suicides*, Eugenides brings us to the final frontier of border anxieties: the threat is not just inside the house; it is a matter of genetic architecture. On one level, by eliding the gap between the "bounded spaces" of the house and the girls' bodies, Eugenides links the erotics of the narrators' voyeurism to the gender politics of suburban surveillance. Yet the convergence of home and body adds another layer of complexity to suburban domesticity, aligning the neighborhood's monitoring of domestic borders with efforts to target and, as with the "murdering fence," root out individual disorder.

A Dying Empire

The communal retelling of the suicides as a threat from within the Lisbon house, or as an effect of the girls' genetic dysfunction, opposes a more common discourse of external threat in suburban history, threats that tend to coalesce around ideas about the domestic and the foreign, viewed through the lens of race or national security and, occasionally, the intersection of the two. In *The Virgin Suicides*, this discourse is understated, interwoven with discussions of the Lisbon girls and the family home, but one of the ways this external threat appears is through the familiar history of racial segregation and violence that shaped postwar residential development. As foreshadowed in the rooftop scene on the night Cecilia dies, suburban neighborhoods obscure, even render invisible, the foreign realm of the inner city and the explicit racial and socio-economic segregation that underwrites modern and contemporary suburban living. In his study of Detroit's postwar racial tension and the culminating urban crisis of 1967, Thomas Sugrue notes that ongoing battles over race, unemployment, and residential boundaries shifted physical and "cognitive" geographies. He writes, "Whites created a cognitive map of the city based on racial classifications and made their decisions about residence and their community action in accordance with their vision of the racial geography of the city."[28] The initial postwar promise of economic and labor opportunities for African Americans gave way to increased unemployment and residential segregation in the 1960s and '70s. According to Sugrue, "Detroit's unassuming tree-lined neighborhoods and their modest single-family homes became the major battlegrounds where blacks and whites struggled over the future of the city."[29]

This history of Detroit's residential geography clarifies our understanding of the novel's retrospective analysis of suburban expansion and its effects on the national landscape. In subtle ways, Eugenides invites the reader to see this 1970s suburb as such a "battleground," where the high stakes and indirect costs of racial segregation and domestic policies remain disguised by a façade of denial and decorum. I would argue that, in *The Virgin Suicides*, race emerges in the interstices of the narrative by design, precisely because the topic of race persists as a kind of fissure in the patterns of suburban domesticity. Just as the built environment of suburbia tries to contain difference, we must read the repressed history of race between the lines and at the margins of the novel. In the postwar era, Detroit's most significant rift occurred in 1967, as a long history of intractable racial tensions resulted in violent outbreaks across the metropolitan region. The narrators first mention the riots in an extended reverie about Belle Isle, "the delicate fig-shaped island, stranded between the American Empire and peaceful Canada," an account that encompasses European colonialism, the displacement of native populations, a Civil War memorial, the 1967 riots, and "the eroding tax base" that has transformed the once-prized Botanical Garden into a "false paradise," sending forth the "aroma of a rotting world" (*VS* 104). They make another oblique reference to the riots on the night of the homecoming dance, and the specter of racial conflict materializes here as yet another way of destabilizing perceptions of suburban privatism and isolation. As they are escorted to the dance, the Lisbon girls comment on each of the houses they pass, narrating their own history of the neighborhood: "They recalled the race riots, when tanks had appeared at the end of our block and National Guardsmen had parachuted into our backyards. They were, after all, our neighbors" (119). Parachuting Guardsmen may be a fabulist's tale—a false history inside a gauzy memory—but the reference to race riots and the tanks positioned to protect white suburbanites echoes the war analogies and allusions present within the novel and, more to the point, extends the analysis of suburban isolationism and "the fetishizing of domestic security."[30]

Since people often experience the suburbs through windshields and side windows, perhaps it is not surprising that this complex portrayal of suburban space takes shape during the drive to the homecoming dance. As the car makes its slow progress, the driver turns "down to Jefferson Avenue, past the Wainwright house with its green historical marker, and toward the gathering lakefront mansions. Imitation gas lanterns burned on front lawns. On every corner a black maid waited for the bus. They drove on, past the glittering lake, and finally under the ragged cover of elms near the school" (*VS* 120). The "black maids" at bus stops mark an absent presence in the novel: they are the transient occupants of the sub-urban domestic sphere whose nightly commutes subtly register the macro-level history of postwar, metropolitan Detroit. As Sugrue contends, Detroit's deindustrialization and decentralization trans-formed the labor market in ways that significantly disadvantaged working-class African Americans. Whether motivated by market concerns or encouraged by government subsidies, decisions to relocate industry or increase automation at plants such as Ford and GM "created a spatial mismatch between urban African Americans and jobs."[31] Deindustrialization and job loss, decades of discrimina-tory "redlining" practices, "blockbusting" realtors, and local efforts by neighborhood associations kept Blacks on one side of a residen-tial line and whites on the other.[32] These suburban bus stops are one of the equivocal spaces where the border anxieties of a multi-racial, regionally intertwined metropolis are brought into sharp relief.

In fact, one of the ancillary effects of the Lisbon tragedy was that it temporarily reversed a persistent concern about race and eco-nomic instability. "While the suicides lasted," the narrators note, "and for some time after, the Chamber of Commerce worried less about the influx of black shoppers and more about the outflux of whites. Brave blacks had been slipping in for years, though they were usually women, who blended in with our maids. The city downtown had deteriorated to such a degree that most blacks had no other place to go. . . . [N]othing shocked us more than the sight of a black person shopping on Kercheval" (*VS* 95). This is the legacy of federal policies and programs from the 1940s and '50s: blighted urban centers and ongoing anxieties about Black "influx" and white flight. As a kind of framing remark, race returns near the end of the novel, after the night of the suicides, at an "Asphyxiation"-themed debutante party where affluence effortlessly blends with a blithe disregard for environmental disaster. "A spill at the River Rouge plant" had threatened to spoil the coming-out season: "The swamp smell that arose was outrageous amid the genteel mansions of the automotive families" (229). Mingling with partygoers sporting "tuxedos and gas masks, evening gowns and astronaut helmets," the narrators recall that "black bartenders in red vests served us alcohol without asking for I.D., and in turn, around 3 A.M., we said nothing when we saw them loading leftover cases of whiskey into the trunk of a sagging Cadillac" (229–30). Their silence repays a night of innocent, if illegal, drinking, but it also makes space for a critique of the way suburban decorum writ large sustains systemic social, economic, and racial inequalities precisely through an impulse to look the other way.

These intrusions of racial invisibility in the novel confront the reader—if not always the Lisbon-obsessed narrators—with the spatial politics of racial containment that underwrite suburban domesticity during the long Cold War era. The "black gates of the remaining millionaires" are barriers as real as the fence upon which Cecilia impaled herself (*VS* 134), but these physical markers of private property also call attention to ambiguous boundaries, like tree lines between cities and suburbs, public shopping districts, and the shifting terrain of racial and economic segregation, keeping Black women waiting at suburbia's (mostly unused) bus stops and Black men tending bar at debutante parties. Although the narrators insistently return to their project of mythologizing the Lisbon girls, these geopolitical undertows pull the reader beyond the boundaries of the Lisbon family home. In these clever ways, *The Virgin Suicides* acknowledges the complex interconnectedness between the suburbs and the larger metropolitan region while exposing the politics of privacy and security in which the borders of the home continually renegotiate the line between the domestic and the foreign.[33]

A second, more overt example of this renegotiation in the novel directly invokes early Cold War–era propaganda, specifically the threat of nuclear war. Having wondered how the family survived during the isolation that precedes the final suicides, the narrators learn "that Mrs. Lisbon kept an abundant supply of canned goods downstairs, as well as fresh water and other preparations against nuclear attack. They had a kind of bomb shelter downstairs, apparently, just off the rec room from which we had watched Cecilia climb to her death" (*VS* 158). While the perceived threat posed by a violent and impoverished urban center occupies a familiar place in suburban history, the threat of a nuclear attack also helped sell the idea of residential sprawl to the American people. The 1956 Interstate Highway Act facilitated the rapid expansion of suburban developments and authorized a "National System of Interstate and Defense Highways," implicitly linking together residential sprawl and national security.[34] From the 1950s through the early 1960s, the fear of atomic war helped to promote the "nuclear family" and the single-family home as the last bastions of safety and security.[35] By the mid-1970s, when "Mrs. Lisbon shut the house in maximum-security isolation" (136), bomb shelters would have been considered passé, as suggested by the narrators' wry remark: "But that was in the days when they expected perils to come from without, and nothing made less sense by that time than a survival room buried in a house itself becoming one big coffin" (158). The external "perils" of atomic war may have passed, but the internal or local threat posed by the Lisbon house-cum-coffin remains. Moreover, the adaptability of the bomb shelter and the persistence of Cold War–era survivalist tactics continue to evoke an image of "nation as home." As Kaplan suggests, these two political realms are connected in their "opposition to everything outside the geographic and conceptual border of the home."[36] The fear of nuclear war may have faded, but Eugenides shows us how the suburban familial household continues to function as an outpost wherein anyone or anything outside those borders represents a potential threat.

In the wake of the final suicides, everyone has a theory about the source of these threats and the precursors to this family tragedy, and each account contributes to an expanding topography of domestic insecurity. The tweedy local communist Mr. Conley points the finger at a capitalist system that "'has resulted in material well-being but spiritual bankruptcy'" (*VS* 226). Other neighbors offer their hypotheses, no less general in their ideological commitments:

> Something sick at the heart of the country had infected the girls. Our parents thought it had to do with our music, our godlessness, or the loosening of morals regarding sex we hadn't even had. Mr. Hedlie . . . put the whole thing down to the misfortune of living in a dying empire. It had to do with the way the mail wasn't delivered on time, and how potholes never got fixed, or the thievery at City Hall, or the race riots, or the 801 fires set around the city on Devil's night. The Lisbon girls became a symbol of what was wrong with the country, the pain it inflicted on even its most innocent citizens . . . .(226)

These varied explanations emerge from a focus on the individual—something "had infected the girls"—but evolve into more systemic concerns. Although the narrators find each conjecture equally unconvincing, if we step outside their obsessive focus there is something persuasive about a communal reading of the suicides as symptomatic of "living in a dying empire," especially when we take into consideration the novel's broader geopolitical contexts.

From the late 1960s and into the 1970s, the Vietnam War, Watergate, economic competition from Japan and Germany, "deep domestic deindustrialization," and increasing urban blight temporarily compromised the United States' global ambitions and threatened to end the "American Century."[37] This temporary eclipse of empire would have been acutely felt in Detroit where the automotive industry was literally dying. James Kunstler notes that "in the early seventies the bottom began to drop out of [Detroit's] car business. The Japanese entered the American market with small, reliable, inexpensive cars just as the [1973] Arab Oil Embargo struck."[38] These are the political and economic conditions against which the Lisbon domestic tragedy unfolds and, significantly, the specific conditions that persist in the wake of the suicides and with which the narrators and the community must come to terms. As Womack and Mallory-Kani contend, Eugenides's novels "afford particular attention to the ways in which the fates of his characters are explicitly yoked to critical factors involving both human nature . . . and cultural history (the demise of the American Dream in direct relation to the automobile industry's economic woes, nascent suburbia, and the Watergate crisis)."[39] The narrators cannot offer a convincing answer to the question of why the girls killed themselves, and they admit they "will never find the pieces to put them back together" (*VS* 243), but these failures should reframe our reading. In the end, the novel's rich and fraught heteroglossia—including the narrators' wistful memories, the other voices in the community that enter the text through interviews and remembered conversations, and the repressed historical narratives that collect in the gaps of the narrative—expands the geographic scales of this domestic tragedy.

Our Nation, Our Way of Life

On the night of the suicides, the narrators reenter the Lisbon house for the first time since Cecilia's party. They quickly assesses the damage: "The living room had a plundered look. The television sat at an angle, its screen removed, Mr. Lisbon's toolbox open in front of it. Chairs were missing arms or legs, as though the Lisbons had been using them for firewood" (*VS* 203). The passing reference to the television with "its screen removed" and resting "at an angle" signals the narrators' failed voyeuristic enterprise to construct a narrative that would correct "the television version of things" purveyed by the media and accepted as dogma by the community (220). The narrators had been invited back into the house to confront their ignorance and the inadequacy of their own designs; the Lisbon girls "had brought [them] here to find that out" (210). Even weeks later, after the house has been cleaned out and opened for viewing, the narrators discover an unsettled space that still refuses to give up the girls' secrets: "It felt as though the house could keep disgorging debris forever, . . . and after sifting through it all we would still know nothing" (224). The repeated acknowledgments of the narrators' incomplete purview should encourage us to read against the grain of their fetishistic narrative and to explore the larger critique the novel posits about nation and home.

As the novel draws to a close, we are once again nudged in this direction. In the early morning hours following the "Asphyxiation" debutante party, where affluent parents offered champagne toasts to the return of "our industry . . . our nation, our way of life" (*VS* 230), the young boys look on as an ambulance carries away the final Lisbon daughter, Mary, who had endured a month longer than her sisters before a second, successful suicide attempt ended her life. She emerges from the house on a stretcher, wearing "a black dress and veil" reminiscent "of Jackie Kennedy's widow's weeds," and the narrators remark that "the final procession out the front door, with two paramedics like uniformed pallbearers, and the sound of postholiday firecrackers going off on the next block over, did call to mind the solemnity of a national figure being laid to rest" (232). A cigarette lighter provides an impromptu, fleeting version of "an eternal flame" (232). Last night's drunken paeans to resurgent nationalism give way in the early dawn to a suburban evocation of a nation in mourning. In the wake of this family tragedy, our narrators can only "gaze up at the whited sepulchre of the former Lisbon house" (239), which now reads as a kind of national memorial.

The Virgin Suicides repeatedly calls upon readers to make a similar turn and "face the house." As I have been arguing, this focal point opens the novel to a wider analysis of domestic borders, the private realm, and the complex regional and national interconnectedness of the single-family home. The isolationism of the Lisbon familial household, the efforts on the part of the town to contain the menace in their midst, the allusions to war and bomb shelters, the persistence of racial tensions and inequalities on the home front, the references to environmental degradation—all these elements in the novel coalesce into a broader, retrospective response to the home's ideological function and the ascension of postwar suburban domesticity. As readers, we can situate the Lisbon tragedy within a comprehensive, postwar historical and environmental context: from the "jungle airstrips" of World War II to the 1967 riots to the "dying empire" of the 1970s; from Detroit's post-war boom to "the continuing decline of [the] auto industry" (*VS* 238) to the contemporary destruction of the "last great automotive mansion ... to put up a subdivision" (240); and from the rotting elm trees to the polluted lake to the current "city air-pollution ordinance" against outdoor grilling (240). The community may interpret the suicides and the decay of the Lisbon house as harbingers of the neighborhood's "demise" (238), but the novel suggests something different. Their tragedy provides the occasion, not the cause, to reassess the place of the suburban home within this more extensive geopolitical framework.

By working across multiple scales at once, *The Virgin Suicides* evokes regionalism's interest in the domestic and the foreign while always positioning the reader to view the local through the prism of global, systemic concerns. According to Michael Kowalewski, regional writing, or what he terms "bioregionalism," "attempt[s] to counter the rootless and displaced character of contemporary American society by illuminating the complex ecology of local environments and how those environments affect the life of those who live within them."[40] Read as regional writing, Eugenides's novel breaks free from traditional perspectives on America's placeless landscapes, inviting us to see how suburban homes and the narrative of a "local" tragedy extend to questions of domesticity, nation, and empire in America across the long Cold War era. That is not to say that the novel or the Lisbon suicides in particular serve as "a refutation of the suburban form," but rather that we must rethink the relationship between suburbs and the environment.[41] During the Cold War era, as Christopher Sellers notes, "the rising clamor over pollution reflected just how many cultural boundaries, seemingly so fundamental and stable before and during World War II, now seem to have been blurred or breached. Among these were the borders between city and country, human bodies and their environments, the natural and the human-made."[42] At the contemporary moment of its production, *The Virgin Suicides* seems to pose a more nuanced question: How do we arrive at a fuller understanding of the ways in which our suburban homes and neighborhoods are situated within the intersecting topographies of region and nation?

From their final vantage point, the narrators can only lament the decay of their "sacred objects" (*VS* 241), the exhibits they have enshrined in a "refurbished tree house in one of [their] last trees"

(240), a sly reference to the neighborhood's continued environmental decline. "In the end," they realize, "we had pieces of the puzzle, but no matter how we put them together, gaps remained, oddly shaped emptinesses mapped by what surrounded them, like countries we couldn't name" (241). They construct their narrative in response to this resistance. Stranded "in the tree house" (243), caretakers to a collection of decomposing artifacts, the narrators have taken us as far as they can, but their failure to fill in the gaps clears the way for our own reading. As Lutz contends, American regional writing "abound[s] with images of failed, partial, incomplete cosmopolitanisms, prompting us to larger and larger overviews."[43] Eugenides works within and against the narrators' limited, nostalgic account of the Lisbon girls to expand the narrative's historical and geographical terrain. In the final analysis, the narrators' account proves only "partial," but the novel's allusive structure opens up space for analysis and critique, leading readers to a multifaceted understanding of place and regional interconnectedness at the end of the twentieth century.

In an essay on sustainability studies, Gillen D'Arcy Wood explains that "[a]cross the global culture, [literature] offers the richest available repository of reflections on human embeddedness in the natural world, a psychological and aspirational guidebook to the dynamics of human and natural systems."[44] *The Virgin Suicides* makes room for such complexity and nuance in its attention to domestic and regional borders, the geographic scale of neighborhoods and communities, the racial repressions and occlusions of the metropolitan region, and the fragile sustainability of local environments. As regional writing, the novel leads us to a capacious understanding of suburban domesticity in an era of tense national and international politics. In the end, we do not retreat into the tree house with the narrators. In the wake of the Cold War, anticipating environmental concerns and local-global tensions that will reverberate across U.S. metro-regions in the new millennium, Eugenides's novel leaves us in an unfinished space, enabling us to work out the implications of our own "embeddedness" in the nation and the larger world.

The novels examined in the second part of this study clarify the effects of neoliberal policies on metropolitan expansion, the uneven geographic development of urban centers and suburban regions, the persistent residential segregation on the basis of race, the environmental consequences of widespread deregulation, and evolving conceptions of the nuclear family and "nation as home" from the 1970s to the early 1990s. *The Virgin Suicides*, *White Noise*, and *The Twenty-Seventh City* explore facets of suburban isolationism and the ideological privileging of privatism—prioritizing both the domestic realm and private or individual interests—while U.S. metropolitan regions were expanding into exurbs and edge cities, propelling the country beyond the era of the commuter suburb. In their engagement with late twentieth-century culture, these novels span the fraught domestic and international politics of the Nixon era, stagflation and deindustrialization, the ascendancy of neoliberalism and Reaganomics, the rise of the unrestricted free market and consumer-citizenship, and the global expansion of U.S. economic power. While *White Noise* is especially adept at evoking transformations to the built environment over this period and the far-reaching consequences posed by new, man-made environmental hazards, *Twenty-Seventh City* and *Virgin Suicides* register the persistent racial antagonism and division that has been an axiomatic component of postwar suburban nation building. Alongside the "airborne toxic event" in *White Noise*, the polluted lake and the dying elms of *The Virgin Suicides* speak to a growing sense of environmental precarity linked to industrial deregulation and patterns of residential development that will lead to more urgent calls for sustainability and smart growth. Although reading these works of realist and late-postmodern suburban fiction through a regionalist lens may seem inherently regressive, I would instead argue that these novels expand our historical and territorial understanding of the work regionalism performs as a literary aesthetic and as a critical response to place and structural inequalities in an era of increasing spatial complexity. By inhabiting regionalism, however loosely, suburban fiction provides a vantage point from which to analyze the contested project to construct and define the nation across the postwar era. The next two chapters will move this inquiry into the twenty-first century.

PART III

Regional Crossroads and the New Millennium

(2000s–2010s)

5

Moving Back, Moving On
Transnational Suburban Regions

"YOU'RE STUCK IN TRAFFIC AGAIN."[1]
This is the opening line of *Suburban Nation: The Rise of Sprawl and the Decline of the American Dream*, the popular New Urbanist text by Andres Duany, Elizabeth Plater-Zyberk, and Jeff Speck, reissued in 2010 with a new preface to commemorate its tenth anniversary. *Suburban Nation* offers a nonacademic introduction to the history of sprawl and urban design. Its authors critique an outmoded, midcentury planning model that has damaged the natural environment, fragmented America's residential communities, and undermined its civic institutions. In place of this dysfunctional system, they promote the philosophy of "smart growth": high-density, mixed-use, neighborhoods; pedestrian-friendly towns with efficient public transportation systems; and "a well-defined public realm supported by buildings reflecting the architecture and ecology of the region" (254). As an approach to residential development, New Urbanism promises to offset the runaway expansion of sprawl and return to a more traditional pattern of neighborhood designs "located within a comprehensive regional plan" for living (187).

While many residents, planners, and scholars find much to admire in the ideal of smart growth, critics have noted that, in practice, New Urbanism often exacerbates class and racial segregation through projects that tend toward gentrification, creating wealthy enclaves like Seaside, Florida, designed by Duany and Plater-Zyberk, which, according to Dolores Hayden, are based on "a nostalgic, idealized view of affluent families and the picturesque enclaves and borderlands of the American past."[2] Jim Lewis echoes Hayden's nostalgia critique, claiming that "[t]o its adversaries, New Urbanism is regressive, authoritarian and hidebound."[3] As residents of these New Urbanist communities negotiate the competing entitlements of private homeownership and communal life, they often find they must surrender basic rights. For example, New Town, a planned community in St. Charles, Missouri—also designed by Duany and Plater-Zyberk—restricts "plastic furniture on front porches," "outdoor clotheslines," "aluminum or vinyl fences," "colored window shades," "storm doors," and "gas lawnmowers," which "are prohibited in part because of their noise."[4] In the wake of Hurricane Katrina, in 2005, Duany and the Congress for New Urbanism were invited to recommend design plans for Gulf Coast redevelopment, but a misunderstanding about affordable housing quickly surfaced. For the devastated, predominantly working-class community of East Biloxi, Duany's estimate of $140,000 seemed blatantly aloof. As Lewis writes, "When I asked Bill Stallworth, a black councilman whose ward includes about half of East Biloxi, he was . . . blunt. 'That's not affordable for this area,' he said. 'Affordability is $65,000 to $95,000.'"[5]

These complex debates about how the financial interests of planners and their design imperatives collide with the exigent needs of a devastated community, like post-Katrina towns and neighborhoods, bring the smart growth movement into the contested history of suburban development, and as a literary scholar, I am especially interested in the discourse of New Urbanism and what it tells us about the relationship between individuals and their lived environments. In other words, I am curious about the ways *Suburban Nation*, as a text, recruits us as readers of smart growth, sustainability, and regional planning. With "close to 100,000 copies" in circulation (ix), *Suburban Nation* offers a unique opportunity to consider the various links among writing, popular readership, social engagement, and residential geography. The opening sentence, "You're stuck in traffic again," immediately confines us within an antagonistic scene: the frustrated, isolated driver at odds with an indifferent, even hostile environment. "You're" trapped in your car, presumably one of the millions of "respectable professionals" making her commute to or from the office (xix), a link in the long chain of brake lights coiling its way across the country's highways. Positioned as the driver within the car—carpooling seems out of the question—the reader of the text is also recruited as a reader within the scene: you're reading an "awful new billboard" advertising "NEW HOMES!," homes that will destroy the land "where you hiked and sledded as a child" because it has now been "zoned for single-family housing" (xix).

This opening maneuver subtly reminds us that the American landscape has been forced to conform to the automobile and the highway system, but the scene the authors set also underscores how much the car's ambiguous privacy shapes the relationship between the individual and the suburbs.[6] The car functions as a mobile unit of private property through which we lay claim to public land, offering drivers a real, if withered, sense of individualism among the collective horde. After all, we are never at fault for the jams we find ourselves in on the road. We call ahead to say, "I'm stuck in traffic," never, "I'm running late because I'm collaborating on a traffic jam." This underlying tension between the individual and the collective, I would argue, defines the authors' efforts to conscript active "citizen urbanists," but it also exposes a fundamental paradox. On the one hand, *Suburban Nation* is a call to action: it tries to recruit a community of civically engaged readers and, in the process, to reform the relationship between the isolated subject and her environment. To make this goal explicit, in both the introduction and the conclusion the authors refer to their text as "a primer" written with the specific intent of "stopping sprawl" (xxiv, 216), suggesting that the act of reading serves as a form—or at least an initial stage—of political commitment.

On the other hand, as the authors also make explicit, the community *Suburban Nation* addresses does not yet seem to exist. The places where most Americans live tend to discourage the kind of communal engagement the text invites. Single-use zoning policies have undermined the political efficacy of the public realm, disenfranchising us as "citizens" in the traditional sense: in the suburbs, we no longer seem to be recognized inhabitants of a specific civic entity. In short, at the same time that the authors invoke a community of readers, they also express deep-seated anxieties about communal engagement. The text poses an implicit question—"Is there a public for this text about public engagement?"—and in this way, it is also a primer on how discourse forms community. In effect, the book is an attempt to create the community it addresses. To co-opt Michael Warner's thinking about the formation of "counterpublics," to address a public is to engage in the social project of imagining a public. Publics must be self-created but, at the same time, their self-organized formation depends upon invocation by discourse.[7] This is the paradoxical relationship *Suburban Nation* both confronts and enacts.

Two passages from the introduction clarify how this discursive social project plays out in the text. In both examples, the authors first isolate the reader and exploit her privileged perspective in order then to recruit a broader collective of citizen-readers. As it turns out, what distinguishes the reader—the "you"—the authors invoke is your experience and insight.

> It's not just sentimental attachment to an old sledding hill that has you upset [about these awful new homes]. It is the expectation, based upon decades of experience, that what will be built here you will detest. It will be sprawl: cookie-cutter houses, . . . mindlessly curving cul-de-sacs, a streetscape of garage doors—a beige vinyl parody of *Leave It to Beaver*. Or, worse yet, a pretentious slew of McMansions, complete with the obligatory gatehouse. You will not be welcome there . . . . (xx)

Although somewhat obscured by the freight of negative language, the passage also includes an appeal to the reader's exceptionalism. The reader is never held to account. Apparently, "you" are part of the traffic jam, supposedly an adherent to the suburban American Dream, but your complicity in the detrimental effects of sprawl is displaced by your keen judgment (xx). You may be unwelcome among these gated communities, but your rejection of suburbia's "mindlessly curving cul-de-sacs" affirms your cultural capital.

"You" know you are an informed citizen-reader, and more importantly, the authors know you know. Duany et al. write, "You are against growth, because you believe that it will make your life worse. And you are correct in that belief, because, for the past fifty years, we Americans have been building a national landscape that is largely devoid of places worth caring about" (xx). This is the key moment in the Introduction to *Suburban Nation*, the shift from "you" to "we," confirming the reader's unique insight while simultaneously implicating all of us—"we Americans"—in the decline of our "national landscape."[8] When subjected to a fine-grained analysis, these passages raise important questions about how the act of reading might inspire, or constitute, a form of social and political action. When it comes to literary studies, the links among reading, writing, and activism have been a shibboleth of the discipline, often at the expense of actual commitment. As Gayatri Chakravorty Spivak writes, "This precarious and temporary transfer of agency, earned through imaginative attention, is how the habit of reading and writing as robust allegories of knowing and doing may come to supplement, fill a hole in as well as add to, the decision-making authority of the social sciences."[9] The authors' rhetorical turn from "you" to "we" transforms the scene of reading from a site of isolation into a space from which we can imagine ourselves as part of a socially engaged collective. Or, as Duany et al. clarify in the concluding chapter: "this book is an appeal to the . . . armchair urbanist," who is presented with "a new opportunity every day to make a constructive contribution to the creation and improvement of the public realm" (241). In this respect, *Suburban Nation* also appeals to a shared narrative history as essential to this call to collective action. As Nicholas Blomley insists, "Narratives are held to be powerful not because they serve as a framework imposed upon social processes, but because they constitute that which they narrate."[10]

This chapter examines how literary narratives shape our thinking about the suburbs and regionalism in the new millennium. At a time when New Urbanism was in vogue, writers could appeal to an "armchair urbanist" reader, and something of a popular groundswell existed around the ideas of smart growth and traditional planning. Antipathy toward suburbia may be as old as suburbanization, but at the turn of the century, a desire on the part of both residents and planners to rein in sprawl coincided with the realization that, according to Peter Calthorpe and William Fulton, "We [were] at a turning point in the life of metropolitan America. We [had] outgrown the old suburban model."[11] Nevertheless, calls to action and efforts to alter the nation's predominant pattern of residential development inevitably confront an unwelcome truth: "In the real world, vested interests and inertia often block needed change."[12]

Perhaps unsurprisingly, the authors of *Suburban Nation* put themselves in a similar bind, evoking the "vested interests" of the past even as they advocate for transformative approaches to urban planning. They strategically deploy, as Hayden notes, a "nostalgic, idealized view" of the suburbs for their (upper-middle-class) readers, those hills "where you hiked and sledded as a child," in order to promote their New Urbanism. Even as they disparage sprawl, "cookie-cutter" cul-de-sacs, and the affected elitism of McMansions, they recall a postwar suburban ideal that was, with few exceptions, the exclusive province of white families. In other words, *Suburban Nation* adopts the aesthetics of nostalgia to envision a new direction for suburban living that ironically rehashes a postwar imaginary cleansed of racist practices such as redlining and restrictive covenants. Unlike, for example, the knowing deployment of nostalgia in *A Raisin in the Sun*, in which Hansberry reimagines the rural ideal of the southern home through an urban framework to disrupt the politics of racial containment, *Suburban Nation* offers a reflexive evocation of a (white) postwar ideal. Interrogating the racial exclusivity of properly designed suburban townships or how their own projects might perpetuate similar exclusions does not seem central to their enterprise.[13]

This chapter reads Chang-rae Lee's *Aloft* (2004) and Richard Ford's *The Lay of the Land* (2006) as novels that show we have, as Calthorpe and Fulton suggest, outgrown the traditional model of suburban planning, and in diverse ways, both Lee and Ford engage with the dialectic of necessary change and the inertia that often thwarts progressive transformation at the turn of the millennium. Although in ways far more nuanced than *Suburban Nation*, each narrative recruits readers for this new era of thinking about suburbanization, this "turning point" in our patterns of suburban living. As I will show, the novels produce complementary responses to the spatial effects of residential sprawl, the indirect costs of domestic privatism, and the contemporary suburb as a uniquely problematic and potentially transformative region. *Aloft* and *Lay of the Land* also help us to reimagine turn-of-the-century suburban fiction as an iteration of regional writing—more specifically, as a kind of "transnational" regionalism attuned to evolving patterns of urban development, suburbia's changing demographics, and the economic and cultural currents that intertwine our suburban homes and neighborhoods with more global trends.

In her study of nineteenth-century regionalism, Stephanie Foote writes "that regional writing was responsive to the nationalizing demands of the era that produced it and that its depiction of regions showed them all to be heterogeneous, founded on the differences that regional writing was assumed to eradicate."[14] *Aloft* and *Lay of the Land* demonstrate how suburban fiction continues this literary tradition into the post-9/11 era, at a time of new "nationalizing demands" and amidst a sprawling housing market wrapped, as Ford writes, in "a big shiny bubble," racing toward collapse.[15] As part of an ongoing response to the project of suburban nation building, these novels help readers to perceive both the standardized spaces of postmodern, capitalist culture *and* the heterogeneity that subverts spatial abstractions and gives the lie to the suburban "nowhere."

A Genuine Neighborhood

Aloft offers a dynamic response to the multiplicity of contemporary suburban living, and the novel affords readers a glimpse at what it might mean to take a more multifaceted and affirmative approach to our suburban nation, especially the country's older suburbs. In the process, the single-family home emerges as the site for a reimagined and recalibrated scale of living. Ultimately, the novel presents an affirmative and capacious view of the suburbs as a cultural formation attuned to local-global tensions and the shifting signifiers of race, class, and place. One of the most obvious ways *Aloft* achieves this effect is through its attention to suburbia's evolving ethnic composition. Since the 1980s, new immigrants to the United States have been moving directly into the suburbs, remapping the history of white flight to make room for the ethnic enclave. As Lawrence Levy notes, "legal and illegal immigrants alike are bypassing that cramped apartment in a central city for a cramped subdivision, or sometimes, a subdivided house in suburbia."[16] This trend has reshaped communities from Orange County, California, to Fairfax County, Virginia, suburban strongholds whose foreign-born residents make up about one-quarter of their respective residential populations.[17] These demographic changes have forced scholars to rethink traditional notions of "spatial assimilation." In the past, "New ethnic groups were expected to concentrate in slums . . . , to re-locate in their second generation to working-class districts with an ethnic character, and finally to aspire to assimilate into the 'Promised Land'" of the suburban frontier.[18] Though aspects of this paradigm have remained intact, increasing diversity among suburban populations has disrupted traditional notions of the homogeneous white suburb, even if suburban neighborhoods themselves remain subject to familiar patterns of segregation.[19]

Lee reworks postwar, suburban white flight through these changing patterns of suburbanization. Set on Long Island, *Aloft* is narrated by an Italian American landscaper turned travel agent, Jerry Battle, and the novel, drawing on a long literary tradition, revolves around his midlife crisis. About twenty-five years earlier, Jerry's Korean wife, Daisy, suffering from bipolar disorder, drowned in the family pool, the result of an excessive ingestion of sedatives and alcohol. In the narrative's present, Jerry's multiethnic children are also working through moments of personal crisis. His daughter, Theresa, has recently learned she is both pregnant and has cancer, and her decision to carry the pregnancy to term will prove fatal. Jack, Jerry's son, has taken over Battle Brothers landscaping and moved the company toward the high-end home remodeling featured on HGTV and favored by his wife, Eunice; in the process, he has overextended the company's finances and run his business and personal life into the ground. Jerry's father, who established Battle Brothers and transformed it from a small bricklaying company into a suburban landscaping empire, struggles against the inevitabilities of old age. And, finally, Jerry's long-term, currently estranged, Puerto Rican girlfriend, Rita Reyes, is set to marry another man. The narrative is equal parts tragedy and farce, and the one constant is Jerry's compulsive urge to take off and fly above it all in his Cessna aircraft.

I have loaded this description with ethnic modifiers to underscore Jerry's preoccupation with race and ethnicity. He describes his family in these terms: "an ethnically jumbled bunch, a grab bag miscegenation of Korean (Daisy) and Italian (us Battles) and English-German (Eunice). . . . As a group, you can't really tell what the hell we are, though more and more these days the very question is apparently dubious, if not downright crass, at least to folks like Theresa and [her fiancé] Paul, whose race-consciousness is clearly quite different from mine."[20] Jerry's "race-consciousness" serves as a foil to Theresa's postmodern identity politics and, in the end, the novel casts suspicions on the intractability of each position. Indeed, Jerry's preoccupation with race might better be described as confusion over the shifting modalities of race, as his traditional views about identity and belonging always exist in an imagined tension with Theresa's racial deconstructions. As Mark C. Jerng notes, "The novel exhibits a strict segregation of where race is: it is a part of Jerry's long diatribes about life, but none of it occurs in the direct speech between him and others. In other words, race is everywhere in the novel but it is never talked about."[21]

The fact that "race is everywhere in the novel" distinguishes *Aloft* from more prototypical suburban narratives, but since it "is never talked about," its force remains indirect, especially when considered alongside Lee's earlier novels, *Native Speaker* (1995) and *A Gesture Life* (1999). In the latter work, "Doc" Hata recalls with mild surprise how, in the 1960s, his new neighbors accepted him into the affluent New York suburb of Bedley Run, "especially given [his] being a foreigner and a Japanese." Hata realizes, however, that this easy acceptance depended on his ability to render his ethnicity invisible by disappearing within the sumptuary codes of suburbia: the "unwritten covenant of conduct . . . , of cordiality and decorum," that deters unwelcome intimacies and sustains the neighborhood's "delicate and fragile balance."[22] In other words, whereas race appears in a more accessible, even predictable way in a novel like *A Gesture Life*, in *Aloft* it operates as one facet of a larger, more subtle narrative project to unsettle our assumptions about suburban insularity. The multicultural becomes a signifier for evolving formulations of regionalist-suburban subjectivity in *Aloft*, a subjectivity that remains attuned to the transitional, turn-of-the-century suburban landscape and produces new responses to place. Lee imagines a form of suburban living open to diversity and adaptable in the face of economic and family crises.

Yet it takes a while for Lee's narrative to get us there. For most of *Aloft*, we are left to contemplate the endgame of suburban living and the conspicuous consumption and over-extension of credit that paved the way for the housing crisis and Great Recession. Even before Jack's financial indiscretions come to light, the bottom begins to fall out, literally, as Jerry recalls his former neighbors, the Guggenheimers, and the odor of "epic rot" emitting from the sinkhole in their backyard (284). Winning the lottery temporarily rescues them, but their good fortune cannot safeguard George Guggenheimer who, after a car accident, slowly withdraws from the world, "airlocked in his private bedroom suite" (287). George's wife divorces him and relocates to a gated community with the kids, and George simply disappears, apparently abandoning the house he still owns. The family's windfall exacerbates the impulse toward insularity, and recalling their story in light of the news about his daughter, Jerry "begin[s] to see this sprawly little realm as laden with situations not simply dangerous and baleful" (288).

Aloft's comprehensive representation of suburban living, however, derives from its varied portrayals of these sprawling terrains: the boom-and-bust era of exurban sprawl paired with a reimagining and remodeling of 1950s suburbia. Having re-conceptualized Battle Brothers around current trends in upscale renovations, Jack reaps the rewards of the boom market. "Every one of those remodels needs new lighting and plumbing fixtures and tiles and cabinetry," he says. "And it's all high-end stuff, exactly our Battle Brothers Excalibur products. How do you think I keep Eunice living in the style to which she's accustomed?" (233). Deflecting compliments about an expensive fixture in his own kitchen, Jack continues, "Eunice got the idea from a show on HGTV" (233). The reference to HGTV cleverly draws attention to the role of popular culture in shaping attitudes about suburban living and domestic space, not unlike *House & Garden* or *House Beautiful* did in the immediate postwar era. As Dante Ciampaglia writes, the origin of HGTV was fortuitously timed, "its popularity mirroring a booming national home repair and renovation market."[23] Since the network's debut in 1994, Ciampaglia continues, "The housing market took off, overheated, exploded into a generation-defining global recession, then rebounded. Interest in interior design intensified, and countless professional and amateur designers colonized and popularized blogs and websites like Etsy."²⁴ By fetishizing "triple-nickel-plated" faucets and other fashionable accouterment (233), HGTV and other media outlets helped to normalize a suburban style of living in the early 2000s, when the market was "overheated," that often exceeded (or soon would) the finances of average homeowners. In the process, home remodeling shows perpetuate the perfect consumer cycle: Jack can live beyond his means because other homeowners either have the means or are equally unconcerned about living beyond theirs.

In *Aloft*, HGTV serves as more than an easy target. The extravagant houses and the networks that promote them point to a pervasive economic and spatial denial in suburbia. While waiting to meet with an administrator at Ivy Acres, the retirement community where the senior Battle resides, Jerry and Paul strike up a conversation around an episode on HGTV. Paul, an Asian-American writer currently struggling with both his writing and his betrothed, launches into a diatribe against the people who finance these expensive remodels: "Everyone is Client Zero. . . . They think they can go anywhere and do anything, as if none of their actions has any bearing except on themselves, like they're in their own mini-biosphere, all needs self-providing, everything self-contained, setting it up like God would do himself. It doesn't matter that there are people on the outside tapping at the glass, saying, 'Hey, hey, I'm here. Look out here'" (298). A perfect combination of the literal and figural, Paul's screed allegorizes his relationship with Theresa while offering a straight critique of suburban privatism, the indirect costs of U.S. residential development, and suburbia's imbrication in global politics. Sitcoms have given way to reality TV shows that disseminate and tacitly endorse this hermetic understanding of place for a new generation of suburbanites.

Throughout the novel, Lee sustains our awareness of the explicit and implicit costs of these "mini-biospheres" by adopting a regionalist approach to the interconnectedness of place. Early in the story, Jerry notes, "Now with the economy in the doldrums [Jack] probably wishes he hadn't built his mega-mini-mansion but he doesn't seem concerned" (25). The previous sentence, though, has already alerted us to a worrisome undertow: "Good for him that for the last four years [Jack] has seemed to be practically printing money, what with all the trucks out every day and him needing to hire extra help literally off the street each morning in Farmingville, where the Hispanic men hang out" (25). The references here are subtle, but the subtlety attests to the invisibility of the practice. As Mike Davis argues, the "hyper-privatized, McMansionized villages" of eastern Long Island depend on a reviled "day-labor workforce [that] has been concentrated into the blue-collar enclave of Farmingville. . . . Hundreds of immigrants shape-up every morning along Horseblock Road in a 'slave market' for local contractors and homeowners."[25] By citing Farmingville and Jack's likely dubious hiring practices, Lee evokes the complex heterogeneity of Long Island, juxtaposing the insularity of "mega-mini-mansions" with the "slave market" that sustains them. Through such clever turns, *Aloft* situates the suburbs as transnational nodes, tethered to the Global South, exposing the "[e]conomic and cultural umbilical cords" that link suburban homes and neighborhoods to the flow of capital and labor.[26] And while "mini-biospheres" and the collapse of Battle Brothers may signify the untenable scale of suburban geopolitics, the novel does not disguise its likely perpetuity. Jack and his family abandon their house and move into Jerry's modest ranch, but they still "[find] a Danish corporate executive on assignment to take a three-year lease on the place for $6000 a month" (355). In this way, Lee points toward two aspects of "the foreign" in his suburban novel: the "slave market" of immigrant labor that drives the profit margins for building and redevelopment, and the foreign executive with access to a deep well of reserves on the real estate market.[27] Space continues to have its beneficiaries.

At such moments, Lee's novel confronts the historical and material fact of suburban sprawl and the pervasive suburban worldview that this now-predominant national region reproduces. In chapter three, I examined the effects of postmetropolitan sprawl on both private homes and metro-regional landscapes during the neoliberal era, a period in which, as Fredric Jameson argues, "the replacement of the old tension between city and country, center and province, by the suburb and by universal standardization" had fundamentally altered our ability "to map" and understand the places we inhabit.[28] In *Aloft*, we find a potential corrective to this sense of the placeless, an effort to "re-map" suburbia as a contested terrain at the crossroads of the local and global. The novel offers a "bioregional" approach to contemporary suburbia that "counteract[s] both an American amnesia about history and a related, often deep-seated unresponsiveness to the places in which Americans live."[29] As a text attuned to the complexity of place, *Aloft* repeatedly challenges this spatial "unresponsiveness," and over the course of the novel, as Jerry becomes more accustomed to the changing structure of his own family and their scale of living, new possibilities for suburban sustainability begin to emerge.

The novel's explicit critiques of sprawl prepare the way for a more compelling, implicit argument to reintegrate older suburban neighborhoods into regional planning designs for the twenty-first century, something that urban planners and historians have long advocated.[30] At the end of the novel, Jerry invites the embattled Battle family into his home: his father; Jack, Eunice, and their two children; Paul and the newborn baby, Barthes. Even Rita has returned, though the terms of her relationship with Jerry remain nebulous. This multiethnic, extended family presents a riposte, as Kristin Jacobson suggests, to "the conventionally segregated, single-family suburban home," and this newly expanded and redefined family leads to the literal rebuilding of the house.[31] To accommodate this influx, Jack begins making additions, and his renovated home, as Kathy Knapp notes, is "a vision of community that is provisional in every sense of the word . . . , but in its recognition that life itself is provisional, it reimagines the suburb as a potential site of renewed social connection that addresses the varied needs of its diverse, changing population."[32] The remodeled ranch introduces an earlier era of multigenerational living to this Levittown-era neighborhood and offers a dynamic antidote to the insular and homogeneous suburb.

In contrast to McMansions and the object fetishism of HGTV, the 1950s suburb emerges as the more authentic mode of living in *Aloft*. During one of his reveries, Jerry remarks that his "aging postwar development [is] just now beginning to look and feel like a genuine neighborhood, the trees finally grown up in a vaulted loom over the weathered ranches and colonials" (231). The novel takes the traditional critique of suburban banality, alienation, and homogeneity and turns it on its head, not through a nostalgic, sentimental version of postwar townships, à la *Suburban Nation*, but by reconstructing that older model to make room for an ethnically diverse, non-nuclear family and the reality of economic hardship. Collectively, Jack's financial overextension, the references to HGTV, and the re-composition of the family illustrate the vast differences between "sitcom suburbia" and contemporary sprawl. Although postwar sitcoms staged and validated the nuclear family and the suburban nation-building project, there remained a degree of fictional, even aspirational distance.[33] *Aloft* critiques a more "dangerous and baleful" era of standardized overconsumption (288), and as a work of regional writing, it encourages a more responsive engagement with the places we inhabit and the nation's changing demographics.

Admittedly, Theresa's death makes for an ambivalent ending, and the last scene depicts Jerry lying underground in the trench carved for the new swimming pool. Yet despite its grave-like connotations, his skyward perspective, "gazing up at a perfect frame of firmament for flights endless, unseen" (364), also frames the novel, bringing us back to the opening sequence in which Jerry cruises over the suburban landscape in his Cessna. *Aloft* works through the familiar, aerial shots of uniform suburbs and brings us to ground, to human scale, where the perspective gets more complicated. The reconstruction projects taking place around Jerry invert the impulse toward insularity, and though it is just one house, the multi-family Battle home invites readers to contemplate a recalibrated, perhaps ultimately more sustainable mode of suburban living.

A More Human Scale

On Thanksgiving day, near the end of Richard Ford's *The Lay of the Land*, Frank Bascombe drives north along the Jersey Shore, to Ortley Beach, hoping to connect with a woman who works at the local bistro. A sign on the door indicates the restaurant is closed, due to a death in the family, and as he turns away, Frank observes "[f]our men in khaki clothing and heavy corduroy jackets wait[ing] at the corner under the Garden State Parkway sign . . . . Mexicans, these are. Illegals—unlike [his] Hondurans—hoping to be picked up for a job across the bridge, unaware today's a holiday" (434). This passing observation segues into an extended meditation on mortality, but in often more explicit terms than *Aloft*, Ford's novel draws attention to the "slave market" of day laborers and those "[e]conomic and cultural umbilical cords" that, as Davis suggests, fasten the project of constructing the suburban nation to transnational pathways of immigration and human capital. Frank is careful to note, here and elsewhere, that his Honduran workforce is "legal," but the novel depicts more broadly a Northeast suburban region ill at ease with its own diversification at the hands of a labor force it depends upon and reviles.

Lay of the Land takes place over three days during Thanksgiving week, in the midst of the contested 2000 presidential election, a few weeks shy of the Supreme Court decision in *Bush v. Gore* and Al Gore's subsequent concession. It is the third in a trilogy of novels, preceded by *The Sportswriter* (1986) and *Independence Day* (1995). *Let Me Be Frank with You*, a collection of four interlinked stories, subtitled "A Frank Bascombe Book," appeared in 2014. All told, the collection covers thirty years in the life of Ford's "everyman," from author-turned-sportswriter in his late thirties, through his transition to suburban realtor and the "Existence Period" in his mid-forties, to the "Permanent Period" of his mid-fifties—where we find him in *Lay of the Land*, living on the Shore and battling prostate cancer—and concludes in the aftermath of Hurricane Sandy, with Frank now in his late-sixties, "enjoying the Next Level of life—conceivably the last."[34] As Frank adjusts to what he calls the "Default Period," Ford also brings his Bascombe collection full circle, returning his protagonist to the suburb of Haddam, New Jersey, where he had lived for some twenty years before moving to Sea-Clift in the early 1990s. Of course, Frank never truly left his suburban past behind. As he notes in *Lay of the Land*, "despite a wholly reframed life, I've kept my Haddam affiliations alive and relatively thriving. A town you used to live in signifies something—possibly interesting—about you: what you were once" (13).

The recent election, "the life-threatening part of which is still unsettled in the Florida court" (433), lends an aura of precarity to the novel, and Ford parallels political doom with the potentially lethal prospects of Frank's cancer. During one of his trips to Haddam, he mentally inventories the yard signs: "Some recidivist

Bush sentiment is alive on a few lawns, but mostly it's solid-for-Gore in this moderate, woodsy, newer section of the township (when Ann and I were young newcomers down from Gotham in 1970, it was woods, not woodsy). . . . In these parts, it's a good time for an insurrection" (31–32). The contested election—Frank confides, "I went for Gore" (31)—simmers beneath encounters, both casual and otherwise. While waiting at a "replica of a Revolutionary War roadhouse tavern" for his associate at Realty-Wise, Mike Mahoney (formerly Lobsang Dhargey from Tibet), Frank gets into a political argument with a fellow patron that leads to a brawl and culminates in a racist tirade from the bartender (170). Pointing to the fingers on his left hand, the bartender says, "This is your Russian. This next one's your spic. This one's your African. This last one's your Arab or your sand nigger—whichever. You got your choice. . . . [f]or what language you want to learn when you vote for fuckin' Gore" (183). When Mike arrives on the scene, he is also dismissed with a racist slur. The bartender's "hateful diatribe," as Knapp notes, captures white resentment toward expanding minority populations in the suburbs and foreshadows the anti-Arab sentiment that would take root in the U.S. after September 11.[35] Staged, as it is, in a "replica" Revolutionary War tavern, this cynical scene also suggests something foundational to the country, or perhaps, as Richard Yates suggested of his novel *Revolutionary Road*, it implies that some cherished ideal or origin story is headed toward a "dead end."

To date, the critical response to *The Lay of the Land* offers two noteworthy and consistent motifs: first, the novel marks a departure from the previous entries in the trilogy, and second, it reaffirms Ford's status as a "post-regional" or "post-southern" writer. I would like to draw on elements of both lines of thinking to argue that the novel reframes our understanding of the suburbs as a transnational region, a contested terrain of local and global interests, of the domestic and the foreign, at a moment of national insecurity. In short, what marks the novel as a departure is Ford's keen awareness that we are at an inflection point in reconfigurations of the suburban region. As noted, critics appear unanimous in their assessment that the third novel marks a distinct shift in tone from *The Sportswriter* and *Independence Day*. Frank exhibits an openness to and a solidarity with his fellow human beings that appeared lacking in the earlier novels, inviting a reevaluation of this suburban everyman. According to Robert Brinkmeyer, "Frank now understands that the expression 'the lay of the land' . . . has less to do with the American myth that by repeatedly moving one can escape one's troubles than it does with the universal condition, the trials and tribulations that we all, as creatures who will one day die, face upon this earth."[36] Knapp offers a similar appraisal as it pertains to shared vulnerability: "The previous two novels assumed, for better or worse, that the suburbs offered residents safety and security. [*Lay of the Land*] is predicated upon the assumption that life, no matter where it is lived, is full of contingency and discontinuity," and in this way, the novel stakes out "a revolutionary path" for suburban fiction.[37] Frank's newfound perspective on life's exigencies includes a reassessment of his vocation and the meaning of place. As Tim Foster writes, "Frank laments the fact that so much of the New Jersey suburban environment is an empty reflection of society's acquiescence to the forces of the late-capitalist economy," but he becomes "convinced that an imaginative engagement with space can generate a spatiality—a nexus of society's spatial practices—that is more than a reflection of acquisitiveness."[38]

A fraught example of this less jaundiced perspective on space comes near the end of the novel, and it offers an oblique connection to the remodeled suburban home in *Aloft*. Having previously sold a property at 118 Timbuktu—to a couple who planned to demolish it in favor of "a new manufactured dwelling . . . [with] all the best built-ins"—Frank negotiates to take the house instead of his typical commission and resettle it on a lot in the "Little Manila section, which has begun gentrifying at an encouraging rate" (364). His description of the now-unmoored house and what it signifies intersects with the essential heterogeneity of Sea-Clift's population. "At 1,300 sq. ft.," he notes, "it'll be bigger than most of its Whitman Street neighbors and be exactly the kind of small American ranch any Filipino who used to be a judge in Luzon, but who over here finds himself running a lawn-care business, would see as a dream come true" (364). Despite the glib account of the socioeconomic demotion that immigration to the U.S. from the Global South often entails, Frank demonstrates an impulse to renew a more modest scale of living in this American ranch, a quintessential suburban

dwelling. At the same time, this instinct for sustainability destabilizes the remaining residents on Timbuktu, "who're made rueful
by the sight of a neighbor house being torn off its foundations and
trucked away," possibly "to be replaced by some frightening new construction" (404). The house, "detached from the sacred ground that
makes it what it is—a place of safety and assurance"—appears fragile,
like "a shell waiting for a tornado to sweep it into the past" (413).

Unlike the remodeled 1950s suburban home at the end of *Aloft*,
the repurposed American ranch in *Lay of the Land* offers both the
potential for the immigrant "dream come true" (with profit for
Frank) and the illusory nature of domestic stability, but Frank's reference to "sacred ground" does point toward a new understanding
of what place can signify. In *Independence Day*, by contrast, Frank
displays a distinctly anti-nostalgic depiction of place attachment, a
lesson he attributes, in part, to his career in real estate. At a time when
Frank harbored ambivalent feelings about *"suburban virtues"* and the
properties he was hawking, he claims that "a patent lesson of the realty
profession [is] to cease sanctifying places. . . . Place means nothing."[39]
Even toward the end of the novel, nearing his idealistic and more
explicitly "sentimental" depiction of a Fourth of July parade, Frank
suppresses a nostalgic urge.[40] Standing before his former house in
Haddam, he asks, "[I]s there any cause to think a place—any place—
with its plaster and joists, its trees and plantings, in its putative essence
ever shelters some spirit ghost of us as proof of its significance and
ours?" His response, a resounding "No!," leads him to conclude: "We
just have to be smart enough to quit asking places for what they can't
provide, and begin to invent other options."[41]

In *The Lay of the Land*, Frank demonstrates a new understanding about what places can signify and provide, and Sea-Clift has
reawakened him to the human need for domestic stability—that
"sacred ground"—and to the pressing need for more sustainable
approaches to living. As the owner of one of the few remaining
houses on this stretch of the Shore, Frank reflects, "Beach erosion,
shoreline scouring, tectonic shifts, global warming, ozone deterioration and normal w&t have rendered all us 'survivors' nothing more
than solemn, clear-headed custodians to the splendid, transitory
essence of everything" (207). It is a reflection on existential imper-
manence that encompasses a broader purview of interconnected

regional patterns: the human behavior and man-made constructions that contribute to erosion, wear and tear, and the threat of
"global warming" that portends disaster everywhere. Living amidst
the "tranquil towny heterogeneity" of Sea-Clift, a demographic
blend "spiced with Filipinos, Somalians and hard-working Hondurans" (267), has enriched Frank's sense of solidarity amidst
transience. Although Sea-Clift is not a suburb in the truest sense,
despite its "pastel split-levels" (266), it epitomizes what Knapp calls
"the 'suburban real'—its population, at once fluid and fragmented,
is loosely bound by the shifting sands of contiguity."[42] This awareness of adjoining borders in flux also recalibrates Frank's vocational
practice. "There was no space to grow *out* to, so my business model
pointed to in-fill and retrench," he notes, "not so different from
Haddam, but on a more human scale. . . . [C]ommerce with no like-
lihood of significant growth or sky-rocketing appreciation seems
like a precious bounty and the opposite of my years in Haddam,
when *gasping increase* was the sacred article of faith" (399).

The recalibrated, human scale stands in stark contrast to the
portrait of Haddam that emerges in *Lay of the Land*. Frank's former
suburb has become a "love-it/hate-it paragon of suburban ampli-
tude gone beyond self-congratulation to the point of entropy" (49).
Frank sketches in details about the housing market in the early
1990s, which post-dates *Independence Day* (set in 1988), during
the boom period that would lead to the bubble that would eventually burst in 2008. Ruthless and systematic gentrification projects
emptied formerly Black neighborhoods for a clientele of wealthy,
"newcomer white Yuppies" (63). By 1991, the "town where [he'd] felt
genuine residence . . . had entered a new, strange and discordant
phase" (84), and that dissonance can, in part, be traced to patterns
of displacement. Frank remarks that "Wallace Hill . . . was designated a Heritage Neighborhood, which guaranteed all the black
folks had to leave because of taxes (many fled down south, though
they'd been born in Haddam)" (84–85). As seen in Sinclair Lewis's
Kingsblood Royal, racist neighborhood associations in the postwar
era resorted to violence and intimidation in the hopes of trigger-
ing a reverse Great Migration. Here, at the end of the century, the
"malign force" of a neoliberal economy and an overheated housing market effect a similar racial and regional displacement (85).

In Frank's retrospective account, the early 1990s and its rapacious real estate economy marked a breaking point. Haddam "stopped being a quiet and happy suburb, stopped being subordinate to any other place and became a *place to itself*" (89); the town "entered its period of era-lessness" (90). Haddam embodies the fruition of the suburb as *national region*: a kind of timeless, topographic formation, spreading imperialistically across the country, advertised and exported as a cultural ideal across the globe.

Alongside the reality of entropic, standardized sprawl, *Lay of the Land* also makes room for a more nuanced and heterogeneous perspective, and I want to suggest this vantage point offers a gentle corrective to the "post-regional" school of thought. To be sure, Richard Ford *qua* writer poses an interesting, even enigmatic challenge to a discussion of regionalism. Although born in Jackson, Mississippi, he has made it a point not to be a "southern writer." To date, only his first novel, *A Piece of My Heart* (1976), has been set in the South, and of course, he remains best known for his Bascombe trilogy, set in the suburban Northeast. For this reason, understandably, a number of scholars have characterized Ford's writing as post-southern or post-regional. Reading Frank as "[t]he avatar of [a] postmodern detachment from place," Matthew Guinn contends that Ford's protagonist demands "a new conception of place . . . a sense of place as literal, straightforward, and knowable—with no mystery to complicate things beyond the tangible, no character beyond the commercial. In short, a postregional landscape."[43] Brinkmeyer arrives at a similar conclusion, contending that Ford's fiction reflects "the waning of regionalism and regional identity in the United States during an age of globalism," a transformation that in turn "has freed the southern literary imagination to explore new forms, issues, and settings."[44] Addressing Frank's attachment to the Northeast, Rubén Peinado Abarrio insists, "[T]he fact that a Mississippi-born citizen can become a convinced Yankee must mean that nationality (or in this case, regional belonging) is to a great extent a performance."[45] As a voluntarily displaced southerner with regional affiliations in the Northeast, by way of the upper Midwest, Frank may, indeed, appear post-regional, though it seems one might equally argue that he is in fact teeming with region or regional sensibility.

The Sportswriter offers an interesting case in point for assessing the supposedly post-regional aesthetic. In that novel, during a visit to Detroit, Frank remarks, "I have read that with enough time American civilization will make the midwest of any place, New York included. And from here that seems not bad at all. Here is a great place to be in love; to get a land-grant education; to own a mortgage; . . . . So much that is explicable in American life is made in Detroit."[46] Read pejoratively, to "make the midwest of any place" suggests a transition to a homogeneous no place, a national "geography of nowhere" in which, as *Suburban Nation* argues, "places worth caring about" have been absorbed within an undifferentiated pattern of sprawl beholden to the standardizing demands of globalism. Sure, that reading remains available, but it is worth noting that Frank intends something far less cynical. His depiction of the Midwest exudes a level of sincerity, an unironic approach characteristic of his early descriptions of Haddam and the suburbs more broadly. As Ford noted after the publication of *Sportswriter*, "The suburbs have been written about ironically so often that I thought it might be a more interesting surgery on the suburbs to talk about them in unironic terms."[47] That straight stance invites more careful scrutiny of the passage's regional undertones, or more precisely, its "regionalizing" projection.

While Ford has liberated himself from the geography of the South, he still operates "within a particular southern literary tradition," according to Fred Hobson, a tradition evident in, among other things, a protagonist who "is keenly attuned to place."[48] From *The Sportswriter* to *The Lay of the Land*, Ford's suburban fiction transcends a narrower definition of regionalism as mere "geographic specificity" and, instead, embodies regionalism as a literary aesthetic attuned to the complex interconnections among home, region, and nation. As noted in the introduction to this study, suburban sprawl (abetted by the homogeny of global capitalism) has transformed the landscape and undermined regional identity in indisputable ways, but "local color" was always only one part of the work regionalism performs as a literary discourse and mode of analysis. *Lay of the Land*, especially, offers a deeper understanding of regional writing as responsive to "nationalizing demands," as Foote argues, at a moment of political instability—not only in the contested election of the novel's present, but as it figuratively inhabits the post-9/11 world where readers encounter it. In its attention to "the foreign," the novel points toward a kind of transnational regionalism that structures and supports the contemporary suburban terrain. As Lee does in *Aloft*, Ford remaps the suburbs at the crossroads of the local and the global and, in the process, intuits the need for a more responsible, sustainable scale of living.

Read from this perspective, *Lay of the Land* appears loaded with regional signifiers. When describing his sartorial preference as "a dedicated solid-South, chinos, cotton shirt, cotton socks 'n loafers wearer," Frank notes that Haddam "has its claque of similarly suited crypto-southerners—old remittance men who trace back to rich Virginia second sons of the nineteenth century and who arrived to seminary study bringing along their colored servants (which is why there was once a stable Negro population in the Wallace Hill section—now gentrified to smithereens)" (145). These umbilical cords connect Haddam to the U.S. South, but the novel also exhibits an awareness of how the global flow of human capital has transformed the broader metropolitan region where older townships and inner-ring suburbs have been, to borrow a phrase from Soja, "edgily filled with diasporic migrants from the world's poorest regions."[49] En route to meet his friend Wade, who notably waits near an "empty sixties-era mall" (293), Frank drives through the "dense and un-centered" suburb of Wall Township, its intersections decorated "with signage indicating Russians, Farsi speakers, Ethiopians and Koreans live nearby and do business" (292). Continuing on past a CPR demonstration at the fire station and a car wash fundraiser, he notes a civic gathering of "tall and skinny Ethiopians, with a few smaller Arabs in non-Arab sweaters" (293). Asbury Park offers perhaps the most pronounced portrait in the novel of suburban diversity riven by legacies of racial segregation and regional displacements. According to Frank, the "monied towns all needed reliable servant reserves a bus ride away, and Asbury was ceded to the task. Hopeful Negroes from Bergen County and Crown Heights, Somalis and Sudanese fresh off the plane, plus a shop-keeper class of Iranis for whom Harlem was too tough, now populate the streets we drive down" (297). As Frank and Wade travel toward their destination, the scheduled implosion of the Queen Regent, signs of encroaching blight lead Frank to conclude that "Asbury Park could be Memphis or Birmingham, and nothing or no one would seem out of place" (297). One might read this uncanny effect as "post-regional," but I would argue instead that *Lay of the Land* presents a thoroughly diversified, if nonetheless segregated, suburban territory suffused with regional ties both to the southern U.S. and the Global South. As limned by Ford, the metropolitan region has not only become more ethnically heterogeneous, but these suburbs are also enmeshed in a network of immigration routes and the transnational flow of capital.

The Queen Regent, Frank and Wade's destination, stands decrepit and alone amidst a "dry, treeless urban-renewal savanna stretching back to the leafless tree line of Asbury" (298). It is the only remaining obstacle within the advertised "PROGRESS ZONE! . . . LUXURY CONDO COMMUNITY COMING!" (299). *The Lay of the Land* stages a conflict between two attitudes toward the twenty-first-century suburb, one beholden to land developers, "progress zones," and a rapacious housing market, and the other attuned to "a more human scale" (399), attentive to sustainability, and aware of one's place within a larger, more heterogeneous network of regional, national, and transnational place connections. It is this human scale that, earlier in the novel, informs Frank's opposition to Mike Mahoney's investment in a McMansion building scheme. "Flattening pretty cornfields for seven-figure mega-mansions isn't, after all, really *helping* people in the way that assisting them to find a modest home they want—and that's already there—helps them," Frank says (198). Over the course of the trilogy, clearer possibilities emerge for human solidarity, for a more sustainable, recalibrated scale of living, and for "sacred ground . . . a place of safety and assurance" (413).

In his introduction to the 2000 edition of *Revolutionary Road*, Richard Ford remarks that the suburbanites who populate Yates's novel are "disabled as doers of right, or incapable of the human affiliations that could weave a fabric of communal spirit strong enough to hold the weak should they falter, or console the despairing when they sound a plea" (xxi). Arguably, both *Aloft* and *The Lay of the Land* offer a corrective to the lack of "human affiliation" that Ford reads in *Revolutionary Road*, and in the end, to differing degrees, each novel features "doers of right" and makes space to comfort the despondent. As suggested in the introduction to this chapter, these novels offer complementary literary models for thinking about the geo-cultural scale of the suburban home and the diversity of our metropolitan regions at the turn of the twenty-first century. As works that attend thoughtfully to the notion that the country has "outgrown the old suburban model," they reimagine and remap the existing suburban topography within a national and even international context. They share a kind of "transnational" regional aesthetic, alert to the increasing heterogeneity of suburbia and the cultural and economic "umbilical cords" that tether our homes and neighborhoods to more complex geographic patterns and routes. Like the authors of *Suburban Nation*, Lee and Ford also test the boundaries of narrative as an act of transformative thinking. Although prone to nostalgic idealization and an underdeveloped interest in race and class, *Suburban Nation* does offer a strident, development-focused call to action in an effort to imagine more sustainable patterns of living. I read a similar, more nuanced and politically savvy impulse in *Aloft* and *Lay of the Land*. These novels construct narrative alternatives—in the sense that narratives "constitute that which they narrate"—for the suburban region, counter to the apocalyptic vision offered by James Kunstler, who believes "[t]he suburbs have three destinies, none of them exclusive: as materials salvage, as slums, and as ruins."[50] The reconstructed Battle house in *Aloft* awakens readers to the latent possibilities of older suburban homes and neighborhoods, an investment in sustainability that Frank Bascombe echoes in his vocation to help people to find "a modest home" that already exists. The path forward remains an open question, both in terms of literary models and U.S. residential geography, and the recent housing crises and economic recession have provided writers with the exigent circumstances to explore the consequences of our sprawling patterns of residential living and the enduring cultural ideal of the suburban home.

6

Housing Crises

Race, History, and Recession-Era Domesticity

"But when smiling lawns and tasteful cottages begin to embellish a country,
we know that order and culture are established."
—ANDREW JACKSON DOWNING,
The Architecture of Country Houses (1850)

"In California it was ridiculous—there were stretches that were just,
you know, For Sale, For Sale, For Sale, For Sale, and we definitely saw some of
these ghostly, ghostly subdivisions where you could see it was built very
recently and mostly unoccupied."
—ANONYMOUS HEDGE FUND MANAGER,
Diary of a Very Bad Year (2010)

ON SEPTEMBER 4, 2008, Keith Gessen of *n+1* sat down for his third interview with the anonymous Hedge Fund Manager (HFM). Major investment banks had recorded substantial second-quarter losses and suspicions were swirling about the viability of the mortgage corporations Fannie Mae and Freddie Mac. On this occasion, Gessen and HFM discussed currency exchange rates, risk-averse investors, and the generally sluggish economic markets, prompting Gessen to ask when we would know if this was simply a natural trough in the financial cycle or if it signaled the end of days. "When you see me selling apples out on the street," HFM replied, "that's when you should go stock up on guns and ammunition."[1] Within days of that interview, Fannie Mae and Freddie Mac would enter into a government-controlled "conservatorship"; by the middle of September, Lehman Brothers would file for bankruptcy and AIG would be "nationalized by the Federal Reserve"; before the end of the month, "a $700 billion Troubled Asset Relief Program (TARP)," a bailout for banks, would be proposed and, initially, voted down in Congress; other banks, including Morgan Stanley and Goldman Sachs, would collapse or be seized by the federal government; and October would bring "the stock market's worst week since the Great Depression."[2] By the middle of October 2008, if I were Gessen, I would have been looking for that apple cart.

Diary of a Very Bad Year collects nine interviews, conducted between 2007 and 2009, in which HFM thinks through, in real time, the subprime mortgage crisis and its deleterious ripple effects. Over the course of their conversations, two clear points emerge: first, the increasing share of mortgage securities held by Wall Street banks shackled the broader economy to the plunging housing market; and second, the growing distance between risky assets (read: mortgages likely to default) and the person carrying that risk in the form of a collateralized debt obligation (CDO) encouraged dubious, ultimately perilous investment practices. As Roger Lowenstein explains, "The CDO thus introduced an additional layer into the process, with the result that the ultimate investor was further removed, and less equipped to scrutinize, the quality of the underlying mortgages."[3] In short, the CDOs were bundled in such a way as to offset, even disguise the dodgy mortgages they contained, prompting a cycle of rash investments. While Wall Street and reckless investors are the objects of well-deserved scorn in this saga, the subprime origin story can be traced to earlier political decisions, including Clinton-era initiatives to expand homeownership levels among lower-income families.[4] Under George W. Bush, following the collapse of the dot-com bubble, the Federal Reserve lowered short-term interest rates to stimulate the economy, which eased access to credit and further increased home buying.[5] "By 2004," according to Lowenstein, "the number of Americans who 'owned' their homes had climbed to an unprecedented 69 percent."[6] This sharp rise in ownership levels drove up housing prices and propelled real estate speculation and investment.

Although the government-sponsored expansion of homeownership to working-class and aspiring-middle-class families was noble in its intent, the result was an increase in high-risk loans for people with few (if any) assets and often spotty credit histories. In the near term, expanding credit in this way provided an expedient solution to increasing economic inequality, but it only postponed the inevitable cost. As Raghuram Rajan writes, "Politicians love to have banks expand housing credit, for credit achieves many goals at the same time. It pushes up house prices, making households feel wealthier, and allows them to finance more consumption. It creates more profits and jobs in the financial sector as well as in real estate brokerage and housing construction. And everything is safe—as safe as houses—at least for a while."[7] In fact, that was the case in the early years of the new millennium, with housing prices increasing steadily until 2006 before the offsetting decline began. In the hedonistic days before the housing bubble burst, there were millions to be made by trading and selling overrated CDOs.

As described in *Diary of a Very Bad Year*, so many investors and traders were accumulating wealth in this manner "that the dynamic flipped around. It was almost as if the demand for that paper [CDOs] created the mortgages."[8] This inverted dynamic was premised on the inevitable rise in real estate values, an assumption that sanctioned short-term thinking about profit margins and encouraged predacious lending schemes. In other words, as viewed from Wall Street, there was a financial incentive to steer homebuyers into high-risk NINA loans (No Income, No Assets) or punitive adjustable rate mortgages (ARMs). Although the evil machinations of investment bankers and hedge fund managers are clear even to a layperson, at the time, investors premised their actions on the belief that continuing low interest rates and rising real estate prices would allow homeowners to refinance those mortgages, withdraw the accumulated equity, and postpone repayment.[9] Even though the public at large may consider such practices ill-informed, if not unethical, as HFM explains, "There's this year's compensation period . . . and then there's the future. And the future is *very* heavily discounted."[10]

As has been well documented, by late-2007, the tab had come due. Escalating defaults and foreclosures created a glut of vacant houses, causing housing prices to plummet and exposing the debt of banks and hedge funds holding those high-risk CDOs. The subprime mortgage crisis triggered the broader economic recession because of the links between homeownership and the general market—what Rajan describes as "fault lines" in the world economy. Rising income inequality prompted the government to lower interest rates and expand access to credit. Yet, as Rajan contends, "when easy money pushed by a deep-pocketed government comes into contact with the profit motive of a sophisticated, competitive, and amoral financial sector, a deep fault line develops."[11] Indeed, the most significant increase in borrowing was among people who lacked the income or assets to qualify for traditional mortgages, effectively inflating the housing bubble on the backs of the most economically vulnerable populations who had been saddled with subprime loans.[12]

Since homeownership occupies such a prominent place within the national imaginary—the American Dream scaled to the geo-cultural level of the single-family home—expanding mortgages for low-income earners or under-qualified borrowers offered an enticing if shortsighted palliative measure, reaffirming the links between upward mobility and a house in the suburbs. As Heather McGhee explains, though, expanding homeownership opportunities for low-income earners was only part of the story. She writes that "the subprime loans we started to see in the early 2000s were primarily marketed to existing homeowners, not people looking to buy."[13] The market for subprime mortgage refinancing had an especially insidious effect, as rapacious lenders persuaded current homeowners to enter into risky, fee-laden, high-interest loans that depleted their previously established reserves of home equity. As McGhee argues, the financial fallout from these predatory loans fell unevenly on Black and Latinx homeowners. "By 2000," she writes, "half of the refinance loans issued in majority-Black neighborhoods were subprime. Between 2004 and 2008, Black and Latinx homeowners with good credit scores were three times as likely as whites with similar credit scores to have higher-rate mortgages."[14] Scholars at the Urban Institute, a nonprofit research organization, report similar findings among African American homebuyers who "bought homes at the peak of the bubble at higher rates than whites and Asians, having often been offered subprime loans even when they qualified for prime loans."[15] Black homeowners suffered greater losses than white, Latinx, or Asian American homeowners, and in a worrisome trend, since 2000, "black homeownership rates have declined to levels not seen since the 1960s, when private race-based discrimination was legal."[16] This targeting of Black homeowners effectively revives the legacy of restrictive covenants and redlining practices under the guise of free market capitalism. It offers a grim reminder of the ways suburban nation building, across more than half a century, has maintained racial barriers and denied African Americans equal access to domestic stability.

By summer 2008, monthly home foreclosure rates had more than tripled prerecession levels, and by summer 2009, foreclosure filings totaled well over 300,000 a month.[17] After the dust had settled, the subprime crisis and the Great Recession resulted in the loss of 8.8 million jobs, and household wealth declined by 19.2 trillion dollars.[18] While there has never been a dearth of popular and scholarly assessments of the suburban home and its mythic status in American culture, the time seemed right for a different sort of revaluation. Suburbia as the "American nightmare" has been a mainstay of postwar literature and cultural criticism, and at least as far back as Sloan Wilson's *Man in the Gray Flannel Suit* (1955), as Catherine Jurca notes, "Ownership of a suburban house is treated . . . as a sign of economic weakness, suspended ambition, the *failure* of the American dream instead of its fruition."[19] The subprime mortgage crisis and the Great Recession, however, brought a newly evident—though not new—material and economic reality to the discourse on suburbia. Not new, of course, because class and race have always been central to the political, social, and cultural development of the suburbs, from redlining to restrictive covenants to discriminatory lending practices. In fact, this recent housing crisis has only exacerbated the historical links between suburbia and racial discrimination. As the first decade of the twenty-first century came to an end, familiar tropes about alienating, figuratively lifeless suburbs gave way to literal foreclosures and abandoned developments—newly iconic symbols, not of a cultural malaise but of a global crisis that reprises long-standing racial inequities.

In the initial run of the television series *Arrested Development* (2003–2006), as discussed in the introduction, the sinking model home, stranded amid plot markers in an unfinished subdivision, serves as a refuge for the idiosyncratic discontents of the Bluth family and a reminder of their financial and legal predicaments. In retrospect, that image also presages the rampant real estate speculation and deleterious investment practices that precipitated the recession, creating a fissure in the historical links among homeownership, upward class mobility, and "ideas about democracy, freedom, and civic order."[20] In this concluding chapter, I will consider two examples of how suburban narratives have begun to address these disrupted links: Patrick Flanery's *Fallen Land* (2013) and Jung Yun's *Shelter* (2016). Their attention to the symbolic value of the home at a watershed moment of residential and economic precarity places the contemporary suburb in direct conversation with political thinking about property rights, homeownership, freedom, and identity. When George W. Bush proclaimed in 2002, during a speech at the Department of Housing and Urban Development, that owning your own home is tantamount to "realizing the American Dream," he was tapping into a deep vein of American ideology.[21] In the eighteenth century, values of autonomy, individuality, and democratic citizenship underwrote Jefferson's celebration of agrarianism, an ideal that can be traced back to the ancient Greeks and that evokes early Edenic characterizations of the land.[22] During a wave of home building and urban-fringe development in the early twentieth century, these beliefs would be repurposed by Herbert Hoover, then Secretary of Commerce, who claimed that "[m]aintaining a high percentage of individual homeowners is one of the searching tests that now challenge the people of the United States."[23] Throughout the 1920s, leading up to the Great Depression, such ideas were called upon to advance questionable political policies that, in turn, encouraged predatory lending and risky borrowing, akin to what we witnessed in the decade preceding the Great Recession.[24]

In *Shelter* and *Fallen Land*, the housing crisis provides an occasion for Yun and Flanery to reflect on and update literary approaches to region, the domestic, the foreign, and the American environment. Each novel explores the historical and ideological legacies of landed property and suburban domesticity at a moment of crisis, both personal and political. We can read these family dramas, in which strained relationships and acts of violence figure prominently, as stand-ins for a more global fault line that disarticulates homeownership from conceptions of domestic stability and national security. In complementary ways, *Shelter* and *Fallen Land* use a regionalist aesthetic to evoke and to critique nineteenth-century ideas about the civilizing and moral influence of homeownership and decoration. In doing so, these novels inhabit regionalism as "a mode of analysis, a vantage point within the network of power relations" that exposes the detrimental endgame of two residential patterns: the isolationism of the domestic sphere that fosters violence, suspicion, and surveillance, and the environmental imperialism of suburban sprawl, which leads to ecological predation and economic unsustainability.[25]

Domestic Excess

Initial reviewers of Jung Yun's debut novel invariably described *Shelter* as a hybrid genre, the family drama-cum-thriller, but some of the more in-depth reviews also unpacked the novel's recession-era backdrop.[26] Writing for the *New York Times*, Rani Neutill notes that "the 2008 housing crisis put the phrase 'safe as houses' to rest. The safety and security that once came with owning a home was replaced with debt, loss, anxiety and even homelessness."[27] These insecurities take various forms in the novel. At the outset of *Shelter*, Kyung Cho and his wife Gillian McFadden confront the unwelcome prospect of selling their home in an upscale Boston suburb. At the height of the real estate market, they refinanced their mortgage and borrowed against the value of the house. Now, after the housing bubble has burst, they find themselves "upside down": overwhelmed with student loans and credit card debt and behind on their mortgage payments, they owe the bank more than the property is worth. Threatened with imminent displacement and long-term financial insolvency, Kyung reflects that "[h]e was raised to believe that owning a home meant something. Losing a home like this—that would mean something too."[28] A second-generation Korean American, Kyung is a biology professor at a local college where he struggles against the demands of the tenure clock and labors in the shadow of his more successful and esteemed father, Jin. In every respect, his immigrant father has achieved the American Dream, even owning a grander, more impressive home in the tonier suburb of Marlboro Heights. Kyung laments his failure to match his father's accomplishments, pointedly underscored by the impending loss of his home, but he also wrestles with his filial duties. When Kyung was a child, his father abused his mother and, in turn, his mother abused Kyung. Riven by violence, the Cho home has never signified the traditional suburban haven.

The novel's recession-era plotline is interrupted by a gruesome act, a home invasion at his parents' house. As Kyung and Gillian discuss a dwindling list of unappealing options with their realtor, Kyung's mother, Mae, appears in the field that abuts their property, naked and bloodied from an as-yet-unknown trauma. The intersection of violence and residential insolvency reframes the narrative around larger questions pertaining to race, family, and definitions of domestic security. In *Shelter*, Yun explores the ways race and ethnicity often narrow pathways to economic and professional success, but she also casts a skeptical eye on the ideological significance of suburban domesticity in American culture, paying attention to the various ways—physical, emotional, and financial—that houses fail to protect their inhabitants. In short, the novel decenters the notion of "home as sanctuary" from the arc of the political narrative that has figured the suburban home as central to national security and a forward-looking America. Working within the genres of family drama and domestic thriller, therefore, *Shelter* also evinces a regional attunement to the ways suburban topographies refract national contestations over race and residential rights amidst an era of economic precarity.

Although Kyung belongs to a generation no longer expected to surpass the financial gains of the previous one, his second-generation status compounds this statistical reality. "If an immigrant could come to this country and make something of himself," Yun writes, "his son would surely continue that line of progress, multiplying the gains of one generation for the next. Kyung, however, hasn't moved the line forward so much as back" (129). The threat of dispossession exposes the failed trajectory of generational progress and belies Kyung's social-class aspirations, yet he seems equally perturbed by the way the financial crisis has made members of the middle and lower classes less distinguishable. During a trip to Walmart, Kyung remarks that he "is no longer bothered by the poor people wandering through the aisles, the train wrecks from the Flats" (80), the latter a reference to a 1950s, working-class suburb where his in-laws reside. In the Flats, "The lots are small, divided and subdivided into narrow rectangles, built up with sad little ranches and Capes" (58). Kyung may not live in Marlboro Heights, as his parents do, but he had supposed his own upscale suburb would protect against casual encounters with residents of the Flats, notwithstanding visits from Gillian's family. What most unsettles Kyung is "the people who look like him—clean and well kempt, dressed in clothes that clearly weren't purchased [at Walmart]. . . . Despite all appearances," he admits, "they have more in common with the poor people than with the rich ones" (80).

The Great Recession casts a long shadow over this novel, and it acts as a catalyst for Kyung's long-standing filial disaffection and psychological insecurity. In this way, *Shelter* might rank among the literary works Kristin Jacobson labels "neodomestic": post-1980s literary texts "that renovate the ideal home's usual depiction by positioning instability—as opposed to stability—as a key structure of quotidian American home life."[29] By "recycling and reinventing" the tradition of domestic literature, Jacobson argues, "neodomestic fiction represents and promotes a politics of instability and hetero-geneity."[30] Building on this idea, I would suggest that *Shelter* offers a portrait of contemporary domesticity at war with its own antebel-lum history, a dialectic of stability and instability that invites us to rethink the cultural capital of the suburban home in the recession and now post-recession eras. To unpack the relevance of the novel to this broader conversation, I want to focus on the figure of Mae, Kyung's mother, and her tendency toward "domestic excess" (122). In addition to Kyung and Gillian's embattled sense of security, Yun offers three variations on the theme of domestic security through the character of Mae: the house in Marlboro Heights, the site of the domestic invasion; the beach cottage on Cape Cod where the extended family goes on a summer retreat; and a clandestine apart-ment above a design studio in Connecticut where Mae had planned to relocate after leaving her abusive marriage.

The home invasion in Marlboro Heights provides the novel's most obvious example of domestic insecurity, and the way Yun narrates the physical abuse and sexual violence in a detached, police procedural voice creates a slow-burn effect that compounds the brutality (62–72). Speaking to the *Chicago Tribune*, Yun recalled the 2007 attack in Cheshire, Connecticut, that provided a model for her novel. She claims the crime "helped [her] to understand something that was really important for the plot of 'Shelter.' . . . Home invasions happen throughout the United States, but the victims in this case were white and lived in a very wealthy suburban community, which . . . is why it got so much press attention. This was a community where people were saying, 'This was never supposed to happen here.'"³¹ This predictable if still striking remark reveals two interrelated ideas about homeownership and, more specifically, the suburban house at stake in Yun's novel. On the one hand, *Shelter* challenges the equation of safety and suburbia as it pertains to race and class. The notion that "this was never supposed to happen here" implicitly argues that there are other spaces (urban, poor, non-white) designated for such horrors. Yun further complicates this notion not only because Mae and Jin are immigrants, whose success and wealth allow them access to this predominantly white, upper-class suburban community, but also because the abusive Cho household never provided the imagined security such neighborhoods are meant to signify. Mae's ethnic identity and her role as homemaker intensify her isolation and vulnerability within this exclusive enclave. Jin often beats her for homemaking missteps—"a lukewarm dinner" (105) or looking "unhappy" during a party (174)—but Mae has no true community or friendship network to turn to outside the confines of the familial household. Moreover, in the eyes of Kyung, the home invaders, Nathan and Dell Perry, represent a regionally intrusive presence, not only because they perpetrated the invasion, but because he associates their names with "backwater," southern "[w]hite trash" whose mere appearance in Marlboro Heights constitutes an economic class violation (31).

On the other hand, *Shelter* contests the historical links between suburban homeownership and personal character. In a telling detail, the narrator notes that the Cho house in Marlboro is "a stunning Queen Anne, built in the 1860s," which Mae has "restored to ornate, expensive perfection" (23). This detail subtly draws the novel's contemporary crisis into conversation with nineteenth-century American beliefs about the civilizing and moral influence of homeownership and decoration, like the kind advocated in Andrew Jackson Downing's 1850 pattern book, *The Architecture of Country Houses*. In his preface, Downing extols the "perception of proportion, symmetry, order, and beauty" in architecture, as well as the associated "refinement of manners which distinguishes a civilized from a coarse and brutal people."[32] The house shapes the moral character of its present inhabitants but also influences successive generations (Downing vi), which perhaps clarifies Kyung's remarks about the hazards of losing a home. Downing also enshrines an assumption that, a century later, would provide the ideological underpinning for suburban sprawl: the ideal of the nuclear family and the detached, single-family home located outside the "battle of life, carried on in cities" (v). He writes, "Whatever new systems may be needed for the regeneration of an old and enfeebled nation, we are persuaded that, in America, not only is the distinct family the best social form, . . . [i]t is the solitude and freedom of the family home in the country which constantly preserves the purity of the nation, and invigorates its intellectual powers" (v). Downing gives voice to architecture as national ideology, in which "the character of every man may be read in his house" (25). This explicit connection between architecture and character will extend well into the twentieth century. As discussed in the first chapter, during and after World War II, popular magazines like *House Beautiful* and *House & Garden* promoted a consumerist ideology of domestic nationalism in which the proper home reflects "the economic and political values" of a forward-looking country and guarantees your fitness as an individual.[33] At least temporarily, the recession disrupts this self-assured vision and halts the suburban nation-building project, and in *Shelter*, Yun uses the home invasion trope to turn these ideas inside out.

Given her belief in the ethics of interior design, it is not surprising that, as soon as she is able, Mae's first priority is to restore the house in Marlboro Heights to its former glory in the hope of selling it, but the project proves illusory. On the surface, as Kyung observes, "the house now resembles its former self, tidy and grand.

. . . [I]t's thanks enough to see things as they were, to pretend— if only for a moment—that the attack never happened because there's no evidence that it did" (154). Nevertheless, indelible signs of trauma remain: "the stains on the drapes that the dry cleaner couldn't remove, the faint discolorations on the walls where so many paintings used to hang, but no longer do" (177). The house becomes a metonym for the Cho family: an object that stands in for the recent attack but also encapsulates the long history of abuse that Kyung and his mother have felt at the hands of Jin. In addition, Yun's attention to the interconnectedness of place across built environments—from Kyung and Gillian's economically threatened suburban house to the wealthy but violable enclave of Marlboro Heights to the working-class ranches in the Flats—lends the novel a sense of regional complexity. In *Shelter*, the recession-era suburban region provides a location within which to critique the discursive history that links the single-family home to the safety, security, and "purity of the nation."

In a tense moment at the Marlboro house, Mae says to Kyung, "This house is my business. . . . You just mind your own" (127). Domesticity as both refuge and vocational work clarifies the tension between security and insecurity in the novel. For Mae, a victim of abuse and an immigrant woman who has struggled for acceptance, the house exacerbates her sense of gendered isolation, even as it serves as a form of well-appointed armor. To have the borders of her home invaded, or even her domestic abilities impugned, is perceived as a violation of the self. As a result, Mae multiplies her attempts at stability by settling a number of domestic spaces into which she can retreat. We see a second example of such a space when the narrative shifts to Cape Cod where Jin and Mae have invited the family, including Gillian's father, for an extended vacation. The beach house in Orleans is described as a beautiful "three-story colonial" (210). Yun writes, "Nearly everything in the house is white. White walls, white ceilings, white furniture. . . . The place looks exactly the way a beach house should. Open and airy, like something out of a magazine" (212). The reference to colonial architecture evokes regional specificity alongside the historical associations of the civilizing and moral influence of homeownership, which popular magazines continue to commodify and disseminate. The repetition of the term "white," though, performs a different kind of work. At its most basic level, the term harkens back to the home invasion that inspired *Shelter* and the way Yun interrogates a sense of communal shock over white victimization. Yet the all-white interior of the beach house also signals the various ways race and ethnicity structure the fault lines that run throughout Yun's narrative.

Kyung's marriage to the Irish American Gillian represents one such fault line. He feels unwelcome in the McFadden family and emasculated by Gillian's father and brother, both police officers straight from central casting. His sense of masculine insecurity is compounded by his upscale suburban setting—"He's not handy like some of the other men in the neighborhood, the ones with toolboxes as big as furniture" (6)—and the threat of dispossession reaffirms his sense of inadequacy. Mae and Jin offer readers access to more deeply embedded topographical crises. Economic wealth has given Jin and Mae access to the predominantly white enclave of Marlboro Heights and to their haven on the Cape, but Mae's gender and ethnicity transform the privileges of domestic security into domestic precarity. The invasion of an immigrant home by "white trash" also offers a grim reminder that, historically, suburbia was premised on maintaining barriers of race, class, and gender to secure middle-class whiteness at the center of the nation's forward-looking vision. Finally, the juxtaposition of colonial-style architecture and whiteness, on Cape Cod no less, recalls the colonizing of America as well as the imperial sprawl of suburban residential development across the nation and of suburban culture around the world. As briefly noted in the introduction, the iconic, single-family postwar suburban house "has its origins in the distinctive imperialist history of Britain's colonization of India," and this history has been "kept alive as American consumerism was subsequently projected into the world with iconic images of suburban bliss."[34]

I would argue that *Shelter* inhabits this interwoven geopolitical history and that Mae's commitment to the ethics of "domestic excess" offers an opportunity to rethink the traditional associations Downing limns between "the family home in the country" and "the purity of the nation." It is here, within the very white interior of the Cape Cod colonial, that Kyung opts to disclose the family's secret history of abuse, a violent outpouring triggered by the façade of hospitality. "[D]on't be fooled by all their nice things and nice manners," he says. "They're not good people" (220). "Nice" seems like a particularly loaded term here, reminiscent of Hemingway's careful deployment of the word in *The Sun Also Rises*, where "nice" indicates proper race and ethnicity, people who "were of good family"—that is, not a "Jew" like Cohn.[35] The shame that Kyung visits upon his family in this scene exposes the illusory nature of the house's moral influence, but the pointed use of "nice" and "good" also appears to impugn their right to the white fantasy of the "pure" nation as home. These derisive comments prove to be the final straw, and the following morning, Mae commits suicide by driving her car at full-speed into a tree. She had, apparently, been planning this for weeks, and in lieu of a note, she leaves a twenty-eight-page inventory, "documenting every item she ever bought for the houses in Marlboro and Orleans," as well as to whom they should be bequeathed (236). It is difficult to imagine a more absolute articulation of the domestic as "business" than this catalog of objects. The note neatly dissects Mae's identity into a collection of things, a fragmented legacy that captures the way her attempts at domestic safety and stability have been undone. The inventory also wryly suggests that the moral or civilizing influence of homeownership and decoration simply gives cover to domesticity as consumerism, as so many images in a magazine.

At his mother's funeral, Kyung learns of a third and final domestic space that Mae kept secret from her family: an apartment in Connecticut above the design studio she had intended to join before the home invasion derailed her plans. The apartment was intended as a "work-week" abode, but there is evidence of a long-term escape plan (253–55). The space is exquisitely decorated and furnished, and Kyung realizes that "[t]he apartment was clearly designed as a refuge, a place for Mae to stay during the week and be the person she wanted to be, a person he didn't know or pay any attention to. . . . She was planning a life for herself here, a small and quiet life" (289). This domestic space would have provided seclusion premised on economic independence, as opposed to dependent and abusive isolation, where Mae could live on her own terms, neither wife nor mother, a refugee from the familial consensus that had galvanized postwar suburban development. In this third abode, Yun offers something more akin to the shelter that Mae had sought but failed to achieve either in Marlboro or on the Cape, a private realm where the dialectic of stability and instability might have resolved itself at last, but significantly the space remains unoccupied and the domestic vision unrealized.

Shelter closes with Jin and Kyung in the Marlboro Heights house, returning us to the site of abuse and violation. Kyung had gone there to kill his father, having learned that the original story of the home invasion was a lie. On the night of the attack, Jin had, in fact, been assaulting Mae; she fled the house in search of help, only to run into the men who would beat and rape her. In confronting his father, Kyung has an epiphany of sorts: "With both of his parents gone, he knows he'll inherit their hopelessness, the same hopelessness that sent his mother headfirst into a tree, that has his father kneeling on the floor, begging for his own life to end" (324). Instead, the two men share an awkward embrace. Kyung "fit[s] his body against the inner curve of his father's . . . his head in the crook of Jin's arm," and they wait for the sun to rise (326). They form a kind of shell, folding in on one another as if to create a space of retreat from which they might rebuild their relationship and find a way forward.[36] While the anticipated sunrise may amplify this sense of rebirth, Yun denies the reader any such certainty, leaving us to contemplate the various ways that *Shelter* has disarticulated the logical connections between home and sanctuary. In 1850, Downing claimed, "The mere sentiment of home, with its thousand associations, has, like a strong anchor, saved many a man from shipwreck in the storms of life" (vi). Early in the twenty-first century, Yun offers a bleak assessment of the home's ability to provide financial, structural, or sentimental shelter. Mae is dead; Kyung's marriage is in jeopardy; and Jin and Kyung, curled on the floor, look shipwrecked, not saved. With its focus on ethnic difference, domestic abuse, and economic precarity, Yun's novel exposes the corrosive effects of "domestic excess" and, if only obliquely, the way the instability of the twenty-first-century suburban home evokes and extends the repressed contestations of nineteenth-century domestic ideals.

Promised Land

Downing's testament to the civilizing and purifying force of home-ownership exerts a more direct influence within Flanery's *Fallen Land*. Downing and his colleague, Alexander Jackson Davis, serve as inspirations for one of the novel's central characters, Paul Krovik, a housing developer who purchased a "hundred-and-sixty-acre parcel of farmland near the western edge of the existing suburbs" to build the planned community of Dolores Woods, a new subdivision on the edge of an unnamed midwestern city.[37] In the novel's present, Krovik is on death row for crimes that the narrative's primary timeline, entitled "Past," will eventually clarify. He had envisioned Dolores Woods as a "kind of sanctuary where a man might forget he lives in the twenty-first century and pretend instead it is the nineteenth" (70). The houses he designs, modeled on Gothic Revival cottages, eschew de rigueur open floor plans in favor of "the more traditional arrangement of domestic space into discrete rooms each with a specific purpose" (72). Flanery's title succinctly foreshadows the postlapsarian aftermath of such idyllic visions. Poor planning, inexpert design, the housing bubble, and the ensuing recession all compromise the realization of Krovik's anachronistic redoubt from the tumult of contemporary life. Citing the classic reversal of the American dream narrative, Flanery writes, "He wanted to build a neighborhood that evoked the country's pastoral history, but he has, he knows, created something closer to a landscape of nightmare" (71).

This nightmare has a long history and, in the end, that history is the novel's central preoccupation. *Fallen Land* is a tale of inheritance and dispossession, framed by death, and deeply entrenched in America's embattled landscapes. The novel begins in the "Red Summer" of 1919 in an unnamed midwestern city and concludes, almost a century later, on the cusp of Krovik's execution. A brief prefatory chapter recounts the lynching of two Black men as "race riots swept through cities across the country" (3). The mob next targets Morgan Priest Wright, the liberal "mayor and gentleman farmer" who had attempted "to intervene on behalf of the men" (3). They hang Mayor Wright from a tree outside of his home on Poplar Farm alongside his lover, George Freeman, a twenty-five-year-old Black man and tenant farmer who was found with the mayor in the storm cellar beneath the house. By the time Freeman's brother arrives on the scene, the mob had burned the mayor's home to the ground and fled, and before he can cut down the bodies, a sinkhole swallows the tree. After consultation with the sheriff, and fearing the wild speculation that would surround the discovery of a white mayor bound together with his Black tenant, they decide to fill the sinkhole with the burnt remains of the house. The opening section concludes: "two small slabs of granite were laid in the ground to mark the place where a tree and two men lie buried in land stark with promise and death" (6).

This scene of racial and domestic violence launches *Fallen Land*, a novel comprised of three interlocking story lines, each narrated from a different character's perspective: Louise Washington, the grandniece of George Freeman; the housing developer, Krovik; and the Noailles family, Nathaniel, Julia, and their seven-year-old son, Copley, who has autism. Except for that prefatory "1919" section, the primary setting is the very recent past, bookended by two shorter sections labeled "Present," but we remain in the same violated space throughout the novel: the landscape of "promise and death," marked by the two "slabs of granite." Per Mayor Wright's last will and testament, which bequeathed his property to George Freeman, Louise Washington inherits Poplar Farm. She represents the third and last generation of the Freeman family to live on "this plot that was supposed to be [her] people's promised land, the new home at the end of their long exodus from the south" (54). A series of bad crop yields and falling prices forced Louise to sell the 160-acre farm to Krovik, clearing the way for the ill-fated Dolores Woods. Although evicted under power of eminent domain, she illegally occupies the house, "an intruder on [her] own land" (253). Louise is the voice against the "infection" of sprawl "spreading, consuming the land" (88), and her chapters include poetic descriptions of bygone pastoralism and lamentations about vanishing nature as trees are uprooted and the ground paved over. More importantly, her narrative attests to the ways race continues to inflect the discourse of ownership and land in America—from slavery to sharecropping and tenant farming, to restrictive covenants and redlining practices, to contemporary gated communities—and she views herself as "the keeper of its tale" (90).

In more explicit terms than *Shelter*, *Fallen Land* demonstrates how contemporary suburban nation building reinforces the relationship between private property, privilege, and domestic security, wedded to a purified version of white residential America. Situated on land christened by a lineage of violence, the aptly named Dolores Woods would appear inevitably doomed, and the financial insolvency and forced eviction of Louise Washington mark only the latest chapter in a history of land and race in this unnamed midwestern metropolis. Once the planned community succumbs to the economic recession and its own inept planning, Krovik declares bankruptcy and the bank forecloses on his house, the crown jewel of the suburb, built on the former spot of Mayor Wright's farmhouse. Although neighbors and creditors assume he has fled the scene, Krovik takes up residence in a secret, underground bunker, just off the house, where he drifts into pathological madness. The Noailles family, recently relocated from Boston, purchase the foreclosed property, a space Krovik continues to haunt and terrorize, escalating from petty vandalism to rape and murder.

Read generously, Krovik's brief rise and swift decline offer a more menacing version of the "failed American Dream" story. His character blends a warped version of Emersonian self-reliance with a sense of sociopathic survivalism that has him always poised for an endless "*state of war*" (41). Yet, for all his criminal deficiencies, his plan reiterates a familiar line of American thought, linking country or suburban architecture to proper, civilized living. Krovik's goal is "to design homes that aspired to a vision of residential America so distilled it could only improve the lives of the people within them" (80). In Downing's own words, "a good house (and by this I mean a fitting, tasteful, and significant dwelling) is a powerful means of civilization" (v), and Krovik's benighted attempt to base his luxury suburban estates on this correspondence between homeownership and a moral citizenry introduces perhaps the novel's most compelling critique, a critical response tied to its embedded regional aesthetic. Flanery transforms Dolores Woods into a vantage point from which to examine the contested roots of suburban topography, a factious history shaped by the fault line of race and residential rights and shrouded by an idealized vision of home.

Given such an unbelievable, multigenerational tale of cursed land, dispossession, duplicity, and violence, readers will not be surprised that Nathaniel Hawthorne's *House of the Seven Gables* (1851) makes a cameo appearance. Following "1919," a brief section entitled "Present" begins with an epigraph from Hawthorne's novel: "In this republican country, amid the fluctuating waves of our social life, somebody is always at the drowning point" (7). If beginning a contemporary, recession-era novel with a prefatory chapter set in 1919 had not already announced Flanery's purpose, then certainly tagging a section marked "Present" with a passage from a mid-nineteenth-century novel about ill-gotten property and retribution ought to remove all doubt. A tragic tale of psychological terror, *Fallen Land* is also a story about the environment, ownership, foreclosures, and evictions that Flanery ties inextricably to a primal scene of racial violence. Or, to borrow from another heavyweight of American literature, the novel argues that "[t]he past is never dead. It's not even past."[38] In *House of the Seven Gables*, in which greed, ownership, and violence push individuals to "the drowning point," Hawthorne explores the darker side of Andrew Jackson Downing's contemporaneous, more benevolent notion that "the perception of proportion, symmetry, order, and beauty, awakens the desire for possession" (v). *Fallen Land* yokes these two ideas together—the "desire for possession" and "the drowning point"—to trouble the romantic link between homeownership and civil society that continues to underwrite assumptions about suburban living.

Despite *Fallen Land*'s outrageous turns, then, the novel adds to a long historical tradition of literary approaches to natural and man-made environments. Flanery encounters and reproduces the American landscape as already written, immersed in a discursive history of personal identity, property rights, and nationalism. At the macrolevel, his recession-era Dolores Woods emerges in direct conversation with early Edenic characterizations of the land and American political thought. At the scale of the single-family home, *Fallen Land* marks a crucial threshold in our thinking about suburban literature, homeownership, and U.S. regional writing. As cited in the introduction, Judith Fetterley and Marjorie Pryse argue, "As both a literary and a political discourse, regionalism . . . becomes the site of contestation over the meaning of region."[39] Flanery's narrative expands upon this critical work. *Fallen Land* serves as a site where the meaning of homeownership and the value of the private realm are contested at a moment of economic precarity, when the correspondence between suburban living and forward-looking national identity seems distinctly at odds. The novel juxtaposes the frontier rhetoric of an ever-expanding, residential American empire—embodied in Krovik's antebellum vision for Dolores Woods, a project that extends the legacy of racial dispossession through land acquisition for private development—with a suburban emphasis on privatism taken to dystopian ends. Alongside the dispossession, economic unsustainability, and ecological predation of sprawl, the novel imagines how the isolationism of suburban domesticity lends itself to a security state of permanent suspicion and surveillance.

To clarify the novel's ideological tensions, I want to focus on two key lines of thought in the novel. The first concerns Julia Noailles and her efforts at home redecoration, a project that lays bare the paradoxical nature of the suburban house; the second addresses EKK, the shadowy security corporation where Nathaniel works, a company with a global "vision of how, from the core of self-professed corporate personhood, a new conception of the body politic can radiate across and subsume the previously blighted urban landscape" (141). If the housing crisis and the Great Recession provide the occasion for *Fallen Land*, the novel also arcs toward a misanthropic, near-future setting—or alternative timeline—in which neoliberal ideology reigns unfettered. EKK envisions a three-tier, global society: "the incarcerated population comprised of the ex-citizen" exists on the third tier; "the ordinary citizen" occupies the second; and, at the top, "governments and corporations, which will become increasingly indistinguishable from each other" (304). Now-familiar references to foreclosures, failed residential developments, and the economic downturn abound alongside allusions to a quasi-dystopian state, protected by a proto-fascist security force, in which personal privacy is not just an illusion but an undemocratic impulse.

Julia's career propels the family's relocation from Boston to the Midwest. She is a successful, sought-after scientist who works in the field of artificial intelligence to develop "assistive technology"

(306). Although both Julia and Nathaniel had hoped to live in the town's historical district, they quickly realized that "[a] simulacrum was the closest they were going to get, and Dolores Woods, however unfinished it might have been, had pretensions to historical awareness that most suburbs lacked" (49). Although Julia is more enthusiastic than Nathaniel about the move and the new house, even she grows wary over the number of unexplained events. She turns to redecoration, not merely as a form of homemaking, but rather to create a fusion between person and home:

> The redecoration of the house has been undertaken according to Julia's belief that domestic space should be both an extension of their own bodies and a protection against the world. "A house is like an oversized and highly complex prosthetic limb," she explained to [her husband], "allowing us to move in ways we couldn't without it, letting us rise through space by means of stairs, helping us remain clean, our temperatures optimal, assisting us in the preparation and storage of food, while at the same time acting as a shell that protects us from the damage of the outside world." (186)

We can read a repressed trace of a Cold War "topological crisis" in this rendering of the home; as previously cited, Deborah Nelson writes that "[a]ll sorts of entities were imagined as bounded spaces: nations, bodies, homes, and minds" in midcentury America.[40] *Fallen Land* updates this "topological crisis" for the recession era when the ideology of "nation as home" evokes a dialectic of instability and stability.

Yet the house as both "prosthesis" and protective "shell" also offers a knowing account of the single-family home as a nexus, connecting individuals to a more complex, public network—namely, as Julia describes in the noted passage, water lines and power grids. Lefebvre addresses this domestic duality, its simultaneous solidity and permeability, by imagining a "critical analysis" that would remove "concrete slabs" and "non-load-bearing walls." With the façade of solidity stripped away, the "house would emerge as permeated from every direction by streams of energy which run in and out of it by every imaginable route: water, gas, electricity, telephone lines, radio and television signals, and so on. Its image of immobility would then be replaced by an image of a complex of mobilities, a nexus of in and out conduits. . . . [T]his piece of 'immovable property' is actually a two-faceted machine analogous to an active body."[41] Certainly, the pleasure of a proper shelter is that one need not constantly ponder its Lefebvrean permeability; when houses are in good repair and functioning well, they conceal their exposure to this "nexus of in and out conduits." *Fallen Land*, however, suggests something more insidious: that the protective isolationism of communities like Dolores Woods fosters an indifference to the indirect costs that sustain suburban residential living. By stripping away the supposed solidity of the Noailles dwelling, Flanery's narrative exposes the home's place within complex regional and national systems, yoked here to the geopolitics of energy production. The novel draws the reader's attention to the house as a nexus of political policies, historical legacies of racism, and ideological assumptions about personhood, property, and privilege in American history.

In similar ways, *Fallen Land*'s compelling if exaggerated critique of domestic security dovetails with macrolevel concerns about privacy, personal property, and, perhaps surprisingly, the scourge of mass incarceration. In the small hours of the night, after the Noailles family has settled into their new house, Nathaniel notices clumps of dirt by the front door and unfamiliar shoe prints on the stairs. He assumes the movers have left the mess, but even this makes him uneasy, "thinking of the menacing men, the way they came and went, the access they had to every corner of the house," and after a moment's additional thought, "he decides to speak with the technicians at work about installing a home security system. Danger is everywhere, especially in the suburbs" (128). This assessment will turn out to be an understatement as the increasingly deranged Krovik begins to haunt and to terrorize the Noailles family, leading to the rape of Julia and culminating in the deaths of Nathaniel and Copley. Although Copley warns his parents that he has seen a man in the house, they refuse to believe him and initially assume he is responsible for rearranging furniture and scrawling graffiti on the walls, exacerbating the already fraught relationship between Nathaniel and his son.

On its face, "dangerous" suburbs and fraught family relationships are such fertile literary ground as to border on cliché, which
Flanery acknowledges through a shrewd evocation of John Cheever,
the dean of suburban letters. Readers familiar with *Bullet Park*
(1969) will recognize the glaring parallels, right down to the characters' names. In Cheever's novel, Eliot Nailles has a strained relationship with his son, Tony, who suffers from an unnamed illness.
The Nailles family is hounded by a psychopath named Paul Hammer, who plots to kill Eliot before shifting his target to the younger
Nailles. As the newspapers report following Tony's rescue, Hammer
"carried Nailles to the church with the object of immolating him in
the chancel. He intended, he claimed, to awaken the world."[42] *Bullet
Park* and *Fallen Land* both end with their respective villains under
state supervision: Paul Hammer is remanded to a psychiatric hospital, and Paul Krovik awaits his execution on death row.

Despite its forthright indebtedness to this Cheever-esque tradition, *Fallen Land* updates these tropes for the contemporary era
of global precarity. When considering the move to the suburbs,
Nathaniel views it as an opportunity to give Copley "a childhood of
trees and lawns before the possibility of houses and yards like the
one they have bought disappears into a future of hot and unpre-
dictable chaos" (117). In Flanery's novel, domestic security exists as
one component within a dystopian world in which "security will
matter more than anything else: not just of person and property but
also of food, water, health, medicine, the environment. Security will
become the defining quality and concern of human existence on
the planet and beyond" (117). EKK, the company Nathaniel works
for, envisions itself at the forefront of a worldwide security system
that will eventually oversee every aspect of the individual's life,
with programs planned to facilitate housing, education, healthcare,
entertainment, employment, and incarceration. That last item falls
under Nathaniel's purview, specifically privatizing the prison system. As his supervisor explains, "Crime is our oyster: it's an amaz-
ing workforce just waiting to be 'rehabilitated' into positive labor
production. Let's not kid ourselves about these people, . . . we know
who they are even before they do" (155). In a country where a zip
code often determines one's fate, EKK promises to capitalize on the
historical correlation between race and social control in the U.S.

through mass incarceration. As Michelle Alexander notes, "Like Jim Crow (and slavery), mass incarceration operates as a tightly networked system of laws, policies, customs, and institutions that operate collectively to ensure the subordinate status of a group defined largely by race."[43] In the imagined world of *Fallen Land*, EKK neither pays lip service to colorblind policies nor disguises its intent to create a permanent "criminal class transformed by legal means into the largest body of slave labor since the great emancipation" (157). This story line brings the novel full circle: the Freeman family's journey from slavery to tenant farmers to property owners serves as prelude to a new arrangement of "slave labor," the contemporary corporate ownership of incarcerated bodies.

While the prison industrial complex may mark the most egregious example of neoliberal privatization in the novel, it is of a piece with the broader, paradoxical program of "global transparency" in which "the ordinary citizen" and their residential dwellings must surrender privacy "for the sake of global stability" (304). In the "topography of the future security landscape," as the CEO explains, "[t]he house *qua* home is no longer a space of privacy. The only privacy that remains must therefore be the privacy of governments and corporations for the good of the public, . . . for the security of the public *qua* franchised citizen living a transparent life" (302–3). In this new global security state, in which the suburb of Dolores Woods exists as an "EKK SafeZone" (397), every security system doubles as a domestic monitoring device. Although such assurances of security are ultimately not enough to save himself or his son, Nathaniel provides a resounding endorsement. "*This*, surely, is what the future should look like," he thinks: "not just governments and private corporations monitoring security, but anyone anywhere checking up on their neighbors, friends, associates, peers, even strangers, to see that everyone is living responsibly" (305). This campaign to privatize the public realm would seem, inevitably, to resolve the earlier paradox of the home's solidity and permeability. As Nathaniel's corporate-speak suggests, only the transparency of the private realm will guarantee its protection.

In the end, readers may find such Orwellian provocations as compelling as they are confounding, leaving them to wonder if Flanery simply does not know what he wants the novel to be. In the author's own words, *Fallen Land* is "a novel about the vulnerability of domestic space, about the ever-widening ideological divide in American life, about dispossession, race, and property as well as the uncanny and the Gothic, set against the backdrop of an age in which the corporate and the carceral seem to be dancing us toward a ghastly, bleak horizon."[44] Indeed, by turns, the narrative is gothic tale, dystopian crime thriller, historical fiction, social realism, and a recent entry in the long tradition of the failed American dream story. Critics have reviewed this mélange with varying degrees of admiration, notwithstanding some apt reservations about a narrative center that does not hold and the novel's drift into caricature.[45] Admittedly, the evil machinations of the multinational EKK border on the cartoonish, and the company's sinister outlook on privacy and personal liberties seems an easy extension of today's saturated social media landscape. Had these corporate-dystopian aspects been its primary focus, *Fallen Land* would have been a lesser work—or it would have been Dave Eggers's *The Circle* (2013), a novel whose characters express eerily similar beliefs in the benefits of living a "transparent life."[46] When read through a regionalist lens, however, the various generic threads of the novel coalesce around a critical response to place and the topographical history of marginalization, dispossession, and containment that have facilitated suburban nation building. The novel evinces deep-seated anxieties about the way property ownership confers rights and privileges and how civil liberties tied to the land have been premised upon the enslavement and, later, disenfranchisement of Black populations. In other words, *Fallen Land* takes this pivotal moment—the housing crisis and the Great Recession—and glances both backward and forward, evoking the historical links between race and real estate while imagining an equally "bleak horizon."

As the novel concludes, Louise Washington recounts the assorted tragedies that have unfolded on this plot of land, dating from the arrival of Morgan Wright's earliest ancestors to the present moment. "This is the history of the land you own," she tells Julia Noailles. "I used to say it was perfect land, redemptive land, but I no longer think this is true. There is no such thing as good land or bad land. There are merely cycles of goodness and badness upon it" (393). That may not count as optimism, but it is a reckoning of sorts, and in that regard *Fallen Land* enacts a kind of literary "un-concealment": an attempt to redeem moments buried beneath the rewritten or paved over landscape and to create, as Lawrence Buell would say, an instance of "environmental awakening—retrievals of physical environment from dormancy to salience."[47] In the wake of the Great Recession, Flanery's novel depicts the suburb as a con-tested site with a deep topographical past, where a local tragedy lays bare the legacies of personhood and property, race and priv-ilege, domesticity and nation that define America's relationship to the land.

The subprime mortgage crisis and the Great Recession introduced new terms of art into popular discourse: subprime, NINA loans, ARMs, CDOs, and credit default swaps. That vernacular may dis-tinguish this crisis from earlier downturns in the housing market or from previous financial recessions, but the current stakes for indi-viduals, neighborhoods, metro-regions, and the country at large have evolved from a long and entangled history of homeownership, race, democratic citizenship, and domestic security. As Roger Keil writes, "In Anglo-American societies, and more pronouncedly in settler democracies of the New World, landed property, and par-ticularly the suburban home, became the symbol of successful arrival, liberation from European shackles of status and class, and self-determination and cultural autonomy of the individual."[48] In their evocation of nineteenth-century ideals about the moral and civilizing roles of domesticity—ideals that, in turn, evoke Jeffer-sonian-era agrarianism and the Edenic New World—*Shelter* and *Fallen Land* unsettle the suburban home's symbolic value and the economic security of landed property, especially, though not exclu-sively, for non-white citizens trying to prosper, or just survive, within "Anglo-American societies." While the recent housing crisis and economic recession provide the occasion for these novels, their authors take aim at a broader matrix of concerns pertaining to sub-urban domesticity and secure personhood: the isolation and abuse of women; economic insecurity; racial violence and displacement; neoliberal privatization; and the creeping threat of environmental decline. *Shelter* and *Fallen Land* work at the intersections among these coextensive fault lines and, in doing so, dispel the notion that "the solitude and freedom of the family home . . . preserves the purity of the nation" (Downing v). As contemporary iterations of regional writing, these recession-era suburban novels serve as sites of contestation over the meaning of privacy, the economic and symbolic value of the suburban home, and the links between domestic and national security at a critical juncture in the country's residential history. Admittedly, they are initial, perhaps inchoate responses to this moment, but they suggest the enduring relevance of a literary discourse attuned to the regional complexities of suburban topography and the enmeshed histories of race, class, and residential rights.

Epilogue

The End of the Suburbs?

"It is time to face the emergence of a postsuburban planet where existing and
new forms of peripheral urbanization interlace in a complex
pattern of urbanity."
—ROGER KEIL,
"The Global Suburb" (2017)

"If Dems win, GOODBYE SUBURBS!"
—@REALDONALDTRUMP,
Twitter (7 Oct. 2020)

DESPITE PROVOCATIVE DECLARATIONS about "the end
of the suburbs" and serious arguments concerning the unsustainability of suburban living, the suburbs as a residential region
do not appear to be going anywhere anytime soon. Responding to
trends in the years after the 2008 housing crisis, Jed Kolko writes,
"Although this century's housing bubble, bust, and recovery caused
wild swings both in the housing market and in residential population growth patterns, there's little evidence of a fundamental or
permanent change in where Americans live."[1] Even younger demographics continue to see some potential for residential life beyond
the city. In a 2017 opinion piece for the *New York Times*, landscape
architect and urban designer Alan Berger turned his attention to

millennials, the continuing appeal of suburbia, and the need for sustainable design and planning. Although one could argue the need to update the existing infrastructure of older, first-ring suburbs presents a more pressing need—a project that would also stimulate the economy and promote a more sustainable future—Berger's forward-looking proposals testify to the continuing relevance of suburban and exurban residential living in the United States. "According to the latest Census Bureau statistics," he writes, "25- to 29-year-olds are about a quarter more likely to move from the city to the suburbs as vice versa; older millennials are more than twice as likely. Their future—and that of the planet—lies on the urban peripheries."[2] Morley Winograd and Michael D. Hais share Berger's enthusiasm about how "the largest generation in US history" will transform the suburbs.[3] Citing Zillow's 2014 Housing Confidence Index, they note "that two-thirds of eighteen-to-thirty-four-year-olds said owning their own home was necessary to live 'the good life' and achieve 'the American Dream,'" but the authors also point out a desire on the part of millennials for "tech-friendly," more energy efficient houses and subdivisions and neighborhoods that promote "social cohesion."[4] The data suggest that eco-friendly demands may push developers to prioritize environmental sustainability and to build communities that challenge the image of suburban anomie.

Twenty-first-century suburbs are also shedding the stereotype of class and racial homogeneity. Perhaps this is why former President Donald Trump's race-baiting gambit fell flat with suburban voters in 2020. In the summer before the election, during a spike in coronavirus infections and amidst widespread racial-justice protests following the murders of Ahmaud Arbery, Breonna Taylor, and George Floyd, former President Trump turned his attention to a sitcom version of suburbia, evoking a nostalgia for the segregated neighborhoods and rigidly enforced gender norms of Cold War domesticity. He addressed a now infamous tweet to "The Suburban Housewives of America," cautioning them about the threat of low-income housing and warning voters that "Biden will destroy your neighborhood and your American Dream."[5] The tweet signaled the president's intent to repeal an Obama-era regulation to combat racial discrimination in American housing and counteract the legacy of residential segregation. The 2015 Affirmatively

Furthering Fair Housing (AFFH) rule intended "to expand housing choices and help make all neighborhoods places of opportunity, providing their residents with access to the community assets
and resources they need to flourish."[6] The tweet is telling, not only
because it traffics in provocative if familiar rhetoric about class, race,
and crime, but also because its message seemed to target a voting
demographic living in the 1950s or 1960s and, as such, revealed the
former president's decidedly anachronistic view of contemporary
suburban communities. (Although, it must be acknowledged, similar race-baiting rhetoric targeting "critical race theory" appeared
to gain traction more recently among some of the same suburban
voters who rejected Trump's message in 2020.)

In the material world, as the country transitioned from the
twentieth to the twenty-first century, "the suburban white population grew by 5 percent while the African American, Latino, and
Asian suburban populations grew by 38 percent, 72 percent, and
84 percent, respectively."[7] Admittedly, despite the diversifying of
suburbia, entrenched, often block-by-block segregation remains a
reality, but opportunities for suburban living have become more
readily available to people of color. As white populations continue
to push further into the postmetropolitan, exurban periphery—or,
in some cases, into gentrified first-ring suburbs or urban neighborhoods—minority populations are moving into older suburban
areas. According to Ali Modarres, "While once again minorities are inheriting the infrastructure left behind by others, it also
means that the suburban promise of homeownership, single-family
homes, larger parks, playgrounds, and amenities for families are
enticements that cut across socioeconomic classes."[8] Yet despite
this promise, poverty rates are on the rise among those first-ring,
majority-minority suburbs.[9] According to a *New York Times* editorial, in the first decades of the twenty-first century, "the number
of people living below the poverty line in the suburbs grew by 66
percent . . . . In 2010, 18.9 million suburban Americans were living
below the poverty line, up from 11.3 million in 2000."[10] As noted in
the last chapter, the housing crisis and ensuing economic downturn
have disproportionately affected Black and Latinx populations.

Ongoing debates about the country's residential future also
seem inextricably tied to recent handwringing about "America's

Millennial Baby Bust," though for now, the most anxious voices on that front seem firmly rooted on the political right.[11] Progressive calls to cancel student debt may continue to make inroads, but in the meantime, that financial burden could discourage millennials and members of Gen-Z from purchasing a house in the near future. The indeterminate, lingering effects of the "COVID-19 recession" and inflation may also prove a deterrent, but in the short term, perhaps unexpectedly, the pandemic has contributed to a recent surge in home building. For some, the newfound ability to work remotely—in spite of its social and psychological costs—has offset concerns about long commutes and recalibrated ideas about where people are willing to live. As Conor Dougherty and Ben Casselman have recently reported, "Would-be homeowners are flocking to the new farthest exurbs, where home builders can meet demand—and together they are again stretching the boundaries of a city and its surrounding sprawl."[12] A shrinking inventory of affordable homes in major metropolitan regions may continue to push developers and prospective homebuyers beyond the fringes of existing edge cities, but this boom in new construction raises significant questions about environmental sustainability and the possibility of another housing bubble.

This generational, economic, and environmental uncertainty notwithstanding, the idea that suburbia will soon vanish from the U.S. residential landscape seems remote. As even Leigh Gallagher acknowledges in *The End of the Suburbs*, "Whatever things look like in ten years—or twenty, or fifty, or more—there's one thing everyone agrees on: there will be more options."[13] Titles like Gallagher's—or, from the 1990s, Kunstler's *The Geography of Nowhere*—will continue to provoke, but regional transformation appears as a more likely future than placeless, dystopian wastelands. For too long, the American Dream has been defined by a singular, predominantly white vision scaled to the geo-cultural ideal of the suburban home, and as a country, we would do well to turn away from the extreme patterns of residential, car-dependent sprawl that have characterized postwar urban history. That said, not everyone can afford to live in the DUMBO neighborhood of Brooklyn, one of the examples Gallagher cites to demonstrate that new construction is moving from suburban to urban locales, nor are "cool" suburban villages, like School Street in Libertyville, Illinois, where bungalows sell for upward of $700,000, quite within the average homeowner's reach.[14]

My critique of "the end of the suburbs" narrative, however, should not be read as an endorsement of the status quo. I am simply more persuaded by planners like Calthorpe and Fulton who argue that "[w]e must leave behind our notion of the metropolis as a series of disconnected places. We must cease viewing problems of suburban sprawl and urban decay as individual problems with no relationship to one another. We must instead think of the metropolitan region as a series of interconnected places—a Regional City— that will not function effectively unless it is consciously designed."[15] As a literary scholar, I also believe in the unique humanistic power of literature to awaken us to the diverse ways we are rooted in these "interconnected places." To once again invoke Gillen D'Arcy Wood, "Across the global culture, [literature] offers the richest available repository of reflections on human embeddedness in the natural world."[16] Spanning nearly seventy-five years of U.S. literary history, *Contested Terrain* has explored this sense of "human embeddedness" through the lens of an updated and expansive understanding of regionalism—that is, as a recognizable literary aesthetic attendant to the varying and intersecting scales of suburban nation building. By examining literature as a site where the meanings of home, neighborhood, community, region, and nation are contested, this project has tried to clarify our place within evolving patterns of residential development, the persistent crisis of racial segregation, the quest for domestic security, and more recent threats to sustainability.

One of the premises of this study has been that the focus on a placeless, "nowhere" suburbia obscures these regional connections and the local-global contestations that underwrite the postwar suburban nation-building project. This brings my examination of suburban fiction into conversation with more recent ecological approaches to suburbia. As Sellers writes, "In seeking to take [environmental] differences seriously, a more ecological narrative of postwar suburbanization must begin with the actual changes wrought not just by a single builder but by multiple types of builders, across an entire suburbanizing region."[17] A consciousness responsive to regional patterns of place connection and the various geographic scales of the lived environment can be a starting point for more sustainable choices. Sarah Jack Hinners offers a complementary perspective on "the potential for conscious intent, for design, to shape these ecosystems" in the suburbs, arguing that communities purposely planned "to reflect and celebrate the native ecology" could, at the very least, provide a remedy for the sense of "placelessness" that plagues suburbia.[18] By inviting readers to image the interconnections of home-region-nation, *Contested Terrain* reflects a concerted effort to counteract this impression of a "placeless" landscape.

As a central part of this project, I have also argued for the continuing relevance of regionalism—as a genre, a critical discourse, and a mode of analysis—and in the process, I have attempted to stretch its traditional literary and territorial parameters to include suburban fiction and topography. Admittedly, reading works as varied as *A Raisin in the Sun* and *White Noise*, or *The Price of Salt* and *Aloft*, as "regional writing" may inevitably trouble the stability of generic categories, but I would argue it does so in generative ways, breaking down borders between often marginalized narratives and so-called "serious fiction." More importantly, though, as a method of analysis, regionalism facilitates meaningful dialogue between suburban literature and the discourses of ecology, environmental studies, and urban planning that try to account for the "entire suburbanizing region." The literary works examined throughout *Contested Terrain* share an aesthetic attunement to this interconnected regional perspective. Contentions over residential rights and racial containment, sexuality and domestic security, sprawl and sustainability have played a pivotal role in constructing and defining the nation, and these conflicts emerge as central to the literature's suburban settings. Works of fiction that clarify the complex history of our built environment can elucidate environmental threats and domestic perils, but they can also imagine new residential and regional futures. Literature can awaken us to the geopolitical and ecocritical significance of the places we inhabit, to those suburban homes and neighborhoods where the majority of Americans still reside and tell their stories.

Notes

Introduction

1. *Mr. Blandings Builds His Dream House*, directed by H. C. Potter (1948; Burbank, CA: Warner Brothers, 2005), DVD. Quotations are from my own transcription.

2. Dolores Hayden writes, "Corporate tie-ins with companies marketing steel, linens, paint, and carpet brought free print advertising to the film. General Electric rushed a new electric kitchen to the set so it could be used in the film. . . . Finally, in the biggest promotion of all, over seventy model Blandings 'dream houses' were constructed around the country and raffled off as publicity for the film." See Hayden, *Building Suburbia: Green Fields and Urban Growth, 1820–2000* (New York: Vintage-Random House, 2003), 150.

3. See Christopher C. Sellers, *Crabgrass Crucible: Suburban Nature and the Rise of Environmentalism in Twentieth-Century America* (Chapel Hill: University of North Carolina Press, 2012), 17. According to Sellers, this pursuit of country life persisted through the postwar years of suburbanization: "Even around the nation's largest and richest cities, many who moved [to the suburbs], even into the newest and most massive subdivisions, were seeking a kind of countryside home, where good health could be had and a semblance of nature could be found" (35).

4. Eric Hodgins, *Mr. Blandings Builds His Dream House*, illus. William Steig (1946; repr., Chicago: Academy Chicago Publishers, 1987), 234, 235.

5. *Arrested Development*, season 1, episode 22, "Let 'Em Eat Cake," directed by Paul Feig, written by Mitchell Hurwitz and Jim Vallely, aired June 6, 2004, in broadcast syndication, 20th Century Fox, 2004, DVD. Quotations are from my own transcription.

6. Lyn Lofland argues that "privatism . . . may, in part, be a creature of antiurbanism and may, once created, loop back and feed the cultural

theme that helped give it birth." See Lofland, *The Public Realm: Exploring the City's Quintessential Social Territory* (New York: Aldine De Gruyter, 1998), 143. Her work focuses on technological, architectural, and social-psychological factors that promote an anti-urban aesthetic and contribute to "the movement of human activity from commonsensically understood 'public' space into commonsensically understood 'private' space" (143).

7. See David Harvey, *A Brief History of Neoliberalism* (New York: Oxford University Press, 2005), 23.

8. William A. Garnett, *Lakewood, California*, gelatin silver prints (1950), permanent collection, J. Paul Getty Museum, Los Angeles, https://www.getty.edu/art/collection/object/108G27. On the suburban "nowhere," see James Howard Kunstler, *The Geography of Nowhere: The Rise and Decline of America's Man-Made Landscape* (New York: Simon and Schuster, 1993).

9. D. J. Waldie, *Holy Land: A Suburban Memoir* (New York: St. Martin's Griffin, 1996), vi. Waldie attributes this insight to Lois Craig, "Suburbs," *Design Quarterly* 132 (1986): 1–32.

10. For example, Bernice M. Murphy writes, "The most characteristic narrative trope of the Suburban Gothic is, of course, the revelation, time and time again, that no matter how picturesque and peaceful a neighborhood, house or family may seem on the surface, dark and usually terrible secrets lie beneath, whether of a psychological, supernatural or familial nature." See Murphy, *The Suburban Gothic in American Popular Culture* (Basingstoke: Palgrave Macmillan, 2009), 200. I tend to agree with Martin Dines's critique: "the gothicity of the suburban gothic becomes redundant; quite simply, it is not being utilized to say anything that is not already well known about the suburbs." See Dines, "Suburban Gothic and the Ethnic Uncanny in Jeffrey Eugenides's *The Virgin Suicides*," *Journal of American Studies* 46, no. 4 (2012): 960.

11. Catherine Jurca, *White Diaspora: The Suburb and the Twentieth-Century Novel* (Princeton, NJ: Princeton University Press, 2001), 7, 19.

12. Robert Beuka, *SuburbiaNation: Reading Suburban Landscape in Twentieth-Century American Fiction and Film* (New York: Palgrave Macmillan, 2004), 235.

13. Citing Foucault's claim that "space is fundamental in any exercise of power" ("Space, Knowledge, and Power," in *The Foucault Reader*, ed. Paul Rabinow [New York: Pantheon, 1984], 252), David Harvey contends, "The implication is that spaces outside of power, heterotopia, are impossible to achieve." See Harvey, "Cosmopolitanism and the Banality of Geographical Evils," *Public Culture* 12, no. 2 (2000): 538.

14. Beuka writes, "But one is tempted to ask what, if any, relevance the postwar view of suburbia as an American dystopia holds today," and he cites Levittown and Lakewood as models that have gone out of fashion. See Beuka, *SuburbiaNation*, 235. Until this point, however, his study adheres to well-worn constructs of "postwar class consciousness" (69), "the crisis of masculinity" (114), a Friedan-esque critique of female "imprisonment" (159–60), and suburban social and racial exclusivity (197–98).

15. Kathy Knapp, *American Unexceptionalism: The Everyman and the Suburban Novel after 9/11* (Iowa City: University of Iowa Press, 2014), xvii.

16. Knapp, *American Unexceptionalism*, xviii.

17. Knapp, xxx.

18. Karen Tongson, *Relocations: Queer Suburban Imaginaries* (New York: New York University Press, 2011), 17.

19. Tongson, *Relocations*, 18.

20. Joseph George, *Postmodern Suburban Spaces: Philosophy, Ethics, and Community in Post-War American Fiction* (Switzerland: Palgrave Macmillan/Springer, 2016), 5.

21. George, *Postmodern Suburban Spaces*, 27.

22. Martin Dines, *The Literature of Suburban Change: Narrating Spatial Complexity in Metropolitan America* (Edinburgh, Scotland: Edinburgh University Press, 2020), 7.

23. Dines, *The Literature of Suburban Change*, 19.

24. Roberto M. Dainotto, *Place in Literature: Regions, Cultures, Communities* (Ithaca, NY: Cornell University Press, 2000), 17.

25. See Judith Fetterley and Marjorie Pryse, *Writing out of Place: Regionalism, Women, and American Literary Culture* (Urbana: University of Illinois Press, 2003), 4.

26. Allen Ginsberg, *Howl and Other Poems* (San Francisco: City Lights Books, 1956), 22. Tom Lutz writes, "By the 1950s, the fate of farmers was not a key concern for the general culture, and suburbia became the milieu that seemed richest for displaying the culture's fault lines." See Lutz, *Cosmopolitan Vistas: American Regionalism and Literary Value* (Ithaca, NY: Cornell University Press, 2004), 190.

27. Lutz, *Cosmopolitan Vistas*, 14.

28. Douglas Reichert Powell, *Critical Regionalism: Connecting Politics and Culture in the American Landscape* (Chapel Hill: University of North Carolina Press, 2007), 19.

29. Lucy R. Lippard, *The Lure of the Local: Senses of Place in a Multicentered Society* (New York: New Press, 1997), 36.

30. Tongson, *Relocations*, 12.

31. Kenneth T. Jackson, *Crabgrass Frontier: The Suburbanization of the United States* (New York: Oxford University Press, 1985), 204.

32. Jackson, *Crabgrass Frontier*, 197. Jackson writes that "HOLC appraisers divided cities into neighborhoods and developed elaborate questionnaires relating to the occupation, income, and ethnicity of the inhabitants and the age, type of construction, price range, sales demand, and general state of repair of the housing stock" (197).

33. See Arnold Hirsch, *Making the Second Ghetto: Race and Housing in Chicago, 1940–1960* (Cambridge: Cambridge University Press, 1983), 268–75. Hirsch writes: "The charges so often leveled at the federal effort—that it neglected the poor; that it was actually anti-poor because of its demolition of low-rent housing and inadequate relocation procedures; that it simply subsidized those who needed aid least; and that it was transformed into a program of 'Negro clearance'— were hardly evidence of a plan gone awry. These were not 'perversions' of the enabling legislation, they were the direct consequences of it" (273).

34. Adam Rome notes that "the single-family home was one of the defining symbols of 'the American way of life.' The issue of homeownership was also tied to ideas about democracy, freedom, and civic order." See Rome, *The Bulldozer in the Countryside: Suburban Sprawl and the Rise of American Environmentalism* (New York: Cambridge University Press, 2001), 7. Rome also provides context for what I am calling the "imperialist land-grab campaign": "The residents of postwar suburbs lived in the midst of one of the most profound environmental transformations in the nation's history. Every year, a territory roughly the size of Rhode Island was bulldozed for urban development" (8). See also Jessica Blaustein, "Counterprivates: An Appeal to Rethink Suburban Interiority," *Iowa Journal of Cultural Studies* 3 (Fall 2003). She argues, "To be a good citizen of a stable nation, it was assumed . . . one must inhabit an autonomous, detached unit with identifiable boundaries that at once announce its contents to the social world and seal, stabilize, and defend them from it" (42).

35. Theodore Martin, *Contemporary Drift: Genre, Historicism, and the Problem of the Present* (New York: Columbia University Press, 2017), 2.

36. Martin, *Contemporary Drift*, 15.

37. Martin, 6.

38. Martin's project focuses on popular and enduring genres, including film noir, the Western, and the detective novel; regionalism does not rank, an indicator, perhaps, of "the conspicuous gendering of genre that continues to dictate . . . how (and which) genres are allowed to

be transformed from objects of popular entertainment to subjects of serious study." See Martin, 11.

39. Kristin J. Jacobson, *Neodomestic American Fiction* (Columbus: Ohio State University Press, 2010), 4.

40. Jacobson, *Neodomestic American Fiction*, 25.

41. Jacobson, 115, 47–48.

42. Jacobson, 155.

43. Hayden, *Building Suburbia*, 3. The 2010 census data supports the trend of continued suburban growth, despite a slight increase in the population of central cities. See Mark Mather, Kevin Pollard, and Linda A. Jacobsen, "First Results from the 2010 Census," *Population Reference Bureau Reports on America* (Population Reference Bureau, 2011), 13, 15, http://www.prb.org/resources/first-results-from-the-2010-census.

44. Hayden writes, "Battles over land underlie the developers and builders' process of production as well as the residents' struggle for a decent house, a connection to nature, and a sense of community." See Hayden, *Building Suburbia*, 245. Rome makes a similar point about building new communities attuned to environmental protection: "Though intended to serve a public purpose, a new community was still a profit-making venture. Unless a developer chose willingly to accept a substandard rate of return, the cost of environmental planning and open-space preservation had to be included in the price of homes and development sites." See Rome, *Bulldozer in the Countryside*, 262.

45. Jon C. Teaford, "The Myth of Homogeneous Suburbia," in Alan M. Berger and Joel Kotkin, eds., *Infinite Suburbia*, with Celina Balderas Guzmán (New York: Princeton Architectural Press, 2017), 127.

46. Peter Calthorpe and William Fulton, *The Regional City: Planning for the End of Sprawl* (Washington: Island Press, 2001), 15.

47. Calthorpe and Fulton write, "The businesses for which we work are typically bound up in a series of economic relationships with vendors and customers that are concentrated on a regional or metropolitan scale. And, even if we do live and work in one small town in the best Gopher Prairie tradition, the ecological fallout of our day-to-day patterns will be felt upstream or downstream throughout the region." See *Regional City*, 15–16.

48. Calthorpe and Fulton, *Regional City*, 16.

49. Reichert Powell, *Critical Regionalism*, 27–28.

50. Fetterley and Pryse, *Writing out of Place*, 6.

51. Roger Keil, "The Global Suburb: Divesting from the World's White Picket Fences," in Berger and Kotkin, *Infinite Suburbia*, 365.

52. Fetterley and Pryse, *Writing out of Place*, 11. They write, "[W]e understand region less as a term of geographical determinism and more as discourse or a mode of analysis, a vantage point within the network of power relations that provides a location for critique and resistance" (11). My understanding of "region" differs insofar as, alongside "a location for critique and resistance," I am also acutely interested in the "geographical determinism" of the suburban region.

53. Lutz, *Cosmopolitan Vistas*, 15.

54. Amy Kaplan, *The Anarchy of Empire in the Making of U.S. Culture* (Cambridge, MA: Harvard University Press, 2002), 1.

55. Kaplan anticipates what I am calling the central tension of postwar suburban development, describing the "double vision of U.S. imperialism as both expansive and contracting, on the one hand, constitutionally capable of boundless expansion, and on the other, narrowly protective of its own borders." See Kaplan, *Anarchy of Empire*, 12.

56. Neil Smith, *American Empire: Roosevelt's Geographer and the Prelude to Globalization* (Berkeley: University of California Press, 2003), 20, 19.

57. Henri Lefebvre argues, "There are beneficiaries of space, just as there are those excluded from it, those 'deprived of space'; this fact is ascribed to the 'properties' of a space, to its 'norms,' although in reality something very different is at work." See Lefebvre, *The Production of Space*, trans. Donald Nicholson-Smith (Malden, MA: Blackwell, 1991), 289.

58. On U.S. military bases "exporting American suburbs," see Mark L. Gillem, *America Town: Building the Outposts of Empire* (Minneapolis: University of Minnesota Press, 2007), xv, 168–70. On how U.S. dependence on foreign oil enables dictatorships around the world, see Thomas L. Friedman, "The First Law of Petropolitics," *Foreign Policy* (May/June 2006): 28–36. On the global impact of America's fast food culture, see Eric Schlosser, *Fast Food Nation: The Dark Side of the All-American Meal* (New York: Perennial, 2002), 225–52.

59. Lawrence Buell, *Writing for an Endangered World: Literature, Culture, and Environment in the U.S. and Beyond* (Cambridge, MA: Harvard University Press, 2001), 18.

60. Smith, *American Empire*, 5. Smith identifies "three formative moments in the U.S. rise to globalism." The first links the "classically colonial wars of 1898" to "Wilson's dream of a global Monroe Doctrine" after World War I. The second follows World War II: "by the war's end the ascendancy of U.S. capital and culture seemed assured. However truncated and transformed by anticolonial struggles and the cold war, it was this American globalism that flowered after 1945" (5). The first

Gulf War and "the advent of a 'new world order'" (6) inaugurate the third moment, which the War on Terrorism—"a war devoted to the completion of the geo-economic globalism of the American Empire" (xiv)—solidifies.

61. Smith, *American Empire*, 345.

62. Harvey, *Brief History of Neoliberalism*, 118. For a fuller discussion of the "uneven geographical developments" of neoliberalism, see 87–119.

63. One casualty of this emphasis on the homogeneous, "nowhere" quality of suburbia is the notion of "suburban nature." Sellers contends that the natural, ecological diversity of suburban developments across the twentieth century has been downplayed or obfuscated in favor of a popular image of banal uniformity. He writes, "Despite the actual variety of suburbs that arose in a place like Long Island, contemporary media blurred all these neighborhood ecologies together as a single 'suburbia.'" See Sellers, *Crabgrass Crucible*, 60.

64. For a brief discussion of anti-labor decisions by the federal courts and the Roberts court, see Sara Nelson, "America's Judges Are Putting My Life on the Line," Sunday Review, *New York Times*, November 11, 2021, https://www.nytimes.com/2021/11/11/opinion/courts-labor-strikes.html.

65. See Harvey, *Brief History of Neoliberalism*, 119. Harvey cites Paul Volcker's tenure as chairman of the U.S. Federal Reserve and Reagan's "deregulation, tax cuts, budget cuts, and attacks on trade union and professional power" as instrumental to the rise of neoliberalism in the United States (23–25), but he claims "[i]t was . . . [Bill] Clinton and then [Tony] Blair who, from the centre-left, did the most to consolidate the role of neoliberalism both at home and internationally" in the mid-1990s (93).

66. See Leigh Gallagher, *The End of the Suburbs: Where the American Dream Is Moving* (New York: Penguin, 2013).

67. Knapp makes a similar observation in her analysis of Richard Ford's Bascombe trilogy: "Indeed, though postwar suburbanization appears to be the result of a final wave of New Deal initiatives, built into the very foundation of these houses are the neoliberal ideals that by the 1970s would be so pervasive as to be unassailable." See Knapp, *American Unexceptionalism*, 6.

68. Calthorpe and Fulton, *Regional City*, 277.

69. Dainotto, *Place in Literature*, 32.

70. Francesco Loriggio, "Regionalism and Theory," in *Regionalism Reconsidered: New Approaches to the Field*, ed. David Jordan (New York: Garland, 1994), 8.

Chapter 1. Moving Out, Moving In: Race, Residential Rights, and Domestic Security

1. "Uncle Sam tells you how to Guard the Value of your Home," Celotex Building Products, advertisement, *House & Garden*, September 1942, 69.
2. May Oil Heating Equipment, advertisement, *House & Garden*, August 1942, 85.
3. Max Horkheimer and Theodor W. Adorno, *Dialectic of Enlightenment: Philosophical Fragments*, ed. Gunzelin Schmid Noerr, trans. Edmund Jephcott (Stanford, CA: Stanford University Press, 2002), 132.
4. On the rise of the "do-it-yourself" ideology in suburbia, see Gary Cross, "The Suburban Weekend: Perspectives on a Vanishing Twentieth-Century Dream," in *Visions of Suburbia*, ed. Roger Silverstone (New York: Routledge, 1997), 108–31.
5. "*House Beautiful* Presents. . . a symbol of what we're fighting for. . . A Fine Home and a Beautiful Garden," *House Beautiful*, January 1944, 29.
6. Hayden, *Building Suburbia*, 8.
7. "A Proper Dream House: For Any Veteran," *House Beautiful*, January 1945, 37.
8. "A Proper Dream House," 34.
9. "A Proper Dream House," 34.
10. "Looking Forward: Help Yourself—and Your Architect—by Keeping Your Mind Open to New Ideas," *House & Garden*, February 1945, 33.
11. See "If Your House Is Too Small," *House & Garden*, February 1945, 34–37; "Stretching the Kitchen," *House & Garden*, February 1945, 46–49.
12. Horkheimer and Adorno, *Dialectic of Enlightenment*, 132.
13. GE All-Electric Kitchen, advertisement, *House & Garden*, February 1945, [121].
14. See William M. O'Barr, *Culture and the Ad: Exploring Otherness in the World of Advertising* (Boulder, CO: Westview Press, 1994), 108.
15. Carol M. Rose and Richard R. W. Brooks, "Racial Covenants and Housing Segregation, Yesterday and Today," in *Race and Real Estate*, ed. Adrienne Brown and Valerie Smith (New York: Oxford University Press, 2016), 162.
16. "FHA Can't Prevent Housing Ban," *New York Times*, March 19, 1949, quoted in Becky M. Nicolaides and Andrew Wiese, eds., *The Suburb Reader* (New York: Routledge, 2006), 327.

17. Craig Thompson, "Growing Pains of a Brand-New City," *Saturday Evening Post*, August 7, 1954, 72.

18. Sellers writes, "Though starting at 20 percent in 1940 (a much lower rate than for whites), home ownership among African Americans had doubled by 1960. On Long Island, as in other suburban areas where they moved, the new black migrants could buy houses in only a few locations." See Sellers, *Crabgrass Crucible*, 53.

19. Andrew Wiese writes that for many African Americans, the suburban home provided "evidence of permanence, a marker of achievement, and the satisfaction of a long-deferred dream in the black South. For others, suburban space represented a means to economic subsistence, even independence. . . . For many, it was a black community, a place of social comfort and cultural affirmation if not racial pride, a 'safe space' in which to nurture families and educate children, a symbol of resistance to white supremacy and a foundation for politics, if not economic and political power." See Wiese, *Places of Their Own: African American Suburbanization in the Twentieth Century* (Chicago: University of Chicago Press, 2004), 8.

20. On urban naturalism, see Kecia Driver McBride, "Fear, Consumption, and Desire: Naturalism and Ann Petry's *The Street*," in *Twisted from the Ordinary: Essays on American Literary Naturalism*, ed. Mary E. Papke (Knoxville: University of Tennessee Press, 2003), 305–22. See also Friederike Hajek, "Richard Wright's *Native Son* and Ann Petry's *The Street*: Problems of Commitment and Authority," in *Looking Inward, Looking Outward: American Fiction in the 1930s and 1940s*, ed. Hans Bak and Vincent Piket (Bochum, Germany: European University Press, 1990), 45–52. For a discussion of *The Street*'s place in the gothic literary tradition, see Keith Clark, *The Radical Fiction of Ann Petry* (Baton Rouge: Louisiana State University Press, 2013), 93–121.

21. Ann Petry, *The Street* (1946; repr., Boston: Houghton, Mifflin, 1974), 28. Subsequent references are cited in the text.

22. See Wiese, *Places of Their Own*, 149.

23. Fetterley and Pryse, *Writing out of Place*, 27, 281.

24. U.S. Supreme Court, *Shelley v. Kraemer*, 334 U.S. 1 (1948), *JUSTIA*, decided May 3, 1948, https://supreme.justia.com/cases/federal/us/334/1/case.html.

25. U.S. Supreme Court, *Shelley v. Kraemer*. It is worth noting that three justices recused themselves from the case, a fact that Rose and Brooks cite among the reasons "for thinking that *Shelley* would not stick. . . . Given the prevalence of racial restrictions at the time, it appeared that at least some of the other three recused themselves because their own

homes had such restrictions." See Rose and Brooks, "Racial Covenants and Housing Segregation," 167. A subsequent Supreme Court decision pertaining to racial covenants, *Barrows v. Jackson* (1953), outlawed the collection of damages from white homeowners who sold their properties to non-whites. It was a 6–1 decision, with two justices recusing themselves from the hearing.

26. Richard R. W. Brooks and Carol M. Rose, *Saving the Neighborhood: Racially Restrictive Covenants, Law, and Social Norms* (Cambridge, MA: Harvard University Press, 2013), 169.

27. "Let Freedom Ring," *Chicago Defender*, May 15, 1948, in Nicolaides and Wiese, *Suburb Reader*, 325, 324. On the legal impact of the case, Rose and Brooks write that "over the years, *Shelley* has had only limited effectiveness as a doctrine that carries over from racially restrictive covenants to other legal areas." See Rose and Brooks, "Racial Covenants and Housing Segregation," 167.

28. "Real Estate: Exclusive . . . Restricted," *U.S. News & World Report*, May 14, 1948, in Nicolaides and Wiese, *Suburb Reader*, 326. Advocated practices included: "Social pressure—that is, a hostile attitude on the part of neighbors to unwanted newcomers"; "Financial pressure" on the part of "[p]rivate lending institutions"; pressure by real estate agents, who "may avoid selling to persons whose presence they think will lower values"; and finally, "Methods of harassment by police and other local authorities may be employed to some extent to maintain residential segregation" (326). See also Rose and Brooks, "Racial Covenants and Housing Segregation," 166.

29. Wiese notes, "In the postwar era, whites of various social classes united along racial lines to restrict the benefits of suburban living to 'Caucasians only.'" See *Places of Their Own*, 95.

30. Sinclair Lewis, *Kingsblood Royal* (New York: Random House, 1947), 110, 256, 268, and 303. Subsequent references are cited in the text.

31. For a detailed discussion of Hansberry's work at *Freedom* from 1951 to 1953, see Judith E. Smith, *Visions of Belonging: Family Stories, Popular Culture, and Postwar Democracy, 1940–1960* (New York: Columbia University Press, 2004), 284–89 and 293–304. For additional perspective on Hansberry's writing at *Freedom*, see Imani Perry, *Looking for Lorraine: The Radiant and Radical Life of Lorraine Hansberry* (Boston: Beacon, 2018), 12–13 and 46–49.

32. Lorraine Hansberry, *A Raisin in the Sun*, intro. Robert Nemiroff (New York: Vintage, 1994), 24. Subsequent references are cited in the text.

33. Edward Watts, "*Kingsblood Royal, The God-Seeker*, and the Racial History of the Midwest," in *Sinclair Lewis: New Essays in Criticism*, ed.

James M. Hutchisson (Troy, NY: Whitston Publishing Co, 1997), 96. Watts grounds his argument in Richard White's history of the Midwest, *The Middle Ground* (1991). Robert Sheckler, also citing White's *Middle Ground*, makes a similar observation: "Lewis hearkens back to this pre-American pluralistic society and hopes that it will serve as a model for the reformation of the modern Midwest, its descendant." See Sheckler, "The Road to Understanding and Reform in *Kingsblood Royal*," *The Sinclair Lewis Society Newsletter* 8, no. 1 (1999): 8.

34. Jennifer Delton, "Before the White Negro: Sin and Salvation in *Kingsblood Royal*," *American Literary History* 15, no. 2 (2003): 318.

35. One consistency throughout the novel, as Steven Michels observes, is that white "characters see race not as one biological characteristic among many, but as the defining characteristic around which all others revolve." See Michels, *Sinclair Lewis and American Democracy* (Lanham: Lexington Books, 2017), 135. Robert L. McLaughlin makes similar point, noting that "the Grand Republic whites have bought into the black/white dichotomy: they believe that each race is defined in opposition to the other and that a person can be in only one of the categories." See McLaughlin, "Deconstructing Culture in *Kingsblood Royal*," *Midwestern Miscellany* 28 (2000): 14.

36. Sarah J. McCullough writes, "The critics were—and are—quick to call Lewis's plot unrealistic and lacking in complexity," adding that "Lewis's artistic techniques run against the grain of modern stylistic biases." She also expresses justified disbelief over the accusation that the novel "oversimplifies American racial prejudice." See McCullough, "*Kingsblood Royal*: A Revaluation," *Sinclair Lewis Newsletter* 4 (1972): 11.

37. James Baldwin, "The Image of the Negro," Books in Review, *Commentary*, April 1948, 378, 379.

38. On the "passing novel," see Robert E. Fleming, "*Kingsblood Royal* and the Black 'Passing' Novel," in *Critical Essays on Sinclair Lewis*, ed. Martin Bucco (Boston: G. K. Hall, 1986), 213–21. On "*transracial* movement," see Andrea K. Newlyn, "Undergoing Racial 'Reassignment': The Politics of Transracial Crossing in Sinclair Lewis's *Kingsblood Royal*," *Mfs* 48, no. 4 (2002): 1047, 1048.

39. Newlyn, "Undergoing Racial 'Reassignment,'" 1056.

40. Delton, "Before the White Negro," 312, 325.

41. See Edward Dauterich, "*Kingsblood Royal*'s Grand Republic: Sundown Town?" *MidAmerica* 39 (2012): 65–81. Dauterich argues that *Kingsblood* "accurately delineates racial policies and occurrences of the time period which are largely forgotten today," and the novel "was very likely an attempt by Lewis to draw attention to those policies and

events as he understood them in Duluth, Minnesota" (68). In terms of initial reactions to the novel, he writes that even reviewers who noted the novel's attention to race "either spend too much time criticizing aesthetics or gloss lightly over the racial issues" (67).

42. Steven Wandler contends that "the novel's central insight into the race problems of the latter half of the twentieth century is this: the rights of a citizen are not something that someone *earns*, they are something that someone *has*." See Wandler, "Race and Citizenship in Sinclair Lewis's *Kingsblood Royal*," *Twentieth-Century Literature* 60, no. 1 (2014): 88.

43. Although Neil has been the controlling consciousness of the novel, it seems fitting that Vestal should get the last word. In the end, she stands by Neil and willingly adopts a Black identity: "Didn't you know I'm a Negro too?" (348). Delton reads this declaration as a harbinger of "the civil rights movement," designating Vestal "a new soldier in a war for a new world," and Sheckler interprets the entire closing scene as indicative of Lewis's belief in "the racial and cultural plurality of the 'middle ground'" and his conviction "that both blacks and whites should fight to topple discriminatory social hierarchies." See Delton, "Before the White Negro," 323; and Sheckler, "The Road to Understanding and Reform in *Kingsblood Royal*," 11.

44. Watts, "*Kingsblood Royal, The God-Seeker*, and the Racial History of the Midwest," 101–2.

45. According to Anita Hill, this monologue was "edited out of the 1959 version but reinstated in the 1983 text"; through this passage "Hansberry shows that what drives Walter is not purely desire for himself, but his dream for his son, Travis. Yet she also shows that even that dream is motivated by Walter's view of manhood and the role that he thinks women should play." See Anita Hill, *Reimagining Equality: Stories of Gender, Race, and Finding Home* (Boston: Beacon Press, 2011), 74–75.

46. See U.S. Supreme Court, *Hansberry v. Lee*, 311 U.S. 32 (1940), *JUSTIA*, decided November 12, 1940, https://supreme.justia.com/cases/federal/us/311/32/case.html. For a more complete discussion of Hansberry's childhood and her experiences with harassment in South Park, see J. Smith, *Visions of Belonging*, 284–89.

47. Hill, *Reimagining Equality*, 58.

48. Arnold R. Hirsch, "Massive Resistance in the Urban North: Trumbull Park, Chicago, 1953–1966," *The Journal of American History* 82, no. 2 (1995): 533.

49. Hirsch, "Massive Resistance in the Urban North," 540, 547. He continues, "When violence erupted in the nearby Calumet Park at the end

of [July], Trumbull Park exploded as well. As white mobs roamed the southeast side of the city, South Deeringites again gathered at the Wisconsin Steel works to attack Blacks. . . . The riot of July 1957 shattered the optimistic illusions held earlier in the year" (548).

50. Houston A. Baker, Jr., *Workings of the Spirit: The Poetics of Afro-American Women's Writing* (Chicago: University of Chicago Press, 1991), 104.

51. Erin D. Chapman links Walter's "patriarchal aspiration"—"I am a man"—to his "monetary ambition," contending that "Walter Lee's patriarchal aspiration and 'money values' blind him to the quest for real freedom." See Chapman, "Staging Gendered Radicalism at the Height of the US Cold War: *A Raisin in the Sun* and Lorraine Hansberry's Vision of Freedom," *Gender & History* 29, no. 2 (2017): 455.

52. J. Smith, *Visions of Belonging*, 283.

53. My examination of home shares some common points of inquiry in terms of citizenship and civil rights with Kristin L. Matthews, "The Politics of 'Home' in Lorraine Hansberry's *A Raisin in the Sun*," *Modern Drama* 51, no. 4 (2008): 556–78. Yet, whereas Matthews's argument focuses more on the Clybourne Park house as a figurative collage of "the viability and vulnerability of the various 'homes' occupied by the Younger family in their attempts to find and express themselves" (557), my interest lies in the way Mama Younger's "rustic suburban vision" and the family's move to Clybourne Park dovetail with the history of black pioneering and midcentury challenges to white suburban supremacy.

54. For some, this remains a nettling issue: Is Clybourne Park a "suburb"? Other scholars refer to Clybourne Park as a "suburb," including Chapman, Hill, and Wiese, but suburbanization and residential pioneering have not been a central focus of the scholarship on the play. In his introduction to the Vintage edition of *Raisin*, Robert Nemiroff, Hansberry's ex-husband and literary executor, insists it is "hardly suburbia, as some have imagined" (11). The offstage neighborhood should not be mistaken for a professional enclave such as Sylvan Park in Lewis's *Kingsblood*. Clybourne Park would also likely not fit the image purveyed by 1950s sitcoms, and it certainly would not jibe with what the term suburbia connoted in 1988, when Nemiroff was drafting his introduction. The Youngers are not moving to a suburb of strip malls and split-level houses, nor into a cul-de-sac of McMansions, but I would argue that in the play's original, postwar context we should read Clybourne Park as a fringe or first-ring suburb, accommodating a predominantly working-class population. It is a suburb in the

most basic sense of the word: a residential community that lies within commuting distance of a downtown or urban center that individuals would depend on for employment and entertainment opportunities.

55. Hill, *Reimagining Equality*, 64.

56. Wiese, *Places of Their Own*, 144.

57. Wiese, 146.

58. See William Murray, "The Roof of a Southern Home: A Reimagined and Usable South in Lorraine Hansberry's *A Raisin in the Sun*," *Mississippi Quarterly* 68, nos.1–2 (2015): 285. Murray argues that Hansberry's "characters embrace a useable Southern history offered by Mama, and this reimagined and reclaimed South gives the family the confidence to move forward with their lives" (282).

59. See "Morgan Park," *Encyclopedia of Chicago*, ed. Janie L. Reiff, Ann Durkin Keating, and James R. Grossman (Chicago: Chicago Historical Society, 2005), http://www.encyclopedia.chicagohistory.org/pages/842.html. The entry notes, "Although the Chicago, Rock Island & Pacific Railroad laid tracks through the area in 1852, regular commuter service to downtown was not established until the suburban line opened in 1888."

60. See "Morgan Park."

61. Will Cooley, "Moving On Out: Black Pioneering in Chicago, 1915–1950," *Journal of Urban History* 36, no. 4 (2010): 487. Cooley argues that "[p]roperty and upward mobility were seen as ways to legitimize black claims to full citizenship. However, 'black pioneers' . . . were caught between a hostile white world and the declining conditions in the jam-packed ghetto" (486).

62. Michelle Gordon discusses the recurrence of rats and roaches in texts by Black writers: "Where there is little or no municipal sanitation or landlord upkeep, rats and roaches thrive. . . . [T]he rat in *A Raisin in the Sun* addresses this callous neglect and economic exploitation of ghettoized communities." See Gordon, "'Somewhat Like War': The Aesthetics of Segregation, Black Liberation, and *A Raisin in the Sun*," *African American Review* 42, no. 1 (2008): 127.

63. GerShun Avilez, "Housing the Black Body: Value, Domestic Space, and Segregation Narratives," *African American Review* 42, no. 1 (2008): 137.

64. Lindner's position echoes an actual refrain used by the *South Deering Bulletin* in the 1950s to oppose racial integration: "White People Must Control Their Own Communities." See Hirsch, "Massive Resistance in the Urban North," 548.

65. Gordon observes that "Mr. Lindner's speech represents only one rhetorical maneuver by which improvement associations defended

segregation in the urban North. Their paternalism was accompanied by two other rhetorical strategies: a battle language of victimization and terrorism, on the one hand, and a language of miscegenation and degeneration, on the other hand." See Gordon, "'Somewhat Like War,'" 129.

66. Hana' Khalief Ghani, "I Have a Dream—Racial Discrimination in Lorraine Hansberry's *A Raisin in the Sun*," *Theory and Practice in Language Studies* 1, no. 6 (2011): 613.

67. Producers expressed concerns about the play's running time and, more generally, feared audiences would not attend a Broadway play about a Black family; as a concession, Hansberry cut the original ending. As Gordon observes, in an earlier draft, the play ended with the Younger family "in their new living room in Clybourne Park, in the dark, armed and waiting for the white mob to come. . . . Ending the action prior to the Youngers' arrival in Clybourne Park supplies Hansberry with the only prospect of keeping it real, so to speak, while breaking the cycles of desegregation and ritualized white violence." See Gordon, "'Somewhat Like War,'" 130. The 1961 film adaptation also ends before the family arrives in Clybourne Park, but it does show the Youngers visiting the house in an earlier scene. The location looks like a modest, first-ring suburban neighborhood. See *A Raisin in the Sun*, directed by Daniel Petrie, performed by Sidney Poitier, Claudia McNeil, Ruby Dee, and Diana Sands (1961; New York: Criterion Collection, 2018), DVD.

68. For a broader discussion of assimilation and integration, as wells as the harsh critiques leveled against *Raisin* in the 1960s, see Yomna Saber, "Lorraine Hansberry: Defining the Line Between Integration and Assimilation," *Women's Studies* 39 (2010): 451–69.

69. Mary Esteve, *Incremental Realism: Postwar American Fiction, Happiness, and Welfare-State Liberalism* (Stanford, CA: Stanford University Press, 2021), 79. In a similar vein, Chapman argues that "Hansberry sets up Walter Lee's desire to affirm his manhood through conspicuous consumption and familial mastery as an aspect of the money values that the women characters insist he must relinquish in order to lead his family responsibly." See Chapman, "Staging Gendered Radicalism," 455.

70. While there is much to admire in Matthews's reading of the play, I take exception to her conclusion that "Mama Younger, in her conflation of her literal house and her personal 'home' or sanctuary in religion, ignores the immediate dangers she and her family will face—dangers in *this* world, announced in the newspaper headlines and intimated by

Mr. Lindner." See Matthews, "The Politics of 'Home,'" 566. To my mind, the play suggests quite the opposite, that Mama has been keenly aware of "*this* world" and its literal deprivations, injustices, and violence, both in the South from which she escaped and in the urban North. While she may take refuge in religion, it does not come at the expense of a knowledge of this world, as suggested by her reply to Mrs. Johnson's remark about the bombings and the "baaaad peckerwoods" of Chicago: "(*Wearily*) We done thought about all that Mis' Johnson" (102).

71. Murray notes that, by accepting the hat, Mama "illustrates that a connection to the South . . . should be understood as simply an affirmation of their family and their legacy." See Murray, "The Roof of a Southern Home," 284.

72. See Laurie Goodman, Alanna McCargo, and Jun Zhu, "A Closer Look at the Fifteen-Year Drop in Black Homeownership," *Urban Wire: Housing and Housing Finance*, Urban Institute, February 13, 2018, https://www.urban.org/urban-wire/closer-look-fifteen-year-drop-black-homeownership.

Chapter 2. Adjustment Culture: Compulsory Domesticity and Its Discontents

1. John Cheever, *The Journals of John Cheever* (1991; repr., New York: Ballantine Books, 1993), 117. Hereafter cited as *J*, with page references appearing in the text.

2. K. A. Cuordileone, *Manhood and American Political Culture in the Cold War* (New York: Routledge, 2005), 138.

3. See my "John Cheever's Shady Hill, Or: How I Learned to Stop Worrying and Love the Suburbs," *Studies in American Fiction* 34, no. 2 (2006): 215–39. On the "familial consensus," see Elaine Tyler May, *Homeward Bound: American Families in the Cold War Era*, rev. ed. (New York: Basic Books, 1999), 14. May explains how the Great Depression and World War II created the conditions during the Cold War for a "widespread endorsement of this familial consensus."

4. Blake Bailey, *Cheever: A Life* (New York: Knopf, 2009), 207.

5. John Cheever, *The Wapshot Chronicle* (1957; repr., New York: Harper Perennial Classics, 2003), 287. Hereafter cited as *WC*, with page references appearing in the text.

6. Bailey identifies "C." as Calvin Kentfield, a writer Cheever had met at Yaddo. See *Cheever*, 289–90.

7. Algis Valiunas, "O Joy! O Sorrow! O Cheever!" *Commentary*, April 2009, 66.
8. On the comparison to Chekhov, see Bailey, *Cheever*, 661; see Richard Gilman, "Dante of Suburbia," *Commonweal*, December 19, 1958, 320.
9. Valiunas, "O Joy!," 68.
10. See James O'Hara, "Cheever's *The Wapshot Chronicle*: A Narrative of Exploration," *Critique: Studies in Contemporary Fiction* 22, no. 2 (1980): 24.
11. William H. Whyte, *The Organization Man* (1956; repr., New York: Doubleday Anchor Books, 1957), 286. One of Whyte's central insights is the way the organization gives rise to a new, universal "Social Ethic" in midcentury America (10). Although a "Protestant Ethic" of individual ability, self-reliance, struggle, and perseverance continues to inform the rhetoric of the American dream (5), this Social Ethic promotes, even indoctrinates, "a belief in the group as the source of creativity" and "a belief in 'belongingness' as the ultimate need of the individual" (7).
12. Fetterley and Pryse, *Writing out of Place*, 320.
13. Nayan Shah, *Contagious Divides: Epidemics and Race in San Francisco's Chinatown* (Berkeley: University of California Press, 2001), 13–14. Shah's work also influences Jacobson's understanding of "queer domesticity." See her *Neodomestic American Fiction*, 17, 154–55.
14. My thinking about domestic ideology here is indebted to Cuordileone who, in turn, is drawing on the work of the political theorist Michael Rogin. The latter "has stressed that in domestic ideology, women were conceded a heightened, if oblique, authority with the home in tacit exchange for their political and economic subordination; when that authority was experienced as too powerful, mothers could become menacing figures in the male imagination." See Cuordileone, *Manhood and American Political Culture in the Cold War*, 132.
15. Whyte, *The Organization Man*, 10.
16. Whyte, 310. Whyte elaborates, "In the chapters on the corporation I argued that it was the very beneficence of the environment that made resistance to it so difficult. So in suburbia" (387).
17. Robert J. Corber, *Homosexuality in Cold War America: Resistance and the Crisis of Masculinity* (Durham, NC: Duke University Press, 1997), 2.
18. "Transcript: Donald Trump Expounds on His Foreign Policy Views," *New York Times*, March 26, 2016, https://www.nytimes.com/2016/03/27/us/politics/donald-trump-transcript.html.

19. See Stephanie Coontz, *The Way We Never Were: American Families and the Nostalgia Trap* (New York: Basic Books, 1992), 24.

20. Coontz, *Way We Never Were*, 28. On the era of "sitcom suburbs," see Hayden, *Building Suburbia*, 128–53.

21. May, *Homeward Bound*, 12.

22. May, 13.

23. Betty Friedan, *The Feminine Mystique* (1963; repr., New York: Norton, 1974), 33, 233.

24. Friedan, *Feminine Mystique*, 16.

25. For one of the most scathing critiques of Friedan and *The Feminine Mystique*, see bell hooks, *Feminist Theory: From Margin to Center* (New York: Routledge, 2015), 1–3. See also Daniel Horowitz, *Betty Friedan and the Making of the Feminine Mystique: The American Left, the Cold War, and Modern Feminism* (Amherst: University of Massachusetts Press, 1998).

26. See *The Decline of the American Male*, by the Editors of *Look*, ill. Robert Osborn (New York: Random House, 1958).

27. Philip Wylie, *Generation of Vipers* (1942; repr., Normal, IL: Dalkey Archive Press, 1996), 198.

28. Wylie, *Generation of Vipers*, 207, 199.

29. J. Robert Moskin, "Why Do Women Dominate Him?" in *The Decline of the American Male*, 14.

30. Moskin, "Why Do Women Dominate Him?" 22.

31. Friedan, *Feminine Mystique*, 274. Clarifying these linked problems, she writes, "Today, when not only career, but any serious commitment outside the home, are out of bounds for truly 'feminine' housewife-mothers, the kind of mother-son devotion which can produce latent or overt homosexuality has plenty of room to expand to fill the time available" (276).

32. Friedan, 261. Friedan argues, "Sex is the only frontier open to women who have always lived within the confines of the feminine mystique" (261). Many scholars have addressed the connections among consumerism, the "organization man," and the suburbs. Corber writes, "Insofar as it promoted the mass consumption of durable goods such as automobiles, televisions, and refrigerators, the rise of the 'organization' man facilitated the transition to a Fordist regime of capital accumulation." See Corber, *Homosexuality in Cold War America*, 6. On consumerism and the suburban home, May writes, "Consumerism was not an end in itself; it was the means for achieving individuality, leisure, and upward mobility." See May, *Homeward Bound*, 12.

33. Cuordileone, *Manhood and American Political Culture in the Cold War*, 136. David Riesman examines the shift from "inner-directed" (cultivating one's own goals and judgement) to "outer-directed" social character (desiring security and acceptance by the group) beginning in the 1950s. He writes, "*What is common to all the other-directed people is that their contemporaries are the source of direction for the individual—either those known to him or those with whom he is indirectly acquainted, through friends and through the mass media*" (emphasis in the original). See Riesman, *The Lonely Crowd: A Study of the Changing American Character* (New Haven, CT: Yale University Press, 1961), 21.

34. Richard Yates, *Revolutionary Road* (1961; repr., New York: Vintage, 2000), intro. by Richard Ford, 219. Subsequent references are cited in the text.

35. Addressing the focus by "modernists and postmodernists" on "the notion of selfhood" and its perpetual "instability," Kate Charlton-Jones writes that "Yates absorbs some of their preoccupations but suggests, as is demonstrated by the narrative view of his characters' performances . . . that there was an authentic self to be uncovered." See Charlton-Jones, *Dismembering the American Dream: The Life and Fiction of Richard Yates* (Tuscaloosa: University of Alabama Press, 2014), 49–50.

36. In her analysis of Sam Mendes's film adaptation, Eleonora Ravizza also notes the performative nature of the scene: "Already set up as a performance—darkness all around them and the car lights shining on them as if they were on an actual stage—the conversation, which started with Frank trying to console April, quickly derails." See Ravizza, "The Politics of Melodrama: Nostalgia, Performance, and Gender Roles in *Revolutionary Road*," in *Poetics of Politics: Textuality and Social Relevance in Contemporary American Literature and Culture*, ed. Sebastian M. Herrmann et al. (Germany: Universitätsverlag Winter, 2015), 70.

37. For a compelling reading of the symbolism of the picture window as it extends "the theme of performativity in the novel" (31), see Rory McGinley, "Playing Suburbia in *Revolutionary Road*," in *Richard Yates and the Flawed American Dream: Critical Essays*, ed. Jennifer Daly (Jefferson, NC: McFarland, 2017), 30–49.

38. See C. Wright Mills, *White Collar: The American Middle Classes* (1951; repr., New York: Oxford University Press, 1956), xii. As Mills elaborates, "But if the work white-collar people do is not connected with its resultant product, and if there is no intrinsic connection between work and the rest of their life, then they must accept their work as meaningless in itself, perform it with more or less disgruntlement,

and seek meanings elsewhere" (228). For a useful critique of "Mills's desire to recover an outmoded form of male identity" (33), see Corber, *Homosexuality in Cold War America*, 30–36.

39. Michael P. Moreno, "Consuming the Frontier Illusion: The Construction of Suburban Masculinity in Richard Yates's *Revolutionary Road*," *Iowa Journal of Cultural Studies* 3 (Fall 2003): 85. Andrew Slade offers a complementary point in his analysis of Sam Mendes's film adaptation, noting how white men at the height of postwar economic power nevertheless "suffer the dissatisfactions of their limits like the grind of the train, the insufferable bosses, the lame tasks of corporate culture." See Slade, "'You are the Most Beautiful Creature': The Ethics of Masculinity in *Revolutionary Road*," *Quarterly Review of Film and Video* 34, no. 7 (2017): 669.

40. Claudia Falk, "'And I Mean Is It Any Wonder All the Men End up Emasculated?' Post-War Masculinities in Richard Yates's *Revolutionary Road* and John Braine's *Room at the Top*," in *Post-World War II Masculinities in British and American Literature and Culture: Towards Comparative Masculinity Studies*, ed. Stefan Horlacher and Kevin Floyd (New York: Routledge, 2016), 64.

41. Moreno, "Consuming the Frontier Illusion," 91.

42. Charlton-Jones writes, "Like the fool in King Lear [*sic*] he speaks with often-impeccable logic as he punctures a fragile social atmosphere by asking questions no one wants to address because to do so is to admit to the fact that there are performances being enacted." See *Dismembering the American Dream*, 64.

43. See Coontz, *Way We Never Were*, 32–33.

44. Corber, *Homosexuality in Cold War America*, 11–12. Citing the similarity in "experts' diagnoses of the bachelor and the homosexual," Cuordileone likewise argues that "having failed to adjust to normative male role requirements, both were assumed to suffer from some combination of the same afflictions." See Cuordileone, *Manhood and American Political Culture in the Cold War*, 146.

45. Charlton-Jones, *Dismembering the American Dream*, 65.

46. Discussing *Modern Woman: The Lost Sex* (1947), by Marynia Farnham and Ferdinand Lundberg, Cuordileone highlights their diagnosis of female discontent—"neurosis stemming from a failure to yield to the female role, as well as 'penis envy'"—noting that such ideas were considered "ridiculously outmoded, even to readers in the late 1940s." See Cuordileone, *Manhood and American Political Culture in the Cold War*, 143.

47. Jill E. Anderson, "'The Whole Imprisoning Wasteland Beyond': Forces of Nature, Ableism, and Suburban Dis-ease in Midcentury Literature," in *Disability and the Environment in American Literature: Toward an Ecosomatic Paradigm*, ed. Matthew J. C. Cella (Lanham, MD: Lexington, 2016), 146.

48. Charlton-Jones cautions, "I do not, and could not, argue that Yates was a protofeminist; he was not. There is a real split between Yates's *intellectual* appreciation of how life is peculiarly difficult for women within marriages that constrain or diminish them and his *emotional* distaste for anything that smacks of a political move to address those issues." See Charlton-Jones, *Dismembering the American Dream*, 154. In response to Sam Mendes's film adaptation, Rubén Cenamor makes a hopeful but strained case for *Revolutionary Road* as a call for progressive gender politics. He writes that the "martyr-like" portrayal of April and Frank's retreat into standard models of midcentury "hegemonic masculinity" makes a progressive case "for alternative models of masculinity which can lead to more gender egalitarian societies." See Cenamor, "What Have We Learnt Since the 1950s? The Return to Conservative Gender Roles in Sam Mendes's Film Adaptation of *Revolutionary Road*," in *Rethinking Gender in Popular Culture in the 21st Century: Marlboro Men and California Gurls*, ed. Astrid M. Fellner et al. (New Castle, U.K.: Cambridge Scholars, 2017), 178.

49. While acknowledging the "gender dynamics of the Eisenhower era," George claims that "April died, in part, because she received no hospitality." See George, *Postmodern Suburban Spaces*, 22. This assessment reflects George's larger project, which "argues that suburban fictions repeatedly imagine a different type of community possible within domestic spaces, one in which critical hospitality refuses individualistic interactions and prompts intersubjective identity construction" (27).

50. Patricia Highsmith, *The Price of Salt* (1952; repr., New York: Norton, 2004), 3. Subsequent references are cited in the text.

51. See Andrew Wilson, *Beautiful Shadow: The Life of Patricia Highsmith* (New York: Bloomsbury, 2003); Joan Schenkar, *The Talented Miss Highsmith: The Secret Life and Serious Art of Patricia Highsmith* (New York: St. Martin's Press, 2009); and Todd Haynes, dir., *Carol*, performed by Cate Blanchett and Rooney Mara (New York: Weinstein Co., 2015).

52. Victoria Hesford has published insightful work on Highsmith's 1950s novels, and she makes a similar point about her fiction more broadly.

See Hesford, "Patriotic Perversions: Patricia Highsmith's Queer Vision of Cold War America in *The Price of Salt, The Blunderer,* and *Deep Water*," *Women's Studies Quarterly* 33, nos. 3–4 (2005): 215–33. She writes, "Highsmith's middle-class families may live in idyllic suburban neighborhoods and enjoy the fruits of economic and social privilege, but a deep undercurrent of inarticulate compulsions and desires always threatens to tear them apart. . . . [Her] characters often act and feel against the heteronormativity of the middle-class home, making the boundaries between the home and 'outside' seem permeable, fragile, and arbitrary" (222–23).

53. Alice M. Kelly contends that this celebrated "happy ending" depends much on the reader's imagination, "a not insubstantial task in a heteronormative mainstream culture that, then as now, has never been designed to sustain such fantasies." See Kelly, "'Lots of Us Are Doing Fine': Femslash Fan Fiction, Happy Endings, and the Archontic Expansions of the *Price of Salt* Archive," *LIT: Literature Interpretation Theory* 31, no. 1 (2020): 43.

54. Victoria J. Hesford, "'A Love Flung Out of Space': Lesbians in the City in Patricia Highsmith's *The Price of Salt*," *Paradoxa* 18 (2003): 125.

55. Derrick King, "The City and the Country: Queer Utopian Spaces in John Rechy's *City of Night* and Patricia Highsmith's *The Price of Salt*," in *Critical Insights: Civil Rights Literature, Past & Present*, ed. Christopher A. Varlack (Ipswich, MA: Salem Press, 2017), 184.

56. Hesford, "Patriotic Perversions," 227. Esteve also sees the "cross-country tour [as] an extension of, rather than an escape from (as some critics suggest), the comfortable life in the suburbs that Carol's estranged husband funds," but she bases this reading on the pervasive nature of consumerism and "consumer agency" in the novel. See Esteve, *Incremental Realism*, 105.

57. Hesford, "Patriotic Perversions," 230.

58. Hesford, 230.

59. King offers a more transcendent reading of the novel's ending: "Her love for Carol breaks free of geography, allowing Therese to imagine a utopia that is not limited to the country. Their love is no longer imagined as an escape from the city; but as a transformation of the world." See King, "The City and the Country," 187. Natalie Prizel makes a similar point in the conclusion to her analysis of lesbian literary history, suggesting that the love between Carol and Therese requires new levels of courage to imagine "radical empathy." She writes, "This is the courage to repair, to regenerate, to imagine, if not a new world, a new way of being in it." See Prizel, "Beside Women: Charles Dickens,

Algernon Charles Swinburne, and Reparative Lesbian Literary History," *GLQ* 24, nos. 2–3 (2018): 285.

60. Sashi Nair, "Loss, Motherhood and the Queer 'Happy Ending,'" *Journal of Language, Literature and Culture* 66, no. 1 (2019): 47. For a less sanguine reading of queer romance and queer motherhood in both the novel and Haynes's film adaptation, *Carol*, see Jenny M. James, "Maternal Failures, Queer Futures: Reading *The Price of Salt* (1952) and *Carol* (2015) against Their Grain," *GLQ* 24, nos. 2–3 (2018): 291–314. Despite her admiration for the intricacies of Carol and Therese's affair, James writes, "I remain disappointed in the narrative's deficient vision of queer kinship that inscribes lesbian desire within neoliberal values while maintaining the lie that family is by definition straight, white, and economically stable" (293).

61. Whyte, *The Organization Man*, 283.

62. John Cheever, *The Wapshot Scandal* (1964; repr., New York: Perennial, 1973), 75. Hereafter cited as *WS*, with page references appearing in the text.

63. See Shah, *Contagious Divides*, 13.

Chapter 3. Serious Fiction: Consumer-Citizenship, Market Logic, and the Postmetropolis

1. Jonathan Franzen, letter to Don DeLillo, June 12, 1995, Harry Ransom Center, University of Texas at Austin.

2. Jonathan Franzen, letter to Don DeLillo, March 31, 1997, Harry Ransom Center, University of Texas at Austin.

3. Jonathan Franzen, letter to Don DeLillo, July 29, 1995, Harry Ransom Center, University of Texas at Austin; Franzen, letter to Don DeLillo, June 12, 1995.

4. Franzen, letter to Don DeLillo, July 29, 1995.

5. Pierre Bourdieu, *The Field of Cultural Production: Essays on Art and Literature*, ed. Randal Johnson (New York: Columbia University Press, 1993), 115.

6. Franzen, letter to Don DeLillo, July 29, 1995.

7. Mitchum Huehls and Rachel Greenwald Smith write that "David Foster Wallace, Jonathan Franzen, Dave Eggers, and other writers who came to adulthood during the late postmodern period . . . often articulated their formal innovations as responses to the literary marketplace, suggesting that reading and writing were activities that should be evaluated according to a market model." See Mitchum Huehls and Rachel

Greenwald Smith, "Four Phases of Neoliberalism and Literature: An Introduction," in *Neoliberalism and Contemporary Literary Culture*, ed. Mitchum Huehls and Rachel Greenwald Smith (Baltimore, MD: Johns Hopkins University Press, 2017), 8.

8. Jonathan Franzen, *How to Be Alone: Essays* (New York: Farrar, Straus, Giroux, 2003), 62. Hereafter cited as *HTBA*, with page references appearing in the text.

9. See Mathias Nilges, "Fictions of Neoliberalism: Contemporary Realism and the Temporality of Postmodernism's Ends," in Huehls and Greenwald Smith, *Neoliberalism and Contemporary Literary Culture*, 105–21. Nilges sees a connection between the "transition into an economic order that since the 1980s and 1990s can be described as dominant neoliberalism and our new economic reality" and "the recent history of the novel. . . . This centrally includes, I argue, the transition away from the experimental forms of high postmodernism and toward the forms of realism that have come to define our moment in literary history" (107). He persuasively suggests that "neoliberalism's transition from utopian fiction to reality is mediated by the rise and exhaustion of postmodernism" (108).

10. Huehls and Greenwald Smith, "Four Phases of Neoliberalism and Literature," 1. The authors provide an excellent overview of the divergent definitions of neoliberalism (2–3), as well as a description of its "four different phases or modes: the economic, the political-ideological, the sociocultural, and the ontological" (3).

11. Michel Foucault, *The Birth of Biopolitics: Lectures at the Collège de France, 1978–1979*, ed. Michel Senellart, trans. Graham Burchell (New York: Picador, 2008), 217.

12. Foucault, *Birth of Biopolitics*, 240.

13. See also Henry A. Giroux, "The Terror of Neoliberalism: Rethinking the Significance of Cultural Politics," *College Literature* 32, no. 1 (2005): 1–19. He argues that "neoliberalism is an ideology, a politics, and at times a fanaticism that subordinates the art of democratic politics to the rapacious laws of a market economy that expands its reach to include all aspects of social life within the dictates and values of a market-driven society" (12).

14. Lisa Duggan, *The Twilight of Equality?: Neoliberalism, Cultural Politics, and the Attack on Democracy* (Boston: Beacon Press, 2003), xi, x.

15. Duggan, *Twilight of Equality*, 10. On the supposedly "apolitical" nature of neoliberalism, Giroux writes, "This is a politics that hides its own ideology by eliminating the traces of its power in a rhetoric

of normalization, populism, and the staging of public spectacles." See Giroux, "The Terror of Neoliberalism," 12.

16. Harvey, *Brief History of Neoliberalism*, 2.
17. Pierre Bourdieu, "The Essence of Neoliberalism," *Le Monde Diplomatique*, December 1998, http://mondediplo.com/1998/12/08bourdieu.
18. Bourdieu, "Essence of Neoliberalism." Discussing Bourdieu's understanding of neoliberalism, Nilges contends, "It is in this way, then, that we can understand neoliberalism as a strategy that moves from the status of fiction to the point of its structural implementation, which profoundly reshapes material and social reality." See Nilges, "Fictions of Neoliberalism," 106.
19. See Harvey, *Brief History of Neoliberalism*, 9.
20. See Harvey, 23.
21. See Huehls and Greenwald Smith, "Four Phases of Neoliberalism and Literature," 7.
22. See Duggan, *Twilight of Equality*, 8. Noting paradoxical conservative arguments in the 1950s and 1960s regarding privacy—more in economic and civil life, less in domestic life—Duggan continues, "In the arena of personal, sexual, and domestic life, conservatives accorded 'privacy' only to the favored form of family life and supported state regulation of intimate relations in the name of social order for all others" (8).
23. Keil, "Global Suburb: Divesting from the World's White Picket Fences," 368.
24. Harvey writes that neoliberalism functions primarily "as a *political* project to re-establish the conditions for capital accumulation and to restore the power of economic elites," aided by tax reforms that favored the wealthy and steep declines in real wages for the working and middle classes. See *Brief History of Neoliberalism*, 19. On the benign face of neoliberalism, Harvey writes, "It has been part of the genius of neoliberal theory to provide a benevolent mask full of wonderful-sounding words like freedom, liberty, choice, and rights, to hide the grim realities of the restoration or reconstitution of naked class power" (119). Duggan similarly argues, "Neoliberalism's avatars have presented its doctrines as universally inevitable and its operations as ultimately beneficial in the long term—even for those who must suffer through poverty and chaos in the short term." See *Twilight of Equality*, xiii.
25. Joel Garreau, *Edge City: Life on the New Frontier* (New York: Doubleday, 1991), 4.

26. Garreau, *Edge City*, 12, 14. Garreau cites Leo Marx, *The Machine in the Garden: Technology and the Pastoral Ideal in America* (1964; repr., New York: Oxford University Press, 2000). Marx claims that "access to undefiled, bountiful, sublime Nature is what accounts for the virtue and special good fortune of Americans. It enables them to design a community in the image of a garden, an ideal fusion of nature with art" (228).

27. Edward W. Soja, *Postmetropolis: Critical Studies of Cities and Regions* (Malden, MA: Blackwell, 2000), xv, 147.

28. Soja, *Postmetropolis*, 148.

29. Soja, 152.

30. Soja, 152. He continues, "In a process that can no longer be simply described as sprawl, post-metropolitan cityspace has been both stretched out and pinned down to cover a much larger regional scale than ever before" (242).

31. Fredric Jameson, *Postmodernism, or the Cultural Logic of Late Capitalism* (Durham, NC: Duke University Press, 1991), 37.

32. See Harvey, *Brief History of Neoliberalism*, 118.

33. Don DeLillo, *White Noise*, (1985; repr., New York: Penguin, 2009), intro. Richard Powers, 5. Subsequent references are cited in the text.

34. Foucault, *Birth of Biopolitics*, 241.

35. Ralph Clare, *Fictions Inc.: The Corporation in Postmodern Fiction, Film and Popular Culture* (New Jersey: Rutgers University Press, 2014), 135.

36. In 1986, Toyota made its "debut as a manufacturer in the United States, with the rollout of the first Toyota car built on American soil." See "Company History," Toyota–USA Newsroom, accessed May 22, 2021, https://pressroom.toyota.com/company-history/. According to the Wikipedia page for Nissan, the "Nissan Motor Manufacturing Corporation USA was established in 1980." See "Nissan," *Wikipedia*, accessed May 22, 2021, https://en.wikipedia.org/wiki/Nissan.

37. Martina Sciolino, "The Contemporary American Novel as World Literature: The Neoliberal Antihero in Don DeLillo's *Cosmopolis*," *Texas Studies in Language and Literature* 57, no. 2 (2015): 210.

38. Some scholars have questioned the "suburban" label in reference to *White Noise*. Dana Phillips notes that Blacksmith is "an unremarkable sprawl of development that could be called 'suburban,' except there is no urban center to which [it] is subjoined." See Phillips, "Don DeLillo's Postmodern Pastoral," in *Reading the Earth: New Directions in the Study of Literature and Environment*, ed. Michael P. Branch et al. (Boise: University of Idaho Press, 1998), 237. Thomas J. Ferraro describes the Gladney home as "a nice house on a quiet street in a

small town that is the suburb of nowhere." See Ferraro, "Whole Families Shopping at Night!," in *New Essays on* White Noise, ed. Frank Lentricchia (Cambridge: Cambridge University Press, 1991), 19.

39. See Edward Soja, *Postmodern Geographies: The Reassertion of Space in Critical Social Theory* (New York: Verso, 1989), 181.

40. See Fredric Jameson, "Postmodernism and Consumer Society," in *The Anti-Aesthetic: Essays on Postmodern Culture*, ed. Hal Foster (Port Townsend, WA: Bay Press, 1983), 124–25. Paula E. Geyh writes, "According to Jameson, cultural postmodernism is defined by certain transformations of material structures of technology, communication, and global economies, which subsequently drive and govern other transformations. Among these transformations are the rise of the computer and other digital technologies (also crucial to Lyotard), and the proliferation of an all-pervasive media culture." See Geyh, "Assembling Postmodernism: Experience, Meaning, and the Space In-Between," *College Literature* 30, no. 2 (2003): 4.

41. Laura Barrett, "Don DeLillo," in *The Cambridge Companion to American Fiction after 1945*, ed. John N. Duvall (Cambridge: Cambridge University Press, 2012), 247.

42. For a different reading of the Gladney's marriage and their post-nuclear family, see George, *Postmodern Suburban Spaces*, 147–57. Drawing on "critical hospitality" theory, George argues, "The fictional family, and the marital pact in particular, though itself a construct or fantasy, provides a schematic of interaction in deadly times, forcing people to recognize their dependence on one another" (149).

43. Regarding the domestic realm in the novel, Frank Lentricchia writes, "In *White Noise*, DeLillo deploys that popular literary form of the private life, but only in order to have his way with it, showing what large and nearly invisible things invade our kitchens, the various coercive environments within which the so-called private life is led." See Lentricchia, "Introduction," in *New Essays on* White Noise, 7. Ferraro also writes: "But it is in the dissent of *White Noise* from the prevailing analysis of how the American family functions—where its 'plight' originates, how actual families manage nevertheless to sustain themselves to the extent that they do, to what else is their operation allied—that DeLillo makes his strongest contribution to our understanding of suburban domesticity." See Ferraro, "Whole Families Shopping at Night!," 19.

44. See Foucault, *Birth of Biopolitics*, 262, n. 11. During his lectures on American neoliberalism, Foucault paraphrases the work of the economist Jean-Luc Migué, whom the editor cites as follows: "One of the

great recent contributions of economic analysis has been the full application to the domestic sector of the analytical framework traditionally reserved for the firm and the consumer. By making the household a unit of production in the same way as the classical firm, we discover that its analytical foundations are actually identical to those of the firm. . . . What in actual fact is the household if not the contractual commitment of two parties to supply specific *inputs* and to share in given proportions the benefits of the household's *output*" (262).

45. Biman Basu reads a sexual ecstasy in Jack's encounter with the ATM: "The passage quite clearly represents a certain pleasure, and given the erotic charge of the word 'entered,' which becomes explicit later in the novel, Jack's 'pleasing interaction' with the machine suggests the interpenetration of man and machine." See Basu, "Reading the Techno-Ethnic Other in DeLillo's *White Noise*," *Arizona Quarterly* 61, no. 2 (2005): 91.

46. See Ferraro, "Whole Families Shopping at Night!," 20–21. Karen Weekes echoes this sentiment, writing that "Jack's experience at the mall also helps him see himself and his existence as part of a larger community, a personal domestic group and a more general capitalist culture." See Weekes, "Consuming and Dying: Meaning and the Marketplace in Don DeLillo's *White Noise*," *Lit: Literature Interpretation Theory* 18, no. 4 (2007): 294.

47. Foucault, *Birth of Biopolitics*, 226.

48. Huehls and Greenwald Smith, "Four Phases of Neoliberalism and Literature," 9. The authors equate this facet of the market with the "*fourth, ontological phase* of neoliberalism" (9), which comes into existence in the 1990s and 2000s. Arguably, *White Noise* anticipates this everyday way of being under neoliberalism.

49 For a more positive take on 1980s mall culture, see Ian Bogost, "When Malls Saved the Suburbs from Despair," *The Atlantic*, February 17, 2018, https://www.theatlantic.com/technology/archive/2018/02/when-malls-saved-cities-from-capitalism/553610/.

50. Soja, *Postmodern Geographies*, 243. Jameson also discusses the Bonaventure; see his *Postmodernism*, 39–44.

51. Soja, *Postmodern Geographies*, 243–44.

52. Cynthia Deitering, "The Postnatural Novel: Toxic Consciousness in Fiction of the 1980s," in *The Ecocriticism Reader: Landmarks in Literary Ecology*, ed. Cheryll Glotfelty and Harold Fromm (Athens: University of Georgia Press, 1996), 196.

53. Deitering, "Postnatural Novel," 198.

54. As Louis Mackenzie notes, "DeLillo denies . . . that spiritual epiphanies can happen only on contact with unmediated nature." See Mackenzie, "An Ecocritical Approach to Teaching *White Noise*," in *Approaches to Teaching DeLillo's* White Noise, ed. Tim Engles and John N. Duvall (New York: Modern Language Association, 2006), 60.

55. Urusla K. Heise, "Toxins, Drugs, and Global Systems: Risk and Narrative in the Contemporary Novel," *American Literature* 74, no. 4 (2002): 753.

56. Jack's father-in-law, Vernon, gives voice to the evocative phrase, "the recesses of the American home." He wryly observes that men no longer need to solicit prostitutes to satisfy unusual sexual proclivities because "[y]ou can get whatever you want in the recesses of the American home" (235). Vernon's image of willing wives and under-employed prostitutes identifies the exchange value of sex as yet another marker of economics and consumerism in the domestic realm.

57. Lawrence Buell, "Toxic Discourse," *Critical Inquiry* 24, no. 3 (1998): 665. Phillips takes a different tack: "The postmodern pastoral, unlike its predecessors, cannot restore harmony and balance of culture with nature, because the cultural distinctions that the pastoral used to make—like that between the city and the country—have become too fluid to have any force and are dissolved in the toxic fog of airborne events." See Phillips, "Don DeLillo's Postmodern Pastoral," 245.

58. Jonathan Franzen, *The Twenty-Seventh City* (New York: Farrar, Straus, Giroux, 1988), v. Hereafter cited as *TSC*, with page references appearing in the text.

59. On the distinction between dispossession and displacement, Nicholas Blomley claims that "[dispossession] refers to the specific processes through which settlers came to acquire title to land historically held by aboriginal people. Displacement, while related, refers to the conceptual removal of aboriginal people from the city, and the concomitant 'emplacement' of white settlers." See Blomley, *Unsettling the City: Urban Land and the Politics of Property* (New York: Routledge, 2004), 109.

60. Nilges, "Fictions of Neoliberalism," 111.

61. This aspect of Franzen's novel is also in keeping with Nilges's argument about the return to realism. He writes that postmodernism "brought about and was actualized in the current stage of capitalism. Once the gap between avant-garde and the quotidian closes, we see a turn to realism and matters of time and temporality to register precisely this transition from fiction to present reality." See Nilges, "Fictions of Neoliberalism," 113. From a different perspective, Jesús Blanco Hidalga claims that there is "a remarkable, unresolved tension between the

two different approaches to the novelistic form, the realist and the postmodernist, which coexist within *The Twenty-Seventh City.*" See Hidalga, "Knowable Conspiracies: A Reassessment of the Formal and Ideological Aspects in Jonathan Franzen's *The Twenty-Seventh City,*" *Miscelánea* 52 (2015): 14.

62. Lefebvre, *Production of Space*, 285.

63. See Blomley, *Unsettling the City*, 67, 122–23. The map as a tool for dispossession and displacement is at the center of Blomley's concerns with space as property—"an external category" or spaces "as 'things'" (67)—and gentrification projects in Vancouver's Downtown Eastside. He writes, "The authoritative production of space through dominant maps . . . has long been used to dispossess: the line between cartographic dispossession and material displacement is a thin one" (68).

64. Jackson discusses St. Louis at some length, citing it as a quintessential example of the crises contemporary cities now face in the midst of sprawling suburban regions, and his data corroborates much of Franzen's historical sketch. See Jackson, *Crabgrass Frontier*, 217.

65. See Amy Stuart Wells and Robert L. Crain, *Stepping over the Color Line: African-American Students in White Suburban Schools* (New Haven, CT: Yale University Press, 1997), 36. They also offer a brief but insightful discussion of Pruitt-Igoe from development to demise (56–57).

66. Gerald Frug, *City Making: Building Communities Without Building Walls* (Princeton, NJ: Princeton University Press, 1999), 80.

67. Ralph J. Poole makes a similar observation, writing that "the novel is an elegiac account of remembering better times and thus is obviously invested in documenting a history of deterioration." See Poole, "Serving the Fruitcake, or Jonathan Franzen's Midwestern Poetics," *Midwest Quarterly* 49, no. 3 (2008): 270.

68. See Carlo Rotella, *October Cities: The Redevelopment of Urban Literature* (Berkeley: University of California Press, 1998), 3.

69. Bourdieu, "The Essence of Neoliberalism."

70. Neil Smith and Setha Low write that, under neoliberalism, "Not only does society merge with the state . . . but it increasingly and forcefully merges with the sphere of private capitalist economic calculation." See Smith and Low, "Introduction: The Imperative of Public Space," in *The Politics of Public Space*, ed. Setha Low and Neil Smith (New York: Routledge, 2006), 15.

71. Robert Beauregard, *Voices of Decline: The Postwar Fate of U.S. Cities*, 2nd ed. (New York: Routledge, 2003), 22. Beauregard argues that the discourse of urban decline does not merely record the physical, social,

and cultural aspects of urban decline, but shapes attitudes toward the city and informs decisions. "In this role, it discursively precedes the deteriorating conditions and bleak future of the city.... Urban decline provides a spatial fix for our more generalized insecurities and complaints and the discourse forestalls their evolution into a more radical critique of American society" (22).

72. Duggan, *Twilight of Equality*, 14–15, emphasis original.

73. See Kenneth M. Reardon, "State and Local Revitalization Efforts in East St. Louis, Illinois," *Annals of the American Academy of Political and Social Science* 551 (May 1997): 247.

74. On demographics, crime rates, and poverty, see Reardon, "State and Local Revitalization Efforts in East St. Louis, Illinois," 235–47. He writes, "Between 1960 and 1990, the African American portion of the population increased from 45 percent to 98 percent, the unemployment rate rose from 10.5 percent to 24.6 percent, the percentage of female-headed households rose from 21 percent to 62 percent, and the percentage of families living in poverty jumped from 11.0 percent to 39.2 percent" (237). Keeping in mind that Franzen's novel was published in 1988, it is worth noting that "[i]n 1990, more than sixty homicides took place in East St. Louis, three-quarters of which were alcohol- or drug-related" (240). On the East St. Louis school system, see Jonathan Kozol, *Savage Inequalities: Children in America's Schools* (New York: Harper Collins, 1992), 7–39.

75. See Duggan, *Twilight of Equality*, 38. For a fuller discussion of "consumer citizenship" and its connection to race, see 37–40.

76. See Colin Hutchinson, "Jonathan Franzen and the Politics of Disengagement," *Critique: Studies in Contemporary Fiction* 50, no. 2 (2009): 194. Hutchinson contends that, like the characters in his first novel, Franzen also capitulates to the inevitability of global capitalism; he fails to deliver on his "professed project of writing a social novel that combines aesthetic achievement with progressive engagement" (194).

77. Like Hutchinson, Ty Hawkins reads the novel's ending as an apathetic dodge and "the undoing of Franzen's text.... Rather than offer the prospect of change—rather than even call for it—*The Twenty-Seventh City* extends an olive branch of irony to the reader, who is encouraged to join Franzen in shaking his or her head in mutual understanding of the nation's intractable awfulness." See Hawkins, "Assessing the Promise of Jonathan Franzen's First Three Novels: A Rejection of 'Refuge,'" *College Literature* 37, no. 4 (2010): 70.

78. On the "sociocultural phase" of neoliberalism and the mandate for "profit maximization," see Huehls and Greenwald Smith, "Four Phases of Neoliberalism and Literature," 8.

79. My reading of the conspiracy's unraveling and the novel's ending shares more in common with Hidalga's assessment than with the harsh critiques leveled by critics such as Hawkins and Hutchinson. Hidalga writes, "Thus, even the corrupt, failed conspiracy of Jammu and her followers furnishes a flickering image of the possibility of public officials acting as revolutionary leaders determinedly taking effective action in favour of the needy, deftly reversing the (generally regarded as irresistible) forces of capitalism, successfully fighting them with their own (financial) weapons." See Hidalga, "Knowable Conspiracies," 22.

80. Soja, *Postmetropolis*, 150.

81. Hidalga makes a similar point about Franzen's "nostalgic yearning" but links it to "the industrial age" and a desire for a vibrant, Habermasian public sphere. See "Knowable Conspiracies," 23.

82. Jonathan Franzen, quoted in Thomas R. Edwards, "Oprah's Choice," *Raritan* 21 (Spring 2002): 77.

83. See David D. Kirkpatrick, "Winfrey Rescinds Offer to Author for Guest Appearance," *New York Times*, October 24, 2001, https://www.nytimes.com/2001/10/24/business/media/winfrey-rescinds-offer-to-author-for-guest-appearance.html.

84. The quotation comes from Janice Radway, who is quoted in "A Novelist, a Talk-Show Host, and Literature High and Low," *Chronicle of Higher Education*, November 30, 2001, https://www.chronicle.com/article/a-novelist-a-talk-show-host-and-literature-high-and-low/. See also Susan Schindehette, "Novel Approach," *People*, November 12, 2001, 83–84; Jeff Giles, "Books: Errors and 'Corrections,'" *Newsweek*, November 4, 2001, https://www.newsweek.com/books-errors-and-corrections-149529. Toni Morrison is quoted in Sarah Bernard, "Jonathan Franzen's Story of O," *New York*, October 5, 2001, https://nymag.com/nymetro/arts/features/5341/. Margo Jefferson summed up the melee "as a fable about the literary class system today," concluding that "[t]he manly conviction that large numbers of women writers and readers signal the decline of literature and the rise of mass-market trash is a few centuries old now." See Jefferson, "On Writers and Writing; There Goes the Neighborhood," *New York Times*, November 25, 2001, https://www.nytimes.com/2001/11/25/books/on-writers-and-writing-there-goes-the-neighborhood.html.

85. Fetterley and Pryse, *Writing out of Place*, 35.

Chapter 4. Containment Culture: Suburban Domesticity and Nation as Home

1. There is an established body of scholarship focusing on these themes in both Eugenides's novel and Sofia Coppola's film adaptation. See Marta Miquel Baldellou, "Inheriting Traditional Roles of American Female Growth: From Louisa May Alcott's *Little Women* to Jeffrey Eugenides's *The Virgin Suicides*," in *New Literatures of Old: Dialogues of Tradition and Innovation in Anglophone Literature*, ed. José Ramón Prado-Pérez and Dídac Llorens Cubedo (New Castle, U.K.: Cambridge Scholars, 2008), 127–35; Ana-Blanca Ciocoi-Pop, "Suicide as Affirmation and Gender as a Conscious Choice: The Deconstruction of Identity in Jeffrey Eugenides's Major Novels," *American, British, and Canadian Studies* 10 (July 2008): 80–90; Clare Hayes-Brady, "'Obviously, doctor, you've never been a thirteen-year-old girl': Problematic Adolescence in *The Virgin Suicides*," in *'Forever Young'? The Changing Images of America*, ed. Philip Coleman and Stephen Matterson (Germany: Universitätsverlag Winter Heidelberg, 2012), 209–18; Bree Hoskin, "Playground Love: Landscape and Longing in Sofia Coppola's *The Virgin Suicides*," *Literature/Film Quarterly* 35, no. 3 (2007): 214–21; Ceri Hovland, "'We Felt That if We Kept Looking Hard Enough, We Might Begin to Understand How They Were Feeling and Who They Were': Point of View and Performance in *The Virgin Suicides*," *Journal of Adaptation in Film and Performance* 3, no. 3 (2010): 259–70; Stephanie McKnight, "Happier with Dreams: Constructing the Lisbon Girls through Nondiegetic Sound in *The Virgin Suicides*," in *True to the Spirit: Film Adaptation and the Question of Fidelity*, ed. Colin MacCabe, Kathleen Murray, and Rick Warner, afterword Fredric Jameson (Oxford: Oxford University Press, 2011), 115–29; Rachael McLennan, "Chasing after the Wind: The Adolescent Aporias of Jeffrey Eugenides," in *Writing America into the Twenty-First Century: Essays on the American Novel*, ed. Elizabeth Boyle and Anne-Marie Evans (New Castle, U.K.: Cambridge Scholars, 2010), 22–38; Kenneth Millard, *Coming of Age in Contemporary American Fiction* (Edinburgh, Scotland: Edinburgh University Press, 2007); and Debra Shostak, "'A story we could live with': Narrative Voice, the Reader, and Jeffrey Eugenides's *The Virgin Suicides*," *Mfs* 55, no. 4 (2009): 808–32. On Eugenides's interest in "impossible voices," see Jeffrey Eugenides, interview by Jonathan Safran Foer, *Bomb* 81 (Fall 2002), https://bombmagazine.org/articles /jeffrey-eugenides.

2. Jeffrey Eugenides, *The Virgin Suicides* (New York: Picador, 1993), 102, 243. Hereafter cited as *VS*, with page references appearing in the text. Eugenides uses the first-person plural "we" to designate the single, coherent perspective of this multiple or collective narrator. For the sake of consistency, however, I will refer to the "narrators" to designate the plurality of this "we" voice in the novel.

3. Shostak, "'A story we could live with,'" 809, 810.

4. Shostak, 826.

5. Kenneth Womack and Amy Mallory-Kani, "'Why don't you just leave it up to nature?': An Adaptationist Reading of the Novels of Jeffrey Eugenides," *Mosaic* 40 (September 2007): 165, 166.

6. Womack and Mallory-Kani, "'Why don't you just leave it up to nature,'" 166. If, as Womack and Mallory-Kani contend, the novel parallels "the demise of the Nixon administration," then their date of "June 13th, 1972" presents a problem. First, the narrators tell us Cecilia's first suicide attempt occurred "on June 16" (*VS* 217). But they also suggest the elapsed time between Cecilia's first suicide attempt and the final Lisbon suicide is "thirteen months" (1), which would be the summer of 1973, not August 1974, when Nixon resigned the presidency.

7. Womack and Mallory-Kani, 158.

8. Martin Dines reads a similar "sense of time being out of joint" in the novel, but his inquiry focuses on the way Eugenides deploys "identifiably gothic motifs and textual strategies" in order to historicize postwar suburbia. See Dines, "Suburban Gothic and the Ethnic Uncanny in Jeffrey Eugenides's *The Virgin Suicides*," 963, 964.

9. See Reichert Powell, *Critical Regionalism*, 19.

10. Lutz, *Cosmopolitan Vistas*, 30.

11. Alan Nadel, *Containment Culture: American Narratives, Postmodernism, and the Atomic Age* (Durham, NC: Duke University Press, 1995), 2–3.

12. See Fetterley and Pryse, *Writing out of Place*, 11.

13. Amy Kaplan, "Homeland Insecurities: Transformations of Language and Space," in *September 11 in History: A Watershed Moment?*, ed. Mary L. Dudziak (Durham, NC: Duke University Press, 2003), 59.

14. See Smith, *American Empire*, 5.

15. Laura Miller, "Family Togetherness and the Suburban Ideal," *Sociological Forum* 10, no. 3 (1995): 415.

16. Blaustein, "Counterprivates," 42.

17. Susan Sontag, *On Photography* (New York: Farrar, Straus and Giroux, 1977), 15.

18. Deborah Nelson, *Pursuing Privacy in Cold War America* (New York: Columbia University Press, 2002), 26.

19. Jeffrey Eugenides, *Middlesex* (New York: Picador, 2002), 242. Hereafter cited as *M*, with page references appearing in the text.

20. Barbara Kelly argues that despite the fact the houses were constructed for veterans and families with working-class incomes, "the Levittown myth" always assigned a middle-class status to the families, signaling an implicit link between suburban homeownership and middle-class standing in postwar America. See Kelly, *Expanding the American Dream: Building and Rebuilding Levittown* (New York: SUNY Press, 1993), 153–54.

21. Hayden, *Building Suburbia*, 132.

22. For an excellent reading of ethnic anxieties as they pertain to questions of whiteness and suburban identity in the novel, see Dines, "Suburban Gothic and the Ethnic Uncanny in Jeffrey Eugenides's *The Virgin Suicides*," 966–73.

23. See Jane Holtz Kay, *Asphalt Nation: How the Automobile Took Over America, and How We Can Take It Back* (Berkeley: University of California Press, 1997), 58.

24. Blaustein, "Counterprivates," 40, 46.

25. Campbell Craig and Fredrik Logevall, *America's Cold War: The Politics of Insecurity* (Cambridge, MA: Belknap-Harvard University Press, 2009), 9, 11.

26. Referring to the war in Vietnam, Craig and Logevall write, "From the prevalent notion of neighboring 'dominoes' falling one by one, it was but a short step to the more sophisticated credibility imperative." In other words, success in Vietnam "was essential lest both allies and adversaries *everywhere* lose faith in America's reliability and resolve." See Craig and Logevall, *America's Cold War*, 274.

27. See Nelson, *Pursuing Privacy in Cold War America*, 87.

28. Thomas J. Sugrue, *The Origins of the Urban Crisis: Race and Inequality in Postwar Detroit* (Princeton, NJ: Princeton University Press, 1996), 229.

29. Sugrue, *Origins of the Urban Crisis*, 177.

30. See Nadel, *Containment Culture*, 3.

31. Sugrue, *Origins of the Urban Crisis*, 141.

32. Sugrue writes, "Whether a neighborhood was covered by a restrictive covenant or not, if it was all white, realtors kept it that way." See *Origins of the Urban Crisis*, 46. The practice of "blockbusting" worked both ways: "helping blacks challenge the city's racial boundaries" on one hand, "while sowing panic among whites" on the other (Sugrue 194–95).

33. Citing "the extreme volatility that characterized the privacy migrations of the late 1950s to the early 1970s," Nelson notes that "[t]he 1980s

witnessed the revival of early cold war containment rhetoric." See *Pursuing Privacy in Cold War America*, xviii. She goes on to argue that in the late 1980s we see a shift "between the final end point of containment privacy . . . and a postcontainment privacy," concluding that "the breakdown of boundaries [between public and private] is rewritten not as pathology but as a process of disruption and repair" (xix).

34. See Hayden, *Building Suburbia*, 166.

35. May writes that "in 1959, two out of three Americans listed the possibility of nuclear war as the nation's most urgent problem. . . . Americans were well poised to embrace domesticity in the midst of the terrors of the atomic age." See May, *Homeward Bound*, 17.

36. Kaplan, "Homeland Insecurities," 59.

37. See Smith, *American Empire*, 5.

38. Kunstler, *Geography of Nowhere*, 195.

39. Womack and Mallory-Kani, "'Why don't you just leave it up to nature,'" 160.

40. Michael Kowalewski, "Bioregional Perspectives in American Literature," in *Regionalism Reconsidered: New Approaches to the Field*, ed. David Jordan (New York: Garland, 1994), 31.

41. See Christian Long, "Running Out of Gas: The Energy Crisis in 1970s Suburban Narratives," *Canadian Review of American Studies* 41, no. 3 (2011): 357. In general, Long's reading of the novel is astute, especially his contention that the unsustainability of "[t]he suburban built environment generates its own destruction" (362), but the suggestion that the suicides were "a refutation of the suburban form, a cry against the suburban development pattern's larger self-destructive logic" (357), attributes a sense of political agency to the girls that the novel does not bear out.

42. Sellers, *Crabgrass Crucible*, 254–55.

43. Lutz, *Cosmopolitan Vistas*, 31.

44. Gillan D'Arcy Wood, "What Is Sustainability Studies?" *American Literary History* 24, no. 1 (2012): 9.

Chapter 5. Moving Back, Moving On: Transnational Suburban Regions

1. Andres Duany, Elizabeth Plater-Zyberk, and Jeff Speck, *Suburban Nation: The Rise of Sprawl and the Decline of the American Dream* (New York: North Point Press, 2010), xix. Subsequent references are cited in the text.

2. Hayden, *Building Suburbia*, 202. Soja uses similar language to describe New Urbanism as "a peculiar postmodern combination of historical urban nostalgia and present-day postsuburbia." See Soja, *Postmetropolis*, 248.

3. Jim Lewis, "Battle for Biloxi," *New York Times Magazine*, May 21, 2006, https://www.nytimes.com/2006/05/21/magazine/21biloxi.html.

4. See Chad Garrison, "Trouble in Paradise," *Riverfront Times*, September 9, 2009, https://www.riverfronttimes.com/news/trouble-in-paradise-new-town-residents-split-over-what-constitutes-loud-2584245.

5. Lewis, "Battle for Biloxi."

6. On the "voracious needs" of the automobile and the "space-grabbing, free-for-all highway," see Kay, *Asphalt Nation*, 58. See especially "The Landscape of the Exit Ramp" (55–78) and "The Road to Environmental Ruin" (79–99).

7. See Michael Warner's *Publics and Counterpublics* (New York: Zone Books, 2002). Warner is specifically interested in the emancipatory potential of counterpublics of sex and gender. Counterpublics always define themselves in tension with the dominant public, but as opposed to the bourgeois public sphere, which consists of individuals whose identities have already been formed in the (heterosexual) context of the private sphere, counterpublics "are scenes of association and identity that transform the private lives they mediate" (57). Warner elaborates seven essential elements for such publics if they are to be viable, including that public discourse must be "poetic," that is invested in the creation of "world-making projects" (67–113).

8. Such attempts can create unintended effects. See Barbara Eckstein, "Making Space: Stories in the Practice of Planning," in *Story and Sustainability: Planning, Practice, and Possibility for American Cities*, ed. Barbara Eckstein and James A. Throgmorton (Cambridge, MA: MIT Press, 2003), 13–36. Regarding the introduction to *Suburban Nation*, Eckstein writes that the "forces shaping the actual reader may in fact be so far outside of the conscription proposed by the story that the reading is a blatantly resistant one" (32). Economic conditions, residential choices, and commuting options may all place an individual outside the windshield-view perspective the authors construct. Elaborating on her own "resistant" reading, Eckstein concludes, "Duany et al. have lost me as a conscriptee" (32).

9. Gayatri Chakravorty Spivak, *Death of a Discipline* (New York: Columbia University Press, 2003), 42.

10. Blomley, *Unsettling the City*, 50–51. Hayden makes a similar case for the relationship between public history's role in remaking the residential landscape: "Interpretation of the history of suburbs is a powerful tool to support reconstruction. Public history can convey the long ideological battle between the suburbs as places of aspiration and hard work and suburbs as places of segregation, stratification, special interests, and profiteering." See Hayden, *Building Suburbia*, 243.

11. Calthorpe and Fulton, *Regional City*, 277.

12. Calthorpe and Fulton, 271.

13. In discussing the history of sprawl, the authors of *Suburban Nation* do acknowledge, in a footnote, that "[t]he strict separation of housing types actually hints at a more insidious cause of sprawl, economic discrimination, or sometimes simple racism" (Duany et al., 10). There is also a passing reference to "racially based white flight" (130), and in a chapter dedicated to "The Inner City," they note, "Racism, redlining, and the concentration of subsidized housing projects destabilized and isolated the poor, while federal home-loan programs, targeting new construction exclusively, encouraged the deterioration and abandonment of urban housing" (153–54).

14. Stephanie Foote, *Regional Fictions: Culture and Identity in Nineteenth Century American Literature* (Madison: University of Wisconsin Press, 2001), 13.

15. Richard Ford, *The Lay of the Land* (2006; repr., New York: Vintage, 2007), 483. Subsequent references are cited in the text.

16. Quoted in Stephen J. Dubner, "What Is the Future of Suburbia? A Freakonomics Quorum," *Freakonomics: The Hidden Side of Everything*, August 12, 2008, www.freakonomics.com/2008/08/12/what-is -the-future-of-suburbia-a-freakonomics-quorum/.

17. For numbers on Orange County, see Adam Nagourney, "Orange County Is No Longer Nixon Country," *New York Times*, August 19, 2010, www.nytimes.com/2010/08/30/us/politics/30orange.html?_r=1 &scp=&st=nyt. On Fairfax County, see David Plotz, "Notes from Tysons Corner; A Suburb All Grown Up and Paved Over," *New York Times*, June 19, 2002, https://www.nytimes.com/2002/06/19/opinions/notes -from-tysons-corner-a-suburb-all-grown-up-and-paved-over.html.

18. Richard D. Alba et al., "Immigrant Groups in the Suburbs: A Reexamination of Suburbanization and Spatial Assimilation," *American Sociological Review* 64, no. 3 (1999): 447.

19. Alba et al., "Immigrant Groups in the Suburbs," 458. See also "The New Ethnic Enclaves in America's Suburbs," Lewis Mumford Center for Comparative Urban and Regional Research, Albany, New York, 2001,

http://mumford.albany.edu/census/suburban/SuburbanReport/page1
.html. The report notes that "[w]hites continue to be the most suburban of major racial and ethnic groups; nationally nearly 71% of whites
now live in suburbs." But the report also notes discernible changes
across several demographics: "More than half of Asians (58%) lived
in suburbs in 2000, up from 53% in 1990, and nearly half of Hispanics
(49%, up from 46%). Lagging behind are African Americans (39%),
though their current situation also represents a marked increase from
1990 (34%)." Nevertheless, segregation remains the norm: "As new
minority residents have entered suburbia, they have been separated
from whites to the same degree as was found ten years before [1990
to 2000]."

20. Chang-rae Lee, *Aloft* (New York: Riverhead, 2004), 72–73. Subsequent
    references are cited in the text.
21. Mark C. Jerng, "Nowhere in Particular: Perceiving Race, Change-rae
    Lee's *Aloft*, and the Question of Asian American Fiction," *Mfs* 56, no. 1
    (2010): 196.
22. Chang-rae Lee, *A Gesture Life* (New York: Riverhead, 1999), 44.
23. Dante A. Ciampaglia, "An Inside Look at How HGTV Became an
    Industry Juggernaut," *Architectural Digest/AD Pro*, July 29, 2019,
    https://www.architecturaldigest.com/story/how-hgtv-became-industry
    -juggernaut.
24. Ciampaglia, "Inside Look at How HGTV Became an Industry
    Juggernaut."
25. Mike Davis, *Magical Urbanism: Latinos Reinvent the US City* (New
    York: Verso, 2001), 80.
26. Davis, *Magical Urbanism*, 96.
27. Jacobson makes a similar observation about the corporate executive,
    writing that "Lee's novel portrays the real trend of foreigners taking
    advantage of increased buying power and a weak dollar by scooping
    up U.S. properties." See Jacobson, *Neodomestic American Fiction*, 132.
28. Jameson, "Postmodernism and Consumer Society," 125, 124–25.
29. See Kowalewski, "Bioregional Perspectives in American Literature," 44.
30. For one example, see Hayden, *Building Suburbia*, 230–48.
31. Jacobson, *Neodomestic American Fiction*, 133.
32. Knapp, *American Unexceptionalism*, 47.
33. See Stephanie Coontz, *The Way We Really Are: Coming to Terms
    with America's Changing Families* (New York: Basic Books, 1997). She
    argues that 1950s viewers "watched [sitcoms] to see how families were
    supposed to live—and also to get a little reassurance that they were
    headed in the right direction" (38).

34. Richard Ford, *Let Me Be Frank with You* (2014; repr., New York: Ecco, 2015), 7. On Frank as suburban "everyman," see Knapp, *American Unexceptionalism*, 1–22. See also Rubén Peinado Abarrio, "Richard Ford's Frank Bascombe as an American Everyman," *Miscelánea* 50 (2014): 49–60.
35. Knapp, *American Unexceptionalism*, 16.
36. Robert H. Brinkmeyer, Jr., "Richard Ford: *The Lay of the Land*," in *Still in Print: The Southern Novel Today*, ed. Jan Nordby Gretlund (Columbia: University of South Carolina Press, 2010), 258.
37. Knapp, *American Unexceptionalism*, 17, 22.
38. Tim Foster, "'A more interesting surgery on the suburbs': Richard Ford's Paean to the New Jersey Periphery," in *New Suburban Stories*, ed. Martin Dines and Timotheus Vermeulen (London: Bloomsbury, 2013), 150.
39. Richard Ford, *Independence Day* (1995; repr., New York: Vintage, 1996), 57, 151–52.
40. Drawing on Svetlana Boym's conception of "restorative nostalgia," Knapp argues that, at the end of *Independence Day*, Ford delivers a "sentimental portrait of a communal history meant to induce in readers a longing for an idealized past. . . . Ford succumbs to the national myth of exceptionalism that reinforces the rampant individualism the novel sought to challenge in the first place." See *American Unexceptionalism*, 14.
41. Ford, *Independence Day*, 442.
42. Knapp, *American Unexceptionalism*, 19.
43. Matthew Guinn, "Into the Suburbs: Richard Ford's Sportswriter Novels and the Place of Southern Fiction," in *South to a New Place: Region, Literature, Culture*, ed. Suzanne Whitmore Jones and Sharon Monteith (Baton Rouge: Louisiana State University Press, 2002), 197, 202.
44. Brinkmeyer, "Richard Ford," 248.
45. Abarrio, "Richard Ford's Frank Bascombe as an American Everyman," 51.
46. Richard Ford, *The Sportswriter* (1986; repr., New York: Vintage, 1995), 115.
47. Wendell Smith, "The Life of the Writer: Lunch with Richard Ford," in *Conversations with Richard Ford*, ed. Huey Guagliardo (Jackson: University Press of Mississippi, 2001), 54.
48. Fred Hobson, "*The Sportswriter*: Post-Faulkner, Post-Southern?" in *Perspectives on Richard Ford*, ed. Huey Guagliardo (Jackson: University Press of Mississippi, 2000), 90, 91.

49. Soja, *Postmetropolis*, 152.
50. On narrative, see Blomley, *Unsettling the City*, 50–51. Kunstler quoted in Dubner, "What Is the Future of Suburbia? A Freakonomics Quorum."

Chapter 6. Housing Crises: Race, History, and Recession-Era Domesticity

1. *Diary of a Very Bad Year: Confessions of an Anonymous Hedge Fund Manager*, interviews with *n+1*, intro. Keith Gessen (New York: Harper, 2010), 53.
2. *Diary of a Very Bad Year*, 63–65.
3. Roger Lowenstein, *The End of Wall Street* (New York: Penguin, 2010), 23.
4. See Raghuram G. Rajan, *Fault Lines: How Hidden Fractures Still Threaten the World Economy* (Princeton, NJ: Princeton University Press, 2010), 36.
5. See Lowenstein, *The End of Wall Street*, 19.
6. Lowenstein, 37.
7. Rajan, *Fault Lines*, 31.
8. *Diary of a Very Bad Year*, 15.
9. Rajan directs some of the blame onto consumers who purchased houses they could not afford. He writes that, during the housing bubble, "rising house prices gave subprime borrowers the ability to keep refinancing into low interest rate mortgages (thus avoiding default) even as they withdrew the home equity they had built up to buy more cars and TV sets. For many, the need to repay loans seemed remote and distant." See Rajan, *Fault Lines*, 5–6.
10. *Diary of a Very Bad Year*, 81. While taking a much broader view of government- and private-sector responsibility for the crisis, Rajan makes a similar point: "the nature of the reward structure in the financial system, whether implicit or explicit, emphasizes short-term advantages and may predispose bankers to take these risks." See Rajan, *Fault Lines*, 17. On the role of the government, Rajan writes, "Without any intent of absolving the brokers and the banks who originated the bad loans or the borrowers who lied about their incomes, we should acknowledge the evidence suggesting that government actions, however well intended, contributed significantly to the crisis" (40).
11. Rajan, *Fault Lines*, 9.
12. Rajan writes that "although housing booms took place around the world, driven by low interest rates, the boom in the United States was especially pronounced among borrowers who had not had prior easy

access to credit, the subprime and Alt-A segments of the market." See *Fault Lines*, 41. Lowenstein also notes, "In 2002, subprime issuance totaled $200 billion. By 2004, it was over $400 billion. As a percentage of annual volume, subprimes now topped 16 percent—up from a mere 8 percent a couple years earlier and hardly anything in the '90s." See *The End of Wall Street*, 19.

13. Heather McGhee, *The Sum of Us: What Racism Costs Everyone and How We Can Prosper Together* (New York: One World, 2021), 70.

14. McGhee, *The Sum of Us*, 70.

15. Laurie Goodman, Jun Zhu, and Rolf Pendall, "Are Gains in Black Homeownership History?" *Urban Wire: Housing and Housing Finance*, Urban Institute, February 15, 2017, https://www.urban.org /urban-wire/are-gains-black-homeownership-history.

16. Goodman, Zhu, and Pendall, "Are Gains in Black Homeownership History?"

17. Lowenstein writes, "By summer [2008], Americans were handing their keys to their bankers at a rate of 280,000 a month, up from a mere 74,000 in 2005." See *The End of Wall Street*, 147. Each interview in *Diary of a Very Bad Year* begins with a set of statistics, including the Dow Jones Industrial Average, the unemployment rate, and foreclosures. For summer 2009 totals, see *Diary of a Very Bad Year*, 181, 209.

18. Department of the Treasury, "The Financial Crisis Response: In Charts," April 2012, https://www.slideshare.net/USTreasuryDept /20120413-financial-crisisresponse

19. Jurca, *White Diaspora*, 134.

20. See Rome, *The Bulldozer in the Countryside*, 7.

21. George W. Bush, "Remarks by the President on Homeownership" (speech, Department of Housing and Urban Development, Washington DC, June 18, 2002). The full quote reads: "I believe when somebody owns their own home, they're realizing the American Dream." Quoted in Rajan, *Fault Lines*, 37.

22. See Thomas Jefferson, Query XIX, *Notes on the State of Virginia* (1787), http://xroads.virginia.edu/~hyper/hns/yoeman/qxix.html. He claims that "Those who labour in the earth are the chosen people of God, if ever he had a chosen people," and he roundly condemns city life: "The mobs of great cities add just so much to the support of pure government, as sores do to the strenth [*sic*] of the human body."

23. Quoted in Rome, *Bulldozer in the Countryside*, 257.

24. Sellers writes, "Echoing the old Jeffersonian rhetoric about the yeoman farmer, the new exponents of home ownership downplayed the debts often incurred, even as the improving terms of the typical

mortgage enabled more speculative and long-term borrowing." See Sellers, *Crabgrass Crucible*, 25.

25. See Fetterley and Pryse, *Writing out of Place*, 11. In part, this chapter adapts and extends their understanding of "region" and "regionalism" in the nineteenth century to the era of the housing crisis and the Great Recession.

26. On the family-thriller genre, see Steph Cha, "Review: Jung Yun's Family Drama 'Shelter' Reads Like a Suspenseful Thriller," *Los Angeles Times*, March, 25 2016, https://www.latimes.com/books /la-ca-jc-jung-yun-20160313-story.html. See also Shalene Gupta, "Review: 'Shelter' Is a Compelling Novel of the Sometimes Chilly Bond between Child and Parents," *National Book Review*, April, 27 2016, https://www.thenationalbookreview.com/features/2016/4/27/kf ccbiuh5hxjk7xhodczcf4nzdo83f.

27. Rani Neutill, "Jun Yun's 'Shelter,'" *New York Times*, March 18, 2016, https://www.nytimes.com/2016/03/20/books/review/jung-yuns-shelter .html.

28. Jung Yun, *Shelter* (New York: Picador, 2016), 12. Subsequent references are cited in the text.

29. Jacobson, *Neodomestic American Fiction*, 2.

30. Jacobson, 14, 4.

31. Kevin Nance, "Jung Yun Interweaves Traditional Parenting, True Crime in Debut Novel 'Shelter,'" *Chicago Tribune*, March 17, 2016, https://www.chicagotribune.com/entertainment/books/ct-prj-shelter -jung-yun-20160317-story.html.

32. Andrew Jackson Downing, *The Architecture of Country Houses* (New York: Appleton, 1850), v. Subsequent references are cited in the text.

33. See "*House Beautiful* presents . . . a symbol of what we're fighting for . . . A Fine Home and a Beautiful Garden," 29+. See also "Looking Forward: Help Yourself—and Your Architect—by Keeping Your Mind Open to New Ideas," 33.

34. See Keil, "Global Suburb: Divesting from the World's White Picket Fences," 365.

35. Ernest Hemingway, *The Sun Also Rises* (1926; repr., New York: Scribner, 2006), 60.

36. In Gaston Bachelard's meditations on domestic spaces, he dedicates a chapter to the metaphor of the shell. He writes, "A creature that hides and 'withdraws into its shell,' is preparing a 'way out.' This is true of the entire scale of metaphors, from the resurrection of a man in his grave, to the sudden outburst of one who has long been silent. If we remain at the heart of the image under consideration, we have the impression

that, by staying in the motionlessness of its shell, the creature is pre-
paring temporal explosions, not to say whirlwinds, of being." See
Bachelard, *The Poetics of Space*, trans. Maria Jolas (1964; repr., Boston:
Beacon Press, 1994), 111.

37. Patrick Flanery, *Fallen Land* (New York: Riverhead Books, 2013), 70.
Subsequent references are cited in the text.

38. William Faulkner, *Requiem for a Nun* (1951; repr., New York: Vintage,
2011), 73.

39. Fetterley and Pryse, *Writing out of Place*, 6.

40. Nelson, *Pursuing Privacy in Cold War America*, 26.

41. Lefebvre, *Production of Space*, 93.

42. John Cheever, *Bullet Park* (New York: Knopf, 1969), 245.

43. Michelle Alexander, *The New Jim Crow: Mass Incarceration in the Age
of Colorblindness*, rev. ed. (New York: New Press, 2012), 13. This proposed system in Flanery's novel provides a historical echo of the "black
codes" and vagrancy laws in the South that, as Alexander writes, were
intended "to establish another system of forced labor" after slavery
had been abolished (28).

44. Patrick Flanery, interview by Christopher Holmes, *Contemporary Literature* 54, no. 3 (2013): 458.

45. The *Guardian* and the *New York Times* offer representative laudatory
reviews, specifically as to the novel's treatment of the American Dream
and the rise of corporate power at the expense of civil liberties. See
John Burnside, "*Fallen Land* by Patrick Flanery–Review," *Guardian*,
April 24, 2013, https://www.theguardian.com/books/2013/apr/24
/fallen-land-patrick-flanery-review; see David Vann, "Company Man,"
review of *Fallen Land*, by Patrick Flanery, *New York Times*, October
4, 2013, https://www.nytimes.com/2013/10/06/books/review/fallen
-land-by-patrick-flanery.html. Despite *Fallen Land*'s provocative
subject matter, the *Telegraph* reads the novel as "an interesting and
intermittently brilliant mess," and in a mostly positive review, the
Boston Globe declares, "there are so many in-your-face portents of
disaster . . . that it sometimes seems as if Flanery is doing a parody
of a textbook foretelling techniques." See James Walton, "Fallen
Land," review of *Fallen Land*, by Patrick Flanery, *Telegraph*, June 8,
2013, https://www.telegraph.co.uk/culture/books/10091434/Fallen
-Land-by-Patrick-Flanery-review.html; Jan Stuart, review of *Fallen
Land* by Patrick Flanery, *Boston Globe*, August 17, 2013, https://www
.bostonglobe.com/arts/books/2013/08/17/shadow-land/X5sKXiD
PRKaZu4MYsl3SiJ/story.html.

46. In Dave Eggers's *The Circle*, the titular corporation—a menacing combination of Google and Facebook—sets its sights on facilitating every aspect of civil, social, and political life. Its "SeeChange" program installs millions of cameras around the world, encouraging both private citizens and public officials to lead "transparent" lives: "As we all know here at the Circle, transparency leads to peace of mind." See Dave Eggers, *The Circle* (New York: Vintage, 2013), 69.

47. Buell, *Writing for an Endangered World*, 18.

48. Keil, "Global Suburb: Divesting from the World's White Picket Fences," 362–64.

Epilogue: The End of the Suburbs?

1. Jed Kolko, "The Continued Suburbanization of America," in Berger and Kotkin, *Infinite Suburbia*, 209. He writes that "recent trends look more cyclical than structural. The bubble favored housing construction and population growth in exurban and rural areas, where there was land to build on and housing prices that remained somewhat affordable . . . . The bust put an end to this low-density hyper-growth. In the recovery, rental apartments have led the construction rebound. But even with this cyclical boost, in 2014 population growth in the densest quartile of counties has once again fallen behind that in the second and third quartiles, the suburbs and exurbs" (211).

2. Alan M. Berger, "The Suburb of the Future, Almost Here," *New York Times*, September 15, 2017, https://www.nytimes.com/2017/09/15/sunday-review/future-suburb-millennials.html.

3. Morley Winograd and Michael D. Hais, "Millennials' Hearts Are in the Suburbs," in Berger and Kotkin, *Infinite Suburbia*, 67.

4. Winograd and Hais, "Millennials' Hearts Are in the Suburbs," 68, 71.

5. Donald J. Trump (@realDonaldTrump), "The Suburban Housewives of America must read this article. Biden will destroy your neighborhood and your American Dream. I will preserve it, and make it even better!" Twitter, July 23, 2020, 11:45 a.m. The tweet is no longer available since the former president's account has been suspended. For a discussion of the tweet's racist subtext, see Annie Karni, Maggie Haberman, and Sydney Ember, "Trump Plays on Racist Fears of Terrorized Suburbs to Court White Voters," *New York Times*, July 29, 2020, https://www.nytimes.com/2020/07/29/us/politics/trump-suburbs-housing-white-voters.html.

6. National Fair Housing Alliance, "Further Fair Housing," National Fair Housing.org (2020), https://nationalfairhousing.org/affirmatively -furthering-fair-housing/. Although the AFFH was included as part of the 1968 Fair Housing Act, it proved largely ineffective due to lack of data gathering, oversight, or consequences for noncompliance. Under President Obama, according to Danielle Kurtzleben, the new policy directs "jurisdictions that receive federal housing funds that they have to assess what patterns of housing discrimination they have and then come up with a plan to diminish them. It also provides a data-based tool for communities to use in doing this assessment." See Kurtzleben, "Seeking Suburban Votes, Trump to Repeal Rule Combating Racial Bias in Housing," *NPR*, July 21, 2020, https://www.npr .org/2020/07/21/893471887/seeking-suburban-votes-trump-targets -rule-to-combat-racial-bias-in-housing.

7. Ali Modarres, "Reexamining Race and Ethnicity in the Suburbs," in Berger and Kotkin, *Infinite Suburbia*, 135.

8. Modarres, "Reexamining Race," 144.

9. Citing a Brookings study, Nicole Stelle Garnett writes "that the number of poor individuals living in suburban neighborhoods where poverty rates exceed 40 percent rose by 63 percent between 2001 and 2010, mostly heavily concentrated in inner suburban communities." See Garnett, "Old Suburbs Meet New Urbanism," in Berger and Kotkin, *Infinite Suburbia*, 676.

10. See "Struggling in the Suburbs," Editorial, *New York Times*, July 7, 2012, https://www.nytimes.com/2012/07/08/opinion/sunday/struggling -in-the-suburbs.html.

11. See "America's Millennial Baby Bust," Editorial, *Wall Street Journal*, May 28, 2019, https://www.wsj.com/articles/americas-millennial-baby -bust-11559086198. See also Ross Douthat, "How Does a Baby Bust End?," *New York Times*, March 27, 2021, https://www.nytimes.com /2021/03/27/opinion/sunday/fertility-population-baby-bust.html.

12. See Conor Dougherty and Ben Casselman, "House Hunters Are Leaving the City, and Builders Can't Keep Up," *New York Times*, May 29, 2021, https://www.nytimes.com/2021/05/29/business/economy/new -home-building-suburbs.html.

13. Gallagher, *End of the Suburbs*, 210.

14. Gallagher, 163–64, 200–2. While Gallagher does acknowledge a rise in suburban poverty levels (16–17, 177–79), the antidotes to decentered, automobile-dependent suburban dwellings she identifies cater to an affluent clientele.

15. Calthorpe and Fulton, *Regional City*, 30.

16. Wood, "What Is Sustainability Studies?" 9.

17. Sellers, *Crabgrass Crucible*, 42.

18. Sarah Jack Hinners, "The Cosmopolitan Ecology of Suburbia," in Berger and Kotkin, *Infinite Suburbia*, 461, 462.

Bibliography

Abarrio, Rubén Peinado. "Richard Ford's Frank Bascombe as an American Everyman." *Miscelánea* 50 (2014): 49–60.

Alba, Richard D., John R. Logan, Brian J. Stults, Gilbert Marzan, and Wenquan Zhang. "Immigrant Groups in the Suburbs: A Reexamination of Suburbanization and Spatial Assimilation." *American Sociological Review* 64, no. 3 (1999): 446–60.

Alexander, Michelle. *The New Jim Crow: Mass Incarceration in the Age of Colorblindness.* Rev. ed. New York: New Press, 2012.

"America's Millennial Baby Bust." Editorial, *Wall Street Journal*, May 28, 2019. https://www.wsj.com/articles/americas-millennial-baby-bust-11559086198.

Anderson, Jill E. "'The Whole Imprisoning Wasteland Beyond': Forces of Nature, Ableism, and Suburban Dis-ease in Midcentury Literature." In *Disability and the Environment in American Literature: Toward an Ecosomatic Paradigm*, edited by Matthew J. C. Cella, 133–49. Lanham, MD: Lexington, 2016.

Avilez, GerShun. "Housing the Black Body: Value, Domestic Space, and Segregation Narratives." *African American Review* 42, no. 1 (2008): 135–47.

Bachelard, Gaston. *The Poetics of Space.* Translated by Maria Jolas. 1964. Reprint, Boston: Beacon Press, 1994.

Bailey, Blake. *Cheever: A Life.* New York: Knopf, 2009.

Baker, Houston A., Jr. *Workings of the Spirit: The Poetics of Afro-American Women's Writing.* Chicago: University of Chicago Press, 1991.

Baldellou, Marta Miquel. "Inheriting Traditional Roles of American Female Growth: From Louisa May Alcott's *Little Women* to Jeffrey Eugenides's *The Virgin Suicides*." In *New Literatures of Old: Dialogues of Tradition and Innovation in Anglophone Literature*, edited by José Ramón Prado-Pérez and Dídac Llorens Cubedo, 127–35. New Castle, U.K.: Cambridge Scholars, 2008.

Baldwin, James. "Image of the Negro." Books in Review. *Commentary*, April 1948, 378–80.

Barrett, Laura. "Don DeLillo." In *The Cambridge Companion to American Fiction after 1945*, edited by John N. Duvall, 244–55. Cambridge: Cambridge University Press, 2012.

Basu, Biman. "Reading the Techno-Ethnic Other in DeLillo's *White Noise*." *Arizona Quarterly* 61, no. 2 (2005): 87–111.

Beauregard, Robert. *Voices of Decline: The Postwar Fate of U.S. Cities*. 2nd ed. New York: Routledge, 2003.

Berger, Alan M. "The Suburb of the Future, Almost Here." *New York Times*, September 15, 2017. https://www.nytimes.com/2017/09/15 /sunday-review/future-suburb-millennials.html.

Berger, Alan M., and Joel Kotkin, eds. *Infinite Suburbia*. With Celina Balderas Guzmán. New York: Princeton Architectural Press, 2017.

Bernard, Sarah. "Jonathan Franzen's Story of O." *New York*, October 5, 2001. https://nymag.com/nymetro/arts/features/5341/.

Beuka, Robert. *SuburbiaNation: Reading Suburban Landscape in Twentieth-Century American Fiction and Film*. New York: Palgrave Macmillan, 2004.

Blaustein, Jessica. "Counterprivates: An Appeal to Rethink Suburban Interiority." *Iowa Journal of Cultural Studies* 3 (Fall 2003): 39–63.

Blomley, Nicholas. *Unsettling the City: Urban Land and the Politics of Property*. New York: Routledge, 2004.

Bogost, Ian. "When Malls Saved the Suburbs from Despair." *The Atlantic*, February 17, 2018. https://www.theatlantic.com/technology /archive/2018/02/when-malls-saved-cities-from-capitalism/553610/.

Bourdieu, Pierre. "The Essence of Neoliberalism." *Le Monde Diplomatique*, December 1998. http://mondediplo.com/1998/12/08bourdieu.

———. *The Field of Cultural Production: Essays on Art and Literature*. Edited by Randal Johnson. New York: Columbia University Press, 1993.

Brinkmeyer, Robert H., Jr. "Richard Ford: *The Lay of the Land*." In *Still in Print: The Southern Novel Today*, edited by Jan Nordby Gretlund, 248–59. Columbia: University of South Carolina Press, 2010.

Brooks, Richard R. W., and Carol M. Rose. *Saving the Neighborhood: Racially Restrictive Covenants, Law, and Social Norms*. Cambridge, MA: Harvard University Press, 2013.

Buell, Lawrence. "Toxic Discourse." *Critical Inquiry* 24, no. 3 (1998): 639–65.

———. *Writing for an Endangered World: Literature, Culture, and Environment in the U.S. and Beyond*. Cambridge, MA: Harvard University Press, 2001.

Burnside, John. "*Fallen Land* by Patrick Flanery–Review." *Guardian*, April 24, 2013. https://www.theguardian.com/books/2013/apr/24/fallen-land-patrick-flanery-review.

Calthorpe, Peter, and William Fulton. *The Regional City: Planning for the End of Sprawl*. Washington: Island Press, 2001.

Cenamor, Rubén. "What Have We Learnt Since the 1950s? The Return to Conservative Gender Roles in Sam Mendes's Film Adaptation of *Revolutionary Road*." In *Rethinking Gender in Popular Culture in the 21st Century: Marlboro Men and California Gurls*, edited by Astrid M. Fellner, Marta Fernández-Morales, and Martina Martausová, 163–84. New Castle, U.K.: Cambridge Scholars, 2017.

Cha, Steph. "Review: Jung Yun's Family Drama 'Shelter' Reads Like a Suspenseful Thriller." *Los Angeles Times*, March 25, 2016. https://www.latimes.com/books/la-ca-jc-jung-yun-20160313-story.html.

Chapman, Erin D. "Staging Gendered Radicalism at the Height of the US Cold War: *A Raisin in the Sun* and Lorraine Hansberry's Vision of Freedom." *Gender & History* 29, no. 2 (2017): 446–67.

Charlton-Jones, Kate. *Dismembering the American Dream: The Life and Fiction of Richard Yates*. Tuscaloosa: University of Alabama Press, 2014.

Cheever, John. *Bullet Park*. New York: Knopf, 1969.

———. *The Journals of John Cheever*. 1991. Reprint, New York: Ballantine Books, 1993.

———. *The Wapshot Chronicle*. 1957. Reprint, New York: Harper Perennial Classics, 2003.

———. *The Wapshot Scandal*. 1964. Reprint, New York: Perennial, 1973.

Ciampaglia, Dante A. "An Inside Look at How HGTV Became an Industry Juggernaut." *Architectural Digest/AD Pro*, July 29, 2019. https://www.architecturaldigest.com/story/how-hgtv-became-industry-juggernaut.

Ciocoi-Pop, Ana-Blanca. "Suicide as Affirmation and Gender as a Conscious Choice: The Deconstruction of Identity in Jeffrey Eugenides's Major Novels." *American, British, and Canadian Studies* 10 (July 2008): 80–90.

Clare, Ralph. *Fictions Inc.: The Corporation in Postmodern Fiction, Film and Popular Culture*. New Jersey: Rutgers University Press, 2014.

Clark, Keith. *The Radical Fiction of Ann Petry*. Baton Rouge: Louisiana State University Press, 2013.

Cooley, Will. "Moving On Out: Black Pioneering in Chicago, 1915–1950." *Journal of Urban History* 36, no. 4 (2010): 485–506.

Coontz, Stephanie. *The Way We Never Were: American Families and the Nostalgia Trap*. New York: Basic Books, 1992.

_____. *The Way We Really Are: Coming to Terms with America's Changing Families*. New York: Basic Books, 1997.

Corber, Robert J. *Homosexuality in Cold War America: Resistance and the Crisis of Masculinity*. Durham, NC: Duke University Press, 1997.

Craig, Campbell, and Fredrik Logevall. *America's Cold War: The Politics of Insecurity*. Cambridge, MA: Belknap-Harvard University Press, 2009.

Craig, Lois. "Suburbs." *Design Quarterly* 132 (1986): 1–32.

Cross, Gary. "The Suburban Weekend: Perspectives on a Vanishing Twentieth-Century Dream." In *Visions of Suburbia*, edited by Roger Silverstone, 108–31. New York: Routledge, 1997.

Cuordileone, K. A. *Manhood and American Political Culture in the Cold War*. New York: Routledge, 2005.

Dainotto, Roberto M. *Place in Literature: Regions, Cultures, Communities*. Ithaca, NY: Cornell University Press, 2000.

Dauterich, Edward. "*Kingsblood Royal's* Grand Republic: Sundown Town?" *MidAmerica* 39 (2012): 65–81.

Davis, Mike. *Magical Urbanism: Latinos Reinvent the US City*. New York: Verso, 2001.

The Decline of the American Male. By the Editors of *Look*. Illustrated by Robert Osborn. New York: Random House, 1958.

Deitering, Cynthia. "The Postnatural Novel: Toxic Consciousness in Fiction of the 1980s." In *The Ecocriticism Reader: Landmarks in Literary Ecology*, edited by Cheryll Glotfelty and Harold Fromm, 196–203. Athens: University of Georgia Press, 1996.

DeLillo, Don. *White Noise*. 1985. Reprint, New York: Penguin, 2009. Introduction by Richard Powers.

Delton, Jennifer. "Before the White Negro: Sin and Salvation in *Kingsblood Royal*." *American Literary History* 15, no. 2 (2003): 311–33.

Diary of a Very Bad Year: Confessions of an Anonymous Hedge Fund Manager. Interviews with *n+1*. Introduction by Keith Gessen. New York: Harper, 2010.

Dines, Martin. *The Literature of Suburban Change: Narrating Spatial Complexity in Metropolitan America*. Edinburgh, Scotland: Edinburgh University Press, 2020.

———. "Suburban Gothic and the Ethnic Uncanny in Jeffrey Eugenides's *The Virgin Suicides*." *Journal of American Studies* 46, no. 4 (2012): 959–75.

Dougherty, Conor, and Ben Casselman. "House Hunters Are Leaving the City, and Builders Can't Keep Up." *New York Times*, May 29, 2021. https://www.nytimes.com/2021/05/29/business/economy/new-home-building-suburbs.html.

Douthat, Ross. "How Does a Baby Bust End?" *New York Times*, March 27, 2021. https://www.nytimes.com/2021/03/27/opinion/sunday/fertility -population-baby-bust.html.

Downing, Andrew Jackson. *The Architecture of Country Houses*. New York: Appleton, 1850.

Duany, Andres, Elizabeth Plater-Zyberk, and Jeff Speck. *Suburban Nation: The Rise of Sprawl and the Decline of the American Dream*. New York: North Point Press, 2010.

Dubner, Stephen J. "What Is the Future of Suburbia? A Freakonomics Quorum." *Freakonomics: The Hidden Side of Everything*, August 12, 2008. www.freakonomics.com/2008/08/12/what-is-the-future-of -suburbia-a-freakonomics-quorum/.

Duggan, Lisa. *The Twilight of Equality?: Neoliberalism, Cultural Politics, and the Attack on Democracy*. Boston: Beacon Press, 2003.

Eckstein, Barbara. "Making Space: Stories in the Practice of Planning." In *Story and Sustainability: Planning, Practice, and Possibility for American Cities*, edited by Barbara Eckstein and James A. Throgmorton, 13–36. Cambridge, MA: MIT Press, 2003.

Edwards, Thomas R. "Oprah's Choice." *Raritan* 21 (Spring 2002): 75–86.

Eggers, Dave. *The Circle*. New York: Vintage, 2013.

Esteve, Mary. *Incremental Realism: Postwar American Fiction, Happiness, and Welfare-State Liberalism*. Stanford, CA: Stanford University Press, 2021.

Eugenides, Jeffrey. Interview by Jonathan Safran Foer. *Bomb* 81 (Fall 2002). https://bombmagazine.org/articles/jeffrey-eugenides.

——. *Middlesex*. New York: Picador, 2002.

——. *The Virgin Suicides*. New York: Picador, 1993.

Falk, Claudia. "'And I Mean Is It Any Wonder All the Men End up Emasculated?' Post-War Masculinities in Richard Yates's *Revolutionary Road* and John Braine's *Room at the Top*." In *Post-World War II Masculinities in British and American Literature and Culture: Towards Comparative Masculinity Studies*, edited by Stefan Horlacher and Kevin Floyd, 55–68. New York: Routledge, 2016.

Faulkner, William. *Requiem for a Nun*. 1951. Reprint, New York: Vintage, 2011.

Feig, Paul, dir. *Arrested Development*. Season 1, episode 22, "Let 'Em Eat Cake." Written by Mitchell Hurwitz and Jim Vallely. Aired June 6, 2004; in broadcast syndication; 20th Century Fox, 2004, DVD.

Ferraro, Thomas J. "Whole Families Shopping at Night!" In *New Essays on White Noise*, edited by Frank Lentricchia, 15–38. Cambridge: Cambridge University Press, 1991.

Fetterley, Judith, and Marjorie Pryse. *Writing out of Place: Regionalism, Women, and American Literary Culture*. Urbana: University of Illinois Press, 2003.

"FHA Can't Prevent Housing Ban." *New York Times*, March 19, 1949. In Nicolaides and Wiese, *Suburb Reader*, 327–28.

Flanery, Patrick. *Fallen Land*. New York: Riverhead Books, 2013.

———. Interview by Christopher Holmes. *Contemporary Literature* 54, no. 3 (2013): 426–58.

Fleming, Robert E. "*Kingsblood Royal* and the Black 'Passing' Novel." In *Critical Essays on Sinclair Lewis*, edited by Martin Bucco, 213–21. Boston: G. K. Hall, 1986.

Foote, Stephanie. *Regional Fictions: Culture and Identity in Nineteenth Century American Literature*. Madison: University of Wisconsin Press, 2001.

Ford, Richard. *Independence Day*. 1995. Reprint, New York: Vintage, 1996.

———. *The Lay of the Land*. 2006. Reprint, New York: Vintage, 2007.

———. *Let Me Be Frank with You*. 2014. Reprint, New York: Ecco, 2015.

———. *The Sportswriter*. 1986. Reprint, New York: Vintage, 1995.

Foster, Tim. "'A more interesting surgery on the suburbs': Richard Ford's Paean to the New Jersey Periphery." In *New Suburban Stories*, edited by Martin Dines and Timotheus Vermeulen, 141–50. London: Bloomsbury, 2013.

Foucault, Michel. *The Birth of Biopolitics: Lectures at the Collège de France, 1978–1979*. Edited by Michel Senellart. Translated by Graham Burchell. New York: Picador, 2008.

———. "Space, Knowledge, and Power." In *The Foucault Reader*, edited by Paul Rabinow, 239–56. New York: Pantheon, 1984.

Franzen, Jonathan. *How to Be Alone: Essays*. New York: Farrar, Straus, Giroux, 2003.

———. Letter to Don DeLillo. June 12, 1995. Harry Ransom Center, University of Texas at Austin.

———. Letter to Don DeLillo. July 29, 1995. Harry Ransom Center, University of Texas at Austin.

———. Letter to Don DeLillo, March 31, 1997. Harry Ransom Center, University of Texas at Austin.

———. *The Twenty-Seventh City*. New York: Farrar, Straus, Giroux, 1988.

Friedan, Betty. *The Feminine Mystique*. 1963. Reprint, New York: Norton, 1974.

Friedman, Thomas L. "The First Law of Petropolitics." *Foreign Policy* (May/June 2006): 28–36.

Frug, Gerald. *City Making: Building Communities Without Building Walls*. Princeton, NJ: Princeton University Press, 1999.

Gallagher, Leigh. *The End of the Suburbs: Where the American Dream Is Moving*. New York: Penguin, 2013.

Garnett, Nicole Stelle. "Old Suburbs Meet New Urbanism." In Berger and Kotkin, *Infinite Suburbia*, 674–81.

Garnett, William A. *Lakewood, California*. 1950. Photograph, gelatin silver prints. J. Paul Getty Museum, Los Angeles. www.getty.edu/art /collection/object/108G27.

Garreau, Joel. *Edge City: Life on the New Frontier*. New York: Doubleday, 1991.

Garrison, Chad. "Trouble in Paradise." *Riverfront Times*, September 9, 2009. https://www.riverfronttimes.com/news/trouble-in-paradise -new-town-residents-split-over-what-constitutes-loud-2584245.

George, Joseph. *Postmodern Suburban Spaces: Philosophy, Ethics, and Community in Post-War American Fiction*. Switzerland: Palgrave Macmillan/Springer, 2016.

Geyh, Paula E. "Assembling Postmodernism: Experience, Meaning, and the Space In-Between." *College Literature* 30, no. 2 (2003): 1–29.

Ghani, Hana' Khalief. "I Have a Dream—Racial Discrimination in Lorraine Hansberry's *A Raisin in the Sun*." *Theory and Practice in Language Studies* 1, no. 6 (2011): 607–14.

Giles, Jeff. "Books: Errors and 'Corrections.'" *Newsweek*, November 4, 2001. https://www.newsweek.com/books-errors-and-corrections-149529.

Gillem, Mark L. *America Town: Building the Outposts of Empire*. Minneapolis: University of Minnesota Press, 2007.

Gilman, Richard. "Dante of Suburbia." *Commonweal*, December 19, 1958, 320.

Ginsberg, Allen. *Howl and Other Poems*. San Francisco: City Lights Books, 1956.

Giroux, Henry A. "The Terror of Neoliberalism: Rethinking the Significance of Cultural Politics." *College Literature* 32, no. 1 (2005): 1–19.

Goodman, Laurie, Alanna McCargo, and Jun Zhu. "A Closer Look at the Fifteen-Year Drop in Black Homeownership." Blog post. *Urban Wire: Housing and Housing Finance*. Urban Institute, February 13, 2018. https://www.urban.org/urban-wire/closer-look-fifteen-year-drop -black-homeownership.

Goodman, Laurie, Jun Zhu, and Rolf Pendall. "Are Gains in Black Homeownership History?" Blog post. *Urban Wire: Housing and Housing Finance*, Urban Institute, February 15, 2017. https://www.urban.org /urban-wire/are-gains-black-homeownership-history.

Gordon, Michelle. "'Somewhat Like War': The Aesthetics of Segregation, Black Liberation, and *A Raisin in the Sun*." *African American Review* 42, no. 1 (2008): 121–33.

Guinn, Matthew. "Into the Suburbs: Richard Ford's Sportswriter Novels and the Place of Southern Fiction." In *South to a New Place: Region, Literature, Culture,* edited by Suzanne Whitmore Jones and Sharon Monteith, 196–207. Baton Rouge: Louisiana State University Press, 2002.

Gupta, Shalene. "Review: 'Shelter' Is a Compelling Novel of the Sometimes Chilly Bond between Child and Parents." *National Book Review,* April 27, 2016. https://www.thenationalbookreview.com /features/2016/4/27/kfccbiuh5hxjk7xhodczcf4nzd083f.

Hajek, Friederike. "Richard Wright's *Native Son* and Ann Petry's *The Street*: Problems of Commitment and Authority." In *Looking Inward, Looking Outward: American Fiction in the 1930s and 1940s,* edited by Hans Bak and Vincent Piket, 45–52. Bochum, Germany: European University Press, 1990.

Hansberry, Lorraine. *A Raisin in the Sun.* Introduction by Robert Nemiroff. New York: Vintage, 1994.

Harvey, David. *A Brief History of Neoliberalism.* New York: Oxford University Press, 2005.

———. "Cosmopolitanism and the Banality of Geographical Evils." *Public Culture* 12, no. 2 (2000): 529–64.

Hawkins, Ty. "Assessing the Promise of Jonathan Franzen's First Three Novels: A Rejection of 'Refuge.'" *College Literature* 37, no. 4 (2010): 61–87.

Hayden, Dolores. *Building Suburbia: Green Fields and Urban Growth, 1820–2000.* New York: Vintage-Random House, 2003.

Hayes-Brady, Clare. "'Obviously, doctor, you've never been a thirteen-year-old girl': Problematic Adolescence in *The Virgin Suicides*." In *'Forever Young'? The Changing Images of America,* edited by Philip Coleman and Stephen Matterson, 209–18. Germany: Universitätsverlag Winter Heidelberg, 2012.

Haynes, Todd, dir. *Carol.* Performed by Cate Blanchett and Rooney Mara. New York: Weinstein Co., 2015.

Heise, Urusla K. "Toxins, Drugs, and Global Systems: Risk and Narrative in the Contemporary Novel." *American Literature* 74, no. 4 (2002): 747–78.

Hemingway, Ernest. *The Sun Also Rises.* 1926. Reprint, New York: Scribner, 2006.

Hesford, Victoria. "'A Love Flung Out of Space': Lesbians in the City in Patricia Highsmith's *The Price of Salt*." *Paradoxa* 18 (2003): 118–35.

———. "Patriotic Perversions: Patricia Highsmith's Queer Vision of Cold War America in *The Price of Salt, The Blunderer,* and *Deep Water.*" *Women's Studies Quarterly* 33, nos. 3–4 (2005): 215–33.

Hidalga, Jésus Blanco. "Knowable Conspiracies: A Reassessment of the Formal and Ideological Aspects in Jonathan Franzen's *The Twenty-Seventh City*." *Miscelánea* 52 (2015): 13–30.

Highsmith, Patricia. *Deep Water*. New York: Harper & Brothers, 1957.

———. *The Price of Salt*. 1952. Reprint, New York: Norton, 2004.

Hill, Anita. *Reimagining Equality: Stories of Gender, Race, and Finding Home*. Boston: Beacon Press, 2011.

Hinners, Sarah Jack. "The Cosmopolitan Ecology of Suburbia." In Berger and Kotkin, *Infinite Suburbia*, 454–62.

Hirsch, Arnold R. *Making the Second Ghetto: Race and Housing in Chicago, 1940–1960*. Cambridge: Cambridge University Press, 1983.

———. "Massive Resistance in the Urban North: Trumbull Park, Chicago, 1953–1966." *The Journal of American History* 82, no. 2 (1995): 522–50.

Hobson, Fred. "*The Sportswriter*: Post-Faulkner, Post-Southern?" In *Perspectives on Richard Ford*, edited by Huey Guagliardo, 83–96. Jackson: University Press of Mississippi, 2000.

Hodgins, Eric. *Mr. Blandings Builds His Dream House*. Illustrated by William Steig. 1946. Reprint, Chicago: Academy Chicago Publishers, 1987.

hooks, bell. *Feminist Theory: From Margin to Center*. New York: Routledge, 2015.

Horkheimer, Max, and Theodor W. Adorno. *Dialectic of Enlightenment: Philosophical Fragments*. Edited by Gunzelin Schmid Noerr. Translated by Edmund Jephcott. Stanford, CA: Stanford University Press, 2002.

Horowitz, Daniel. *Betty Friedan and the Making of the Feminine Mystique: The American Left, the Cold War, and Modern Feminism*. Amherst: University of Massachusetts Press, 1998.

Hoskin, Bree. "Playground Love: Landscape and Longing in Sofia Coppola's *The Virgin Suicides*." *Literature/Film Quarterly* 35, no. 3 (2007): 214–21.

"*House Beautiful* presents . . . a symbol of what we're fighting for . . . A Fine Home and a Beautiful Garden." *House Beautiful*, January 1944, 29+.

Hovland, Ceri. "'We Felt That if We Kept Looking Hard Enough, We Might Begin to Understand How They Were Feeling and Who They Were': Point of View and Performance in *The Virgin Suicides*." *Journal of Adaptation in Film and Performance* 3, no. 3 (2010): 259–70.

Huehls, Mitchum, and Rachel Greenwald Smith. "Four Phases of Neoliberalism and Literature: An Introduction." In *Neoliberalism and Contemporary Literary Culture*, edited by Mitchum Huehls and Rachel Greenwald Smith, 1–18. Baltimore, MD: Johns Hopkins University Press, 2017.

Hutchinson, Colin. "Jonathan Franzen and the Politics of Disengagement." *Critique: Studies in Contemporary Fiction* 50, no. 2 (2009): 191–207.

Jackson, Kenneth T. *Crabgrass Frontier: The Suburbanization of the United States*. New York: Oxford University Press, 1985.

Jacobson, Kristin J. *Neodomestic American Fiction*. Columbus: Ohio State University Press, 2010.

James, Jenny M. "Maternal Failures, Queer Futures: Reading *The Price of Salt* (1952) and *Carol* (2015) against Their Grain." *GLQ* 24, nos. 2–3 (2018): 291–314.

Jameson, Fredric. *Postmodernism, or the Cultural Logic of Late Capitalism*. Durham, NC: Duke University Press, 1991.

———. "Postmodernism and Consumer Society." In *The Anti-Aesthetic: Essays on Postmodern Culture*, edited by Hal Foster, 111–25. Port Townsend, WA: Bay Press, 1983.

Jefferson, Margo. "On Writers and Writing; There Goes the Neighborhood." *New York Times*, November 25, 2001. https://www.nytimes .com/2001/11/25/books/on-writers-and-writing-there-goes-the -neighborhood.html.

Jerng, Mark C. "Nowhere in Particular: Perceiving Race, Change-rae Lee's *Aloft*, and the Question of Asian American Fiction." *Mfs* 56, no. 1 (2010): 183–204.

Jurca, Catherine. *White Diaspora: The Suburb and the Twentieth-Century Novel*. Princeton, NJ: Princeton University Press, 2001.

Kaplan, Amy. *The Anarchy of Empire in the Making of U.S. Culture*. Cambridge, MA: Harvard University Press, 2002.

———. "Homeland Insecurities: Transformations of Language and Space." In *September 11 in History: A Watershed Moment?*, edited by Mary L. Dudziak, 55–69. Durham, NC: Duke University Press, 2003.

Karni, Annie, Maggie Haberman, and Sydney Ember. "Trump Plays on Racist Fears of Terrorized Suburbs to Court White Voters." *New York Times*, July 29, 2020. https://www.nytimes.com/2020/07/29/us /politics/trump-suburbs-housing-white-voters.html.

Kay, Jane Holtz. *Asphalt Nation: How the Automobile Took Over America, and How We Can Take It Back*. Berkeley: University of California Press, 1997.

Keats, John. *The Crack in the Picture Window*. Boston: Houghton Mifflin, 1956.

Keil, Roger. "The Global Suburb: Divesting from the World's White Picket Fences." In Berger and Kotkin, *Infinite Suburbia*, 360–73.

Kelly, Alice M. "'Lots of Us Are Doing Fine': Femslash Fan Fiction, Happy Endings, and the Archontic Expansions of the *Price of Salt* Archive." *LIT: Literature Interpretation Theory* 31, no. 1 (2020): 42–59.

Kelly, Barbara. *Expanding the American Dream: Building and Rebuilding Levittown*. New York: SUNY Press, 1993.

King, Derrick. "The City and the Country: Queer Utopian Spaces in John Rechy's *City of Night* and Patricia Highsmith's *The Price of Salt*." In *Critical Insights: Civil Rights Literature, Past & Present*, edited by Christopher A. Varlack, 174–90. Ipswich, MA: Salem Press, 2017.

Kirkpatrick, David D. "Winfrey Rescinds Offer to Author for Guest Appearance." *New York Times*, October 24, 2001. https://www.nytimes.com/2001/10/24/business/media/winfrey-rescinds-offer-to-author-for-guest-appearance.html.

Knapp, Kathy. *American Unexceptionalism: The Everyman and the Suburban Novel after 9/11*. Iowa City: University of Iowa Press, 2014.

Kolko, Jed. "The Continued Suburbanization of America." In Berger and Kotkin, *Infinite Suburbia*, 208–17.

Kowalewski, Michael. "Bioregional Perspectives in American Literature." In *Regionalism Reconsidered: New Approaches to the Field*, edited by David Jordan, 29–46. New York: Garland, 1994.

Kozol, Jonathan. *Savage Inequalities: Children in America's Schools*. New York: Harper Collins, 1992.

Kunstler, James Howard. *The Geography of Nowhere: The Rise and Decline of America's Man-Made Landscape*. New York: Simon and Schuster, 1993.

Kurtzleben, Danielle. "Seeking Suburban Votes, Trump to Repeal Rule Combating Racial Bias in Housing." *NPR*, July 21, 2020. https://www.npr.org/2020/07/21/893471887/seeking-suburban-votes-trump-targets-rule-to-combat-racial-bias-in-housing.

Lee, Chang-rae. *Aloft*. New York: Riverhead, 2004.

———. *A Gesture Life*. New York: Riverhead, 1999.

Lefebvre, Henri. *The Production of Space*. Translated by Donald Nicholson-Smith. Malden, MA: Blackwell, 1991.

Lentricchia, Frank. "Introduction." In *New Essays on* White Noise, edited by Frank Lentricchia, 1–14. Cambridge: Cambridge University Press, 1991.

"Let Freedom Ring." *Chicago Defender*, May 15, 1948. In Nicolaides and Wiese, *The Suburb Reader*, 324–25.

Lewis, Jim. "Battle for Biloxi." *New York Times Magazine*, May 21, 2006. https://www.nytimes.com/2006/05/21/magazine/21biloxi.html.

Lewis, Sinclair. *Kingsblood Royal*. New York: Random House, 1947.

Lippard, Lucy R. *The Lure of the Local: Senses of Place in a Multicentered Society*. New York: New Press, 1997.

Lofland, Lyn. *The Public Realm: Exploring the City's Quintessential Social Territory*. New York: Aldine De Gruyter, 1998.

Long, Christian. "Running Out of Gas: The Energy Crisis in 1970s Suburban Narratives." *Canadian Review of American Studies* 41, no. 3 (2011): 342–69.

"Looking Forward: Help Yourself—and Your Architect—by Keeping Your Mind Open to New Ideas." *House & Garden*, February 1945, 33.

Loriggio, Francesco. "Regionalism and Theory." In *Regionalism Reconsidered: New Approaches to the Field*, edited by David Jordan, 3–27. New York: Garland, 1994.

Lowenstein, Roger. *The End of Wall Street*. New York: Penguin, 2010.

Lundberg, Ferdinand, and Marynia Farnham. *Modern Woman: The Lost Sex*. New York: Harper & Brothers, 1947.

Lutz, Tom. *Cosmopolitan Vistas: American Regionalism and Literary Value*. Ithaca, NY: Cornell University Press, 2004.

Mackenzie, Louis. "An Ecocritical Approach to Teaching *White Noise*." In *Approaches to Teaching DeLillo's* White Noise, edited by Tim Engles and John N. Duvall, 50–62. New York: Modern Language Association, 2006.

Martin, Theodore. *Contemporary Drift: Genre, Historicism, and the Problem of the Present*. New York: Columbia University Press, 2017.

Marx, Leo. *The Machine in the Garden: Technology and the Pastoral Ideal in America*. 1964. Reprint, New York: Oxford University Press, 2000.

Mather, Mark, Kevin Pollard, and Linda A. Jacobsen. "First Results from the 2010 Census," *Population Reference Bureau Reports on America*. Population Reference Bureau, 2011. http://www.prb.org/resources /first-results-from-the-2010-census.

Matthews, Kristin L. "The Politics of 'Home' in Lorraine Hansberry's *A Raisin in the Sun*." *Modern Drama* 51, no. 4 (2008): 556–78.

May, Elaine Tyler. *Homeward Bound: American Families in the Cold War Era*. Rev. ed. New York: Basic Books, 1999.

McBride, Kecia Driver. "Fear, Consumption, and Desire: Naturalism and Ann Petry's *The Street*." In *Twisted from the Ordinary: Essays on American Literary Naturalism*, edited by Mary E. Papke, 305–22. Knoxville: University of Tennessee Press, 2003.

McCullough, Sarah J. "*Kingsblood Royal*: A Revaluation." *Sinclair Lewis Newsletter* 4 (1972): 10–12.

McGhee, Heather. *The Sum of Us: What Racism Costs Everyone and How We Can Prosper Together*. New York: One World, 2021.

McGinley, Rory. "Playing Suburbia in *Revolutionary Road*." In *Richard Yates and the Flawed American Dream: Critical Essays*, edited by Jennifer Daly, 30–49. Jefferson, NC: McFarland, 2017.

McKnight, Stephanie. "Happier with Dreams: Constructing the Lisbon Girls through Nondiegetic Sound in *The Virgin Suicides*." In *True to the Spirit: Film Adaptation and the Question of Fidelity*, edited by Colin MacCabe, Kathleen Murray, and Rick Warner, 115–29. Afterword by Fredric Jameson. Oxford: Oxford University Press, 2011.

McLaughlin, Robert L. "Deconstructing Culture in *Kingsblood Royal.*" *Midwestern Miscellany* 28 (2000): 7–16.

McLennan, Rachael. "Chasing after the Wind: The Adolescent Aporias of Jeffrey Eugenides." In *Writing America into the Twenty-First Century: Essays on the American Novel,* edited by Elizabeth Boyle and Anne-Marie Evans, 22–38. New Castle, U.K.: Cambridge Scholars, 2010.

Michels, Steven. *Sinclair Lewis and American Democracy.* Lanham: Lexington Books, 2017.

Millard, Kenneth. *Coming of Age in Contemporary American Fiction.* Edinburgh, Scotland: Edinburgh University Press, 2007.

Miller, Laura. "Family Togetherness and the Suburban Ideal." *Sociological Forum* 10, no. 3 (1995): 393–418.

Mills, C. Wright. *White Collar: The American Middle Classes.* 1951. Reprint, New York: Oxford University Press, 1956.

Modarres, Ali. "Reexamining Race and Ethnicity in the Suburbs." In Berger and Kotkin, *Infinite Suburbia,* 134–45.

Moreno, Michael P. "Consuming the Frontier Illusion: The Construction of Suburban Masculinity in Richard Yates's *Revolutionary Road.*" *Iowa Journal of Cultural Studies* 3 (Fall 2003): 84–95.

"Morgan Park." *Encyclopedia of Chicago.* Edited by Janie L. Reiff, Ann Durkin Keating, and James R. Grossman. Chicago: Chicago Historical Society, 2005. http://www.encyclopedia.chicagohistory.org/pages/842.html.

Moskin, J. Robert. "Why Do Women Dominate Him?" In *The Decline of the American Male,* 3–24.

Murphy, Bernice M. *The Suburban Gothic in American Popular Culture.* Basingstoke: Palgrave Macmillan, 2009.

Murray, William. "The Roof of a Southern Home: A Reimagined and Usable South in Lorraine Hansberry's *A Raisin in the Sun.*" *Mississippi Quarterly* 68, nos. 1–2 (2015): 277–93.

Nadel, Alan. *Containment Culture: American Narratives, Postmodernism, and the Atomic Age.* Durham, NC: Duke University Press, 1995.

Nagourney, Adam. "Orange County Is No Longer Nixon Country." *New York Times,* August 19, 2010. www.nytimes.com/2010/08/30/us/politics/30orange.html?_r=1&scp=&st=nyt.

Nair, Sashi. "Loss, Motherhood and the Queer 'Happy Ending.'" *Journal of Language, Literature and Culture* 66, no. 1 (2019): 46–58.

Nance, Kevin. "Jung Yun Interweaves Traditional Parenting, True Crime in Debut Novel 'Shelter.'" *Chicago Tribune,* March 17, 2016. https://www.chicagotribune.com/entertainment/books/ct-prj-shelter-jung-yun-20160317-story.html.

Nelson, Deborah. *Pursuing Privacy in Cold War America*. New York: Columbia University Press, 2002.

Nelson, Sara. "America's Judges Are Putting My Life on the Line." Sunday Review, *New York Times*, November 11, 2021. https://www.nytimes.com/2021/11/11/opinion/courts-labor-strikes.html.

Neutill, Rani. "Jun Yun's 'Shelter.'" *New York Times*, March 18, 2016. https://www.nytimes.com/2016/03/20/books/review/jung-yuns-shelter.html.

"The New Ethnic Enclaves in America's Suburbs." Lewis Mumford Center for Comparative Urban and Regional Research, Albany, New York, 2001. http://mumford.albany.edu/census/suburban/SuburbanReport/page1.html.

Newlyn, Andrea K. "Undergoing Racial 'Reassignment': The Politics of Transracial Crossing in Sinclair Lewis's *Kingsblood Royal*." *Mfs* 48, no. 4 (2002): 1041–74.

Nicolaides, Becky M., and Andrew Wiese, eds. *The Suburb Reader*. New York: Routledge, 2006.

Nilges, Mathias. "Fictions of Neoliberalism: Contemporary Realism and the Temporality of Postmodernism's Ends." In *Neoliberalism and Contemporary Literary Culture*, edited by Mitchum Huehls and Rachel Greenwald Smith, 105–21. Baltimore, MD: Johns Hopkins University Press, 2017.

"A Novelist, a Talk-Show Host, and Literature High and Low." *Chronicle of Higher Education*, November 30, 2001. https://www.chronicle.com/article/a-novelist-a-talk-show-host-and-literature-high-and-low/.

O'Barr, William M. *Culture and the Ad: Exploring Otherness in the World of Advertising*. Boulder, CO: Westview Press, 1994.

O'Hara, James. "Cheever's *The Wapshot Chronicle*: A Narrative of Exploration." *Critique: Studies in Contemporary Fiction* 22, no. 2 (1980): 20–30.

Perry, Imani. *Looking for Lorraine: The Radiant and Radical Life of Lorraine Hansberry*. Boston: Beacon, 2018.

Petrie, Daniel, dir. *A Raisin in the Sun*. 1961. Performed by Sidney Poitier, Claudia McNeil, Ruby Dee, and Diana Sands. New York: Criterion Collection, 2018, DVD.

Petry, Ann. *The Street*. 1946. Reprint, Boston: Houghton, Mifflin, 1974.

Phillips, Dana. "Don DeLillo's Postmodern Pastoral." In *Reading the Earth: New Directions in the Study of Literature and Environment*, edited by Michael P. Branch, Rochelle Johnson, Daniel Patterson, and Scott H. Slovic, 235–46. Boise: University of Idaho Press, 1998.

Plotz, David. "Notes from Tysons Corner; A Suburb All Grown Up and Paved Over." *New York Times*, June 19, 2002. http://www.nytimes .com/2002/06/19/opinions/notes-from-tysons-corner-a-suburb -all-grown-up-and-paved-over.html.

Poole, Ralph J. "Serving the Fruitcake, or Jonathan Franzen's Midwestern Poetics." *Midwest Quarterly* 49, no. 3 (2008): 263–83.

Potter, H. C., dir. *Mr. Blandings Builds His Dream House*. 1948; Burbank, CA: Warner Brothers, 2005. DVD.

Prizel, Natalie. "Beside Women: Charles Dickens, Algernon Charles Swinburne, and Reparative Lesbian Literary History." *GLQ* 24, nos. 2–3 (2018): 267–89.

"A Proper Dream House: For Any Veteran." *House Beautiful*, January 1945, 34+.

Rajan, Raghuram G. *Fault Lines: How Hidden Fractures Still Threaten the World Economy*. Princeton, NJ: Princeton University Press, 2010.

Ravizza, Eleonora. "The Politics of Melodrama: Nostalgia, Performance, and Gender Roles in *Revolutionary Road*." In *Poetics of Politics: Textuality and Social Relevance in Contemporary American Literature and Culture*, edited by Sebastian M. Herrmann, Carolin Alice Hofmann, Katja Kanzler, Stefan Schubert, and Frank Usbeck, 63–80. Germany: Universitätsverlag Winter, 2015.

"Real Estate: Exclusive . . . Restricted." *U.S. News & World Report*, May 14, 1948. In Nicolaides and Wiese, *Suburb Reader*, 325–26.

Reardon, Kenneth M. "State and Local Revitalization Efforts in East St. Louis, Illinois." *Annals of the American Academy of Political and Social Science* 551 (May 1997): 235–47.

Reichert Powell, Douglas. *Critical Regionalism: Connecting Politics and Culture in the American Landscape*. Chapel Hill: University of North Carolina Press, 2007.

Riesman, David. *The Lonely Crowd: A Study of the Changing American Character*. New Haven, CT: Yale University Press, 1961.

Rome, Adam. *The Bulldozer in the Countryside: Suburban Sprawl and the Rise of American Environmentalism*. New York: Cambridge University Press, 2001.

Rose, Carol M., and Richard R. W. Brooks. "Racial Covenants and Housing Segregation, Yesterday and Today." In *Race and Real Estate*, edited by Adrienne Brown and Valerie Smith, 161–76. New York: Oxford University Press, 2016.

Rotella, Carlo. *October Cities: The Redevelopment of Urban Literature*. Berkeley: University of California Press, 1998.

Saber, Yomna. "Lorraine Hansberry: Defining the Line Between Integra-
    tion and Assimilation." *Women's Studies* 39 (2010): 451–69.
Schenkar, Joan. *The Talented Miss Highsmith: The Secret Life and Serious
    Art of Patricia Highsmith*. New York: St. Martin's Press, 2009.
Schindehette, Susan. "Novel Approach." *People*, November 12, 2001, 83–84.
Schlosser, Eric. *Fast Food Nation: The Dark Side of the All-American Meal*.
    New York: Perennial, 2002.
Sciolino, Martina. "The Contemporary American Novel as World Liter-
    ature: The Neoliberal Antihero in Don DeLillo's *Cosmopolis*." *Texas
    Studies in Language and Literature* 57, no. 2 (2015): 210–41.
Sellers, Christopher C. *Crabgrass Crucible: Suburban Nature and the Rise
    of Environmentalism in Twentieth-Century America*. Chapel Hill:
    University of North Carolina Press, 2012.
Shah, Nayan. *Contagious Divides: Epidemics and Race in San Francisco's
    Chinatown*. Berkeley: University of California Press, 2001.
Sheckler, Robert. "The Road to Understanding and Reform in *Kingsblood
    Royal*." *The Sinclair Lewis Society Newsletter* 8, no. 1 (1999): 3, 8–11.
Shostak, Debra. "'A story we could live with': Narrative Voice, the Reader,
    and Jeffrey Eugenides's *The Virgin Suicides*." *Mfs* 55, no. 4 (2009):
    808–32.
Slade, Andrew. "'You Are the Most Beautiful Creature': The Ethics of Mas-
    culinity in *Revolutionary Road*." *Quarterly Review of Film and Video*
    34, no. 7 (2017): 664–77.
Smith, Judith E. *Visions of Belonging: Family Stories, Popular Culture, and
    Postwar Democracy, 1940–1960*. New York: Columbia University
    Press, 2004.
Smith, Neil. *American Empire: Roosevelt's Geographer and the Prelude to
    Globalization*. Berkeley: University of California Press, 2003.
Smith, Neil, and Setha Low. "Introduction: The Imperative of Public
    Space." In *The Politics of Public Space*, edited by Setha Low and Neil
    Smith, 1–16. New York: Routledge, 2006.
Smith, Wendell. "The Life of the Writer: Lunch with Richard Ford." In
    Conversations with Richard Ford, edited by Huey Guagliardo, 49–57.
    Jackson: University Press of Mississippi, 2001.
Soja, Edward W. *Postmetropolis: Critical Studies of Cities and Regions*.
    Malden, MA: Blackwell, 2000.
———. *Postmodern Geographies: The Reassertion of Space in Critical Social
    Theory*. New York: Verso, 1989.
Sontag, Susan. *On Photography*. New York: Farrar, Straus and Giroux,
    1977.

Spivak, Gayatri Chakravorty. *Death of a Discipline*. New York: Columbia University Press, 2003.

"Struggling in the Suburbs." Editorial. *New York Times*, July 7, 2012. https://www.nytimes.com/2012/07/08/opinion/sunday/struggling-in-the-suburbs.html.

Stuart, Jan. Review of *Fallen Land*, by Patrick Flanery. *Boston Globe*, August 17, 2013. https://www.bostonglobe.com/arts/books/2013/08/17/shadow-land/X5sKXiDPRKaZu4MYsl3SiJ/story.html.

Sugrue, Thomas J. *The Origins of the Urban Crisis: Race and Inequality in Postwar Detroit*. Princeton, NJ: Princeton University Press, 1996.

Teaford, Jon C. "The Myth of Homogeneous Suburbia." In Berger and Kotkin, *Infinite Suburbia*, 126–32.

Thompson, Craig. "Growing Pains of a Brand-New City." *Saturday Evening Post*, August 7, 1954, 26–27, 71–72.

Tongson, Karen. *Relocations: Queer Suburban Imaginaries*. New York: New York University Press, 2011.

"Transcript: Donald Trump Expounds on His Foreign Policy Views." *New York Times*, March 26, 2016. https://www.nytimes.com/2016/03/27/us/politics/donald-trump-transcript.html.

U.S. Supreme Court. *Hansberry v. Lee*, 311 U.S. 32 (1940). *JUSTIA*. Decided November 12, 1940. https://supreme.justia.com/cases/federal/us/311/32/case.html.

———. *Shelley v. Kraemer*, 334 U.S. 1 (1948). *JUSTIA*. Decided May 3, 1948. https://supreme.justia.com/cases/federal/us/334/1/case.html.

Valiunas, Algis. "O Joy! O Sorrow! O Cheever!" *Commentary*, April 2009, 66–70.

Vann, David. "Company Man." Review of *Fallen Land*, by Patrick Flanery. *New York Times*, October 4, 2013. https://www.nytimes.com/2013/10/06/books/review/fallen-land-by-patrick-flanery.html.

Waldie, D. J. *Holy Land: A Suburban Memoir*. New York: St. Martin's Griffin, 1996.

Walton, James. "Fallen Land." Review of *Fallen Land*, by Patrick Flanery. *Telegraph*, June 8, 2013. https://www.telegraph.co.uk/culture/books/10091434/Fallen-Land-by-Patrick-Flanery-review.html.

Wandler, Steven. "Race and Citizenship in Sinclair Lewis's *Kingsblood Royal*." *Twentieth-Century Literature* 60, no. 1 (2014): 79–98.

Warner, Michael. *Publics and Counterpublics*. New York: Zone Books, 2002.

Watts, Edward. "*Kingsblood Royal, The God-Seeker*, and the Racial History of the Midwest." In *Sinclair Lewis: New Essays in Criticism*, edited by James M. Hutchisson, 94–109. Troy, NY: Whitston Publishing Co., 1997.

Weekes, Karen. "Consuming and Dying: Meaning and the Marketplace in Don DeLillo's *White Noise*." *Lit: Literature Interpretation Theory* 18, no. 4 (2007): 285–302.

Wells, Amy Stuart, and Robert L. Crain. *Stepping over the Color Line: African-American Students in White Suburban Schools*. New Haven, CT: Yale University Press, 1997.

Whyte, William H. *The Organization Man*. 1956. Reprint, New York: Doubleday Anchor Books, 1957.

Wiese, Andrew. *Places of Their Own: African American Suburbanization in the Twentieth Century*. Chicago: University of Chicago Press, 2004.

Wilhite, Keith. "John Cheever's Shady Hill, Or: How I Learned to Stop Worrying and Love the Suburbs." *Studies in American Fiction* 34, no. 2 (2006): 215–39.

Wilson, Andrew. *Beautiful Shadow: The Life of Patricia Highsmith*. New York: Bloomsbury, 2003.

Winograd, Morley, and Michael D. Hais. "Millennials' Hearts Are in the Suburbs." In Berger and Kotkin, *Infinite Suburbia*, 66–72.

Womack, Kenneth, and Amy Mallory-Kani. "'Why don't you just leave it up to nature?': An Adaptationist Reading of the Novels of Jeffrey Eugenides." *Mosaic* 40 (September 2007): 157–73.

Wood, Gillan D'Arcy. "What Is Sustainability Studies?" *American Literary History* 24, no. 1 (2012): 1–15.

Wylie, Philip. *Generation of Vipers*. 1942. Reprint, Normal, IL: Dalkey Archive Press, 1996.

Yates, Richard. *Revolutionary Road*. 1961. Reprint, New York: Vintage, 2000. Introduction by Richard Ford.

Yun, Jung. *Shelter*. New York: Picador, 2016.

Index

Abarrio, Rubén Peinado, 180, 258n34

adjustment culture, 60, 65, 67, 69, 71, 75, 82, 91

Adorno, Theodor, 27, 30

Affirmatively Furthering Fair Housing (AFFH), 213–14, 264n6

Alexander, Michelle, 208, 262n43

Aloft (Lee): consumerism in, 170–71; ethnicity and race in, 167–69, 174; HGTV in, 170–71, 173–74; immigrant labor in, 172; and impending recession, 170; multigenerational living in, 173–74; and post-9/11 era, 167; as regional writing, 166–67, 171, 173–74, 184; remodeled house in, 170, 173–74, 184; suburb in, 167–74; transnational region in, 167, 172, 184

Anderson, Jill E., 81

Anderson, Sherwood, *Winesburg, Ohio*, 90

Anonymous Hedge Fund Manager (HFM), 185–87. See also *Diary of a Very Bad Year*

architecture: and anti-urbanism, 219–20n6; and country living, 2, 202; and imperialism, 197; moral influence of, 22, 195–96, 202; and New Urbanism, 161; postmodern, 112–13; and post-World War II planning, 28–30.

See also Downing, Andrew Jackson

Arrested Development (television series), 2–4, 190

Avilez, GerShun, 56

Bachelard, Gaston, 261–62n36

Bailey, Blake, 61–62, 234n6, 235n8

Baker, Houston A., Jr., 50

Baldwin, James, 38–39

Barrett, Laura, 108

Beauregard, Robert, 125, 248–49n71

Berger, Alan M., 212–13

Beuka, Robert, 6, 221n14

Black middle class: compared to Black working class, 32; and East St. Louis, 127; in *Kingsblood Royal*, 35, 42–44, 46; in *A Raisin in the Sun*, 51, 54; and suburban life, 31–32, 52

Blaustein, Jessica, 140, 145–46, 222n34

Blomley, Nicholas, 120, 165, 247n59, 248n63, 259n50

Bourdieu, Pierre, 98, 102, 123–24, 129, 243n18

Brinkmeyer, Robert H., Jr., 177, 180

Brooks, Richard R. W., 31, 34, 227n25, 228nn27–28

Brown v. The Board of Education of Topeka, Kansas, 50, 55–56

Buell, Lawrence, 16, 116–17, 210

Pryse, Marjorie, 13–14, 33, 65, 133, 203, 224n52, 261n25

queerness: and construction of normal, 60, 65–66; and motherhood, 84, 88, 91, 241n60; and national security and surveillance, 18–19, 82, 90–91; and regionalism, 6, 19, 65–66, 71, 90, 93; and suburban domesticity, 12, 19, 67, 77, 84, 88, 90–91, 93. *See also* homosexuality

race issues: and homeownership, 31, 58–59, 67, 188–89, 194, 210, 214; and housing policies, 9–10, 129, 143–44, 222n32; and neighborhood associations, 32, 36, 45–48, 50, 53, 55–57, 150, 179, 232–33n65; and residential segregation, 18, 35, 56–57, 129, 132, 144, 149, 158, 213–14, 228n28; and white flight, 99, 127, 151, 167–168, 256n13. *See also* redlining; restrictive covenants
Radway, Janet, 132, 250n84
A Raisin in the Sun (Hansberry): and assimilation, 52, 54, 57, 233n68; Chicago in, 18, 35–36, 48, 52–53; class divisions in, 51–52, 54; desire for home in, 36, 48, 50, 52–53, 57; film adaptation, 233n67; gender issues in, 51–52, 57–58; kitchenette in, 49, 54; neighborhood associations in, 55–57; nostalgia in, 52, 58; race issues in, 48–58; as regional writing, 33, 36, 58; and residential pioneering, 19, 52–53, 57, 59; segregation in, 18, 55–56; South in, 52–53; suburb

in, 36, 48–49, 52, 54, 56–58; threat of violence in, 50–51, 56–58; and whiteness, 18, 33, 52, 55, 56, 59
Rajan, Raghuram G., 187–88, 259nn9–10, 259–60n12
Reagan, Ronald, 18, 103, 129–30, 158, 225n65
redlining, 10, 32, 59, 150, 166, 189, 201, 256n13
regional writing. *See* regionalism
regionalism: as critical response to place, 4, 8–10, 12–14, 16, 20, 23, 100, 105, 117, 127, 134, 144, 155–57, 178–79, 181, 192, 209, 211; as genre, 5, 7–8, 11–12, 15, 81, 137, 157, 180, 216–17; and literary value, 7–9, 100, 132–33, 222–23n38; local-global concerns in, 12, 14, 137, 156, 167, 182, 184; as methodology, 9, 13–14, 158, 191, 203, 216–17; and queerness, 65–66, 71, 90; and race issues, 33, 40, 47, 52, 59, 169, 183; and suburban fiction, 10–11, 13–14, 19–23, 33, 36, 40, 45, 52, 58, 65–66, 71, 81, 89–90, 93, 100, 105–06, 133–34, 137, 155–58, 166–67, 171, 173–74, 181–82, 184, 190–92, 196, 203, 209, 211; tropes of, 19–20, 52, 65, 71, 89–90; and urban planning, 13–14, 21, 161–62, 165, 173, 216–17, 223n47, 244n30
Reichert Powell, Douglass, 9, 13
residential pioneering, 19, 36, 52–53, 57, 59, 231nn53–54, 232n61
residential rights, 11, 18, 33, 36, 40, 47, 54–59, 65, 84, 192, 202, 211, 217. *See also* race issues
restrictive covenants, 18, 31–35, 38,

nation-building, 4, 9, 12–13,
15, 17–19, 21–23, 28–29, 32–33,
40, 47, 58–59, 64–66, 70–71, 84,
93, 101, 103, 105, 109, 135, 137,
143, 158, 167, 170, 174, 189, 195,
202, 209, 216; poverty rates in,
214, 264n9, 264n14; promotion
of, 27–30, 32–33, 109, 152, 195,
219n2; as regulatory terrain,
19, 65–66, 74, 82–83, 87–91,
93; single-family home in, 10,
12, 14, 16, 18, 22, 31, 33, 37–38,
54, 58–59, 65, 92, 103, 109, 146,
149, 152, 155, 163, 167, 173, 188,
195–97, 203, 205, 214, 222n34;
and standardization, 5, 8, 12,
81, 120, 131, 167, 172, 180–81;
and sustainability, 4, 11, 21,
136, 157–58, 162, 173–74, 178–79,
182–84, 191, 204, 212–13, 215–17,
254n41. *See also* race issues
Suburban Nation: appeals to
reader in, 162–65, 255n8; as
call to action, 163, 165; class
privilege in, 162, 166; and New
Urbanism, 161–62, 165; nostalgia in, 161–62, 166, 173–74, 184;
and racial blind spots, 166, 184,
256n13
Sugrue, Thomas J., 149–50, 253n32

Teaford, Jon C., 12
Tongson, Karen, 6–7, 9
Trump, Donald J., 18, 67, 212–14,
263–64nn5–6
Twain, Mark, 8; *The Adventures of
Huckleberry Finn*, 90
The Twenty-Seventh City
(Franzen): civic apathy in,
118, 121, 129–30; as coun-
terfactual history, 118, 121,

129–30; discourse of decline
in, 122, 124–25; East St. Louis
in, 127–28; and free-market
ideology, 106, 121, 124, 126,
129; and maps, 119–21, 127, 131;
and neoliberalism, 20, 100–01,
105–6, 119, 121, 123, 126, 129–30;
nostalgic impulses in, 20, 119,
131; and postmetropolis, 100,
105, 131; postmodern elements
in, 106, 119; race issues in, 20,
101, 119–20, 122, 125–29, 132, 144,
158; as realist novel, 101, 105, 119,
121, 130–31; as regional writing,
20, 100, 105–06, 133–34, 158; St.
Louis in, 105, 118–22, 124–28,
130–31; suburb in, 118, 124–25,
127–28

U.S. News & World Report, 34–35,
228n28

Valiunas, Algis, 63–64
Vietnam War, 143, 153, 253n26
The Virgin Suicides (Eugenides):
and American empire, 138, 144,
149, 153, 156; and Cold War era,
135–37, 146–47, 152, 156–57; and
containment culture, 136–37,
146, 150, 155; critical responses
to, 135; Detroit in, 20, 135, 144,
149–50; environmental threats
in, 140, 142, 146, 151, 155–58; and
the foreign, 138–41, 145–46, 148,
152, 156; and narrative voice, 135,
154–55, 157, 252n2; and nostalgia, 20–21, 136–37, 144, 157;
privacy and privatism in, 137,
142, 145–47, 152, 158; race issues
in, 136, 140, 144, 148–51, 155, 158;
as regional writing, 20–21, 137,

155–58; suburb in, 21, 135–38,
141–42, 145, 147–48, 150–51,
155–56; World War II references
in, 142, 144–45, 155–56

Waldie, D. J., 5
War in Afghanistan, 15
Warner, Michael, 164, 255n7
Watts, Edward, 37, 47, 228–29n33
white middle class: and everyman,
6; and homeownership rates,
67, 186; and neighborhood
control, 34–35, 50, 55–56; as normative force, 64–65, 68, 78–79,
88, 239–40n52; and suburban
living, 10, 15, 22, 28, 30–33,
67–68, 70, 103, 108, 143, 166, 187,
197, 210, 253n20; and victimization, 5–6. See also organization
culture
White Noise (DeLillo): consumerism in, 105–14, 116, 131, 247n56;
domestic realm in, 108–11,
113–14, 116–17, 131; environmental threats in, 20, 101, 105, 109,
115–17, 131, 158; and late capitalism, 101, 107–08, 110, 115, 131;
as late postmodernism, 100,
106–07; and media culture,
108–10, 114, 117; and neoliberalism, 20, 100, 105–08, 112, 115–16;
and postmetropolis, 20, 100–01,
105–06, 108–09, 112–13, 115–17,
119, 131, 158; post-nuclear family
in, 108–10, 117, 131; as regional

writing, 20, 100, 105–06, 134, 158;
shopping mall in, 111–14; suburb
in, 108, 112, 114, 117, 131
"Why Bother? (The *Harper's*
Essay)" (Franzen), 98–99, 117–18
Whyte, William H., 65–66, 81, 91;
The Organization Man, 5, 60,
235n11, 235n16
Wiese, Andrew, 52, 227n19,
228n29, 231n54
Wilson, Sloan, *Man in the Gray
Flannel Suit*, 189
Winfrey, Oprah, 117, 132–33
Winograd, Morley, 213
Womack, Kenneth, 136, 154, 252n6
Wood, Gillen D'Arcy, 157, 216
World War II: and emergence of
U.S. globalism, 4, 16–17, 143,
224–25n60; and familial con-
sensus, 234n3; as leveraged in
popular magazines, 27–30, 42,
59, 195; and New Deal pro-
grams, 9–10, 143; and postwar
suburban home building, 3,
9–10, 16, 22, 31, 42
Wright, Richard, *Native Son*, 50
Wylie, Philip, *Generation of
Vipers*, 69–70

Yates, Richard: on authentic self,
237n35; and feminism, 239n48.
See also *Revolutionary Road*
Yun, Jung: on home invasion in
Cheshire, CT, 194. See also
Shelter

The New American Canon

Half a Million Strong: Crowds and Power from Woodstock to Coachella
by Gina Arnold

Violet America: Regional Cosmopolitanism in U.S. Fiction since the Great Depression
by Jason Arthur

The Meanings of J. Robert Oppenheimer
by Lindsey Michael Banco

Neocolonial Fictions of the Global Cold War
edited by Steven Belletto and Joseph Keith

Workshops of Empire: Stegner, Engle, and American Creative Writing during the Cold War
by Eric Bennett

Places in the Making: A Cultural Geography of American Poetry
by Jim Cocola

The Legacy of David Foster Wallace
edited by Samuel Cohen and Lee Konstantinou

Race Sounds: The Art of Listening in African American Literature
by Nicole Brittingham Furlonge

Postmodern/Postwar—and After: Rethinking American Literature
edited by Jason Gladstone, Andrew Hoberek, and Daniel Worden

After the Program Era: The Past, Present, and Future of Creative Writing in the University
edited by Loren Glass

Hope Isn't Stupid: Utopian Affects in Contemporary American Literature
by Sean Austin Grattan

It's Just the Normal Noises: Marcus, Guralnick, No Depression, *and the Mystery of Americana Music*
by Timothy Gray

Wrong: A Critical Biography of Dennis Cooper
by Diarmuid Hester

Reverse Colonization: Science Fiction, Imperial Fantasy, and Alt-victimhood
by David M. Higgins

Art Essays: A Collection
edited by Alexandra Kingston-Reese

Contemporary Novelists and the Aesthetics of Twenty-First Century American Life
by Alexandra Kingston-Reese

American Unexceptionalism: The Everyman and the Suburban Novel after 9/11
by Kathy Knapp

Visible Dissent: Latin American Writers, Small U.S. Presses, and Progressive Social Change
by Teresa V. Longo

Pynchon's California
edited by Scott McClintock and John Miller

Richard Ford and the Ends of Realism
by Ian McGuire

Novel Subjects: Authorship as Radical Self-Care in Multiethnic American Narratives
by Leah A. Milnes

William Gibson and the Futures of Contemporary Culture
edited by Mitch R. Murray and Mathias Nilges

Poems of the American Empire: The Lyric Form in the Long Twentieth Century
by Jen Hedler Phillis

Reading Capitalist Realism
edited by Alison Shonkwiler and Leigh Claire La Berge

Technomodern Poetics: The American Literary Avant-Garde at the Start of the Information Age
by Todd F. Tietchen

Contested Terrain: Suburban Fiction and U.S. Regionalism, 1945–2020
 by Keith Wilhite

Ecospatiality: A Place-Based Approach to American Literature
by Lowell Wyse

How to Revise a True War Story: Tim O'Brien's Process of Textual Production
by John K. Young